ABUSED BOYS

The Neglected Victims
of Sexual Abuse

by

MIC HUNTER

Lexington Books

D.C. Heath and Company · Lexington, Massachusetts · Toronto

Library of Congress Cataloging-in-Publication Data

Hunter, Mic.
    Abused boys : the neglected victims of sexual abuse / by Mic Hunter.
      p. cm.
    Includes index.
    ISBN 0–669–20866–3 (alk. paper)
    1. Child molesting—Case studies. 2. Boys—Abuse of—Case studies.   3. Sexually
abused children—Case studies.   4. Adult child sexual abuse victims—Case studies.
I. Title.
HQ71.H85   1990
362.7'6—dc20

89–33906
CIP

Published simultaneously in Canada
Printed in the United States of America
Casebound International Standard Book Number: 0–669–20866–3
Library of Congress Catalog Card Number: 89–33906

The paper used in this publication meets
the minimum requirements of American National Standard
for Information Sciences—Permanence of Paper
for Printed Library Materials, ANSI Z39.48–1984.

Year and number of this printing:

90 91 92 8 7 6 5 4 3

This work is dedicated to:
my favorite person and wife Kate An;
the people who first taught me
about recovery from sexual abuse,
Richard and Nickey;
and the members of my
Wednesday afternoon therapy group
and my Thursday night support groups

Contents

Preface and
Acknowledgments

THIS year, as in every year, tens of thousands of boys will be sexually abused in the United States. They will be damaged physically, emotionally, mentally, and spiritually. Every aspect of their lives will be affected. When they become adults they will be plagued with sexual dysfunctions, troubled relationships, a poor sense of self-worth, and intimacy difficulties. Many will become drug addicts. Some will destroy themselves. Most of them will suffer from the effects of sexual abuse without ever realizing that they were victimized. When they read or hear programs about sexual abuse they probably will not hear about male victims. They will call what happened to them many things, but rarely will they think of themselves as victims. To add to the tragedy, those who seek professional help from mental health centers, treatment programs, and therapists will often be misdiagnosed: the sexual abuse will be overlooked or not taken seriously. The symptoms of the abuse may be treated but not the underlying cause. The stereotypes and myths that surround sexual abuse and males will prevent them from getting adequate help. Victimized as boys, they will be neglected as men.

Not long ago, our society thought that sexual abuse was very rare. But the survivors, both female and male, have begun to speak out. Their cries have become too loud and their numbers too great to ignore. They are demanding to be heard and to be believed. They are insisting that something be done. The time has come for us to open our eyes to the reality that we are surrounded by victimized people. It is time to notice their pain.

I never planned to focus my clinical attention on sexual abuse; I was compelled to by my clients. They insisted that I become aware of the effects of sexual abuse. I found that working with people meant that I was going to work with sexual abuse victims. My search of the literature turned up very few resources for male victims and their partners. It was then that I decided to begin this book. I use two terms that require some explanation. Usually I refer to boys and men who have been sexually abused as *victims* rather than as *survivors*. I will discuss my reasoning in more detail later, but the first task of a male who has been seriously mistreated is to accept the fact that he has been victimized; only then can he move on to view himself as a survivor. When referring to adults in relationships with men who were sexually abused I have used the term *partner*. I wanted to be sensitive to those people not married as well as to gay couples. Partner is my all-inclusive term to replace *spouse, lover* (too sexual), or *significant other* (too clinical).

I am grateful for the people who contributed their stories. All names have been changed to ensure the privacy of the authors and their families. Several of the contributors are former clients and so already had a trusting relationship with me, but many others took the risk of contacting me after reading about this project in magazine articles. Many more started their stories only to find that it was too painful, and they decided to stop. I am thankful for their efforts as well.

As I read over what I have written during these last two years, I am aware that my anger showed up in several sections. I have decided to leave these sections as they came out. There is much to be angry about when it comes to the topic of sexual abuse. My anger has served me well in the past, and I hope it has done the same for this project. As our society has focused on the various types of abuse, racism, sexism, classism, and sexual abuse, there has been a need for anger: it gets things done and leads to important changes. I hope you will find just enough anger to accomplish what you need to.

As you read through the text, you will periodically be asked questions. Many of these questions were given to the people who contributed their stories to help them think about what they wanted to include in their writing. The questions are designed to help you to personalize the material. I encourage you actually to write out your responses. Writing your experiences makes them seem more real and helps you to access more emotions and memories. This can be a very painful experience, so I advise you to go slowly and keep in contact with supportive people. If you are in a group, such as Survivors of Incest Anonymous, Al-Anon, Alcoholics Anonymous, Adult Children of Alcoholics, Sex Addicts Anonymous, Overeaters Anonymous, or any of the other groups that are based on the Twelve Steps, you may want to let your sponsor and other group members know what issue you are addressing. Let them know that you will be vulnerable for a while and will need extra attention and comforting. In addition, recovering from sexual abuse can be such an overwhelming process that it is best done with the assistance of a professional therapist who has specialized training. Since trust is so important when talking about sexual abuse and its impact, be sure to interview several therapists, ask about their training, what their goals are for treatment, and what methods they use. Only work with someone who seems safe to you. (See the section "How to Choose a Therapist" in chapter 6.)

Those of you who are reading this to understand better a loved one will also want to respond to these questions. It is important that your needs be addressed too. Healing from sexual abuse is a long, stressful process, but it can be made easier if you have some understanding of what to expect in the coming months from your loved one and from yourself.

I have included the personal stories of recovering men and their partners because the examples taken from my clinical experience cannot fully describe the impact of sexual abuse. They are actual histories, not composites, and are written in the words and style of the people whose lives they describe. Some of the authors chose to use graphic language to make their point. These stories cover a broad range of experiences, types of abuse, and stages of recovery. I encourage you to read all of them, since each has something to teach you. As you read them look for the similarities to your story rather than the differences. None of them is pleasant to read, but I believe they will offer you hope in your recovery.

My thanks to Marilyn Solberg, Ph.D., at Saint Mary's Graduate Center, for her help and support when this book was merely a short graduate paper; Kristie Lange, formerly of the Macalester College Library, for her efforts in locating materials for me; the members of my monthly support group for therapists who work with male sexual abuse survivors, especially Peter Dimock for organizing it; Margaret Zusky at Lexington Books, who believed in this project from our first conversation; Kathe and Michael Gendel, for welcoming me into their home so I could write for a week without being distracted, as well as for their support when my word processor erased a day's worth of effort; and the authors who came before me who wrote about sexual abuse. We often have different views, but our aim is the same: healing the wounds of sexual abuse. I also wish to acknowledge Lynda LaBounty, Ph.D., L.C.P. (my Macalester adviser/instructor, H.A.S. cotherapist, and Gestalt Institute colleague); Richard B. Adams, M.A., L.P., and Rob Berger, M.A. (wise and gentle men both), for taking time to review an early draft of this book. They provided valuable comments and support. This book has been a team effort. May you learn as much about yourself reading it as I learned about myself writing it. May this be the beginning of the end of your suffering.

What Is Sexual Abuse?
Definitions and
Recovery Issues

1

Understanding Sexual Abuse

Defining Sexual Abuse

When a person uses tricks, power, threats, or violence to have sexual contact with another adult, it is called rape or sexual assault.[1] When the victimized person is a child, people often use the phrase *child molesting*. When a child is molested by a relative, it is called incest.

Sexual abuse is in fact a sexual act. That cannot be ignored. Yet it is much more than merely a sexual act. If the adults who are sexual with children merely wanted sex, there are many lower-risk methods of obtaining it. In most cases it is not the touch itself that is harmful but the meaning behind the touch that hurts. Sexual abuse can be an expression of power, compulsiveness, a desire for control, or an act of vengeance, which often comes masked as an act of love.

Many authors have attempted to define what constitutes sexual abuse. David Walters gives one definition: "Sexual abuse of a child is the utilization of the child for sexual gratification or an adult's permitting another person to so use the child."[2] When I use the phrase *sexual abuse,* I am usually referring to any sexual act that an adult does to a child. In order to avoid getting bogged down in debating what constitutes a sexual act or sexual gratification, I have incorporated Judith Lewis Herman's concept that any touch or other behavior between the child and the adult that must be kept secret will be considered abuse.[3] Violence or threats may or may not be overt components of the abuse. In other words, the adult can behave in a gentle manner, but the sexual contact is still abusive. Adults infrequently need to resort to actual physical violence to be sexual with children. More often, enticement, rewards, misuse of authority, or misrepresentation of what is taking place is used instead.[4]

This is a broad definition; some will say too broad. For example, Walters writes:

> Determining sexual abuse requires much more in the way of judgment, and great latitude in behavior and events are noted. It is clearly sexual abuse when a father has sexual relations with his daughter. But is it abuse if a father does not respect his daughter's desire for privacy while dressing, or if he honestly complains because his daughter, who is entering puberty, no longer wishes to bathe with him? Most people would agree that the second father is an unwise parent, but charging abuse is quite a different matter.[5]

My answer to Walter's question is yes; intentional, repeated invasion of privacy is abuse. Just because some people wouldn't agree that it is abuse doesn't mean that it isn't. There are many behaviors that have been considered acceptable behavior in the past that are no longer viewed as appropriate. For example, in the not-too-distant past, boys were castrated in order to preserve their soprano voices for church choirs,[6] and it has only been relatively recently that we have enacted child labor laws to prevent the exploitation of children in factories. The father is placing his desires over the rights of the daughter to decide who views and touches her body. The adult is viewing his wants as more significant than the child's needs. It is irrelevant if the father is "honestly" objecting. Sexual abuse is abusive regardless of the adult's intention. Many adults, when confronted with the consequences of their abusive behavior, will state, "I never intended to hurt anyone." This may be true, but it does not change the fact that harm was done, nor does it eliminate their responsibility for their actions.

What I choose to call sexual abuse is based on how I choose to spend my time. I am a clinician. But I am not writing about data or evidence in the legal sense. I am writing about people and their pain. My definition is based on what people have told me hurt them. It is important to define sexual abuse clearly because what we call something determines how we react to it. As Finkelhor says, "What people think sexual abuse is and how seriously they take it affects how they behave. For example, it may affect what kinds of sexual behaviors get reported to authorities. Researchers have noted ← sexual activities involving adults and boys get reported less often than sexual behaviors involving adults and girls. They have speculated that this is because people see sexual activities with girls as more serious and more abusive than the same activity with boys."[7]

There are two broad categories of abuse: overt and covert. Overt sexual abuse is openly sexual and apparent. Although there may be an attempt to deny that what is being done is *abusive,* there is no attempt to hide the fact that it is *sexual* in nature. For example, a parent gets into a child's bed and fondles his genitals, making no effort to disguise that a sexual act is taking place.

Covert abuse is more insidious, and therefore is harder to identify, because the *sexual* nature of the action is disguised. The person acts as if he or she is doing something nonsexual when in reality he or she is actually being sexual. The betrayal is twofold: the child is abused and then deceived about it. It is this dishonesty that can make covert abuse difficult to identify and therefore difficult to recover from. The victim is led to believe that the event was not sexual, that he has not been abused, and that he should not trust his emotions or perceptions of those around him. The unreal or surreal sense that accompanies all abuse experiences is further increased when the child is tricked into disbelief. Since covert abuse involves deceit, it is important to focus on the *reason* for the behavior rather than on the behavior itself: on the *why* rather than merely on the *what.*

For example, I have had several clients who reported that a parent would require periodic "bug checks," which consisted of the boy's removing his clothes and the parent's running her or his hands over the boy's body, lifting his penis and scrotum, and inserting a finger into his anus. Although these inspections were supposedly held to protect the child from insect-related problems, they did not take place when the child had been playing in the woods but more often when the child had not been out of the house.

Another example of covert sexual abuse can be seen in the story of the adult client who told me that he was sure he had never been sexually abused, although he had many of the symptoms of a sexual abuse victim. "How could I have been? The only time my mother ever saw me without clothes was when she bathed me," he said. So far, this sounds an appropriate, nonabusive behavior. Seeking more details, I asked, "At what age did you start bathing yourself?"

A. About fourteen or so, I guess. [*Matter of factly*]

Q. Who bathed you when your mother wasn't around?

A. I did it myself, of course.

Q. Prior to age fourteen did you or your mother ever suggest that you no longer needed her assistance in keeping yourself clean?

A. Yeah, I remember saying I could do it without her, but she would just say that it was her way of showing that she loved me. I didn't want to hurt her, so I let her keep doing it.

Q. How long does it take you today to completely bathe yourself?

A. About fifteen or twenty minutes if I'm not in a hurry.

Q. How long did it take your mother to bath you?

A. I don't know. [*Quietly*]

Q. Think about it.

A. Half hour, maybe more. [*Softly*]

Q. I wonder what the reason is that she took at least twice as long to wash you.

A. I don't know. [*Very softly*]

Q. Who washed your penis and scrotum?

A. I told you, she washed me. [*Sharply*]

Q. How long does it take you to wash your genitals as an adult?

A. Less than a minute, and I know what your next question is. She took much longer than a minute to wash me down there.

Q. Did you get an erection?

A. [*After a long pause*] Yes, sometimes. [*Pause*] I'm such a pervert. [*Angrily*]

Q. How do you feel?

A. It felt good. [*Shamefully*][8]

Q. What did your mother say when you got an erection?

A. I don't remember. [*Flatly*]

Q. You don't remember or you don't want to tell me what she said?

A. I've never told anyone before. [*Sadly*]

Q. It must be painful.

A. She said my penis was bigger than any of my brothers'
or my Dad's, and that I would make some woman very happy
one day.

The reason that this man's mother was bathing him was not for *his* personal hygiene but rather for *her* sexual pleasure. Rather than openly state that she wished to be sexual with him, she pretended that she was doing her motherly duty. The abuse was twofold in that she was sexual with him and deceived him about it.

Another form of covert incest is the parent sexualizing the relationship. Although the behavior looks appropriate, the adult brings to the interaction his or her sexual needs. Many of my clients have reported that they had a parent who would come in to "tuck them into bed" at night and would rub their backs. This was not a pleasant childhood memory of the physical expression of affection between parent and child; rather, it was recalled as a confusing and frightening ritual. Although no additional physical contact took place, these clients reported that there was an intense tension in the room during these back rubs and that they were confused and thought that "something else might happen," even though they weren't sure what this "something" would be.

Another destructive dynamic is when the adult treats the child as a pseudo- or surrogate spouse.[9] This is sometimes referred to as nonsexual incest.[10] The child is treated as an equal, a peer, rather than as a child. The abusive dynamic of the behavior is that the child is being used by the adult to meet the needs of the adult. There is an intensity and exclusiveness that prevents the child from forming relationships with his true peers and his other parent. The effect of being "married" to a parent is that the child has no siblings because he has been placed in a role that is more like that of a parent than a brother in relation to the other children in the family. If this relationship is with the mother, the child doesn't really have a mother since he is acting as her husband. He is also denied a father since his father is his rival. These relationships are often explained as a result of the child's Freudian Oedipus complex, and the relationship is viewed as originating from the child and his wishes for the mother, rather than coming from the mother's desires.[11] It is common in these relationships for the parent to refer to the child as "lover," "my little man," "the man of the house," or by pet names that are more appropriate in romantic relationships than between parent and child. Often in these relationships the child has access to information about his parents that is inappropriate, such as sexual performance. The boy is often invited into the parent's bed when the *parent* is in need of comfort or protection. Although there may not be actual sexual contact, there will be sexual tension, which will change the relationship between the boy and his parents. Ruth and Henry Kempe describe the consequences of such relationships for the child:

> One noteworthy and largely unmentioned relationship between fathers and daughters and mothers and sons and which does not involve any physical or technical incestuous behavior is, rather, a type of symbiotic or mutually dependent state. The growing child and one parent each finds the other the most important person in his/her life, a relationship that often strains the parents' marriage and tends to delay or to make it impossible to form a lasting relationship with anyone else by the maturing child. The young adults' marriages tend to fail, and fail again, or they never attempt marriage.[12]

Questions to help identify your thoughts and emotions:

> In the past, what has been your definition of sexual abuse or incest?

> Does your definition differ from what was done to you (or your loved one)? If so, in what way?

> In what ways has your definition helped you not to have feel the full impact of your (your loved one's) abuse?

> How does what was done to you (your loved one) fit the definition of abuse I have described?

Types of Sexual Abuse

Specifically, sexual abuse includes any of the following behaviors:

> The adult sexually touching the child[13]

> Having the child touch the adult sexually[14]

Photographing the child for sexual purposes[15]

Sexualized talk[16]

Showing the child pornographic materials or making them available to the child

Making fun of or ridiculing the child's sexual development, preferences, or organs[17]

The adult exposing his or her genitals to the child for sexual gratification[18]

Masturbating or otherwise being sexual in front of the child

Voyeurism[19]

Forcing overly rigid rules on dress or overly revealing dress

Stripping to hit or spank, or getting sexual excitement out of hitting

Verbal and emotional abuse of a sexual nature

Having the child be sexual with animals

Engaging the child in prostitution

Witnessing others being sexually abused

In my experience, I have found it rare for a child to be subjected to only one type of sexual abuse. This list of types of sexual abuse is not complete, and undoubtedly there are other ways that sexual abuse can take place. The more clients I work with, the more amazed I am at the ability of the human mind to generate seemingly endless ways to mistreat children.[20]

The Adult Sexually Touching the Child

A common form of sexual touch is fondling, where the adult manipulates the child's genitals or other erotic areas, such as the buttocks, anus, or nipples. This touch can also come in the form of sexual hugs or rubbing, where the adult rubs her or his body against the child or otherwise uses the child's body for stimulation. This may be done with or without clothing on. Some adults will bathe or shower with a child, and then rub their genitals or breasts against him. Some parents will insert their finger into the child, stating they are doing so in order to clean the child. The adult may sexually grab at or pinch the child when he goes by. The adult may "accidentally" bump into the child or brush against him.

Sexual kisses are another form of touch. Examples of inappropriate kisses between adults and children include long kisses on the mouth or with tongues. Oral sex, where the adult kisses, licks, bites, or sucks on the child's body for sexual gratification, also represents an inappropriate use of the child's body. The most invasive type of touch is sexual penetration with objects, such as fingers, vibrators, pencils, enemas, and in actual intercourse.

Again, it is important to remember that much of the sexual abuse takes place in a covert manner. The adult touches the child for sexual gratification, while excusing the behavior by saying it is not sexual in nature. Enemas can be an example of this covert sexual abuse. The penetration of the child's rectum is done not for the physical health of the child but rather for the sexual excitement of the adult. Another example can be seen in the case of the mother who for years regularly examined her son's penis "to insure that it was growing properly." This inspection consisted of several minutes of the mother stroking her son's penis while kneeling in front of him. The son was placed in a double bind by his mother. If he did not obtain an erection, she would tell him that he was not maturing properly, so further and more frequent inspections would be necessary. However, if he did become erect, she would state that he was being "dirty" and thinking "nasty thoughts about his mother."

HAVING THE CHILD TOUCH
THE ADULT SEXUALLY

The adult can have the child touch the adult in any of the just-mentioned ways. Victims of this type of abuse frequently think that they are responsible for what happened because it appears that they are being more active than the adult(s). They repress or deny the coercion they experienced or do not realize that adults are responsible for setting and maintaining appropriate boundaries with children, regardless of the desires of the child.

PHOTOGRAPHING THE CHILD FOR SEXUAL PURPOSES

These images can be still photos, movies, or videotapes. The most extreme example of this type of photography is child pornography. The key phrase here is *for sexual purposes*. Many parents will photograph their child bathing or exploring the house without clothing, but the reason for the photo is documentary, to record memories, not for the purpose of stimulating sexual fantasies to use during masturbation. Prior to the 1978 federal law that made the sale of child pornography illegal, more than 250 different child porno magazines were available in the United States.[21]

Once an adult has a pornographic photo of a child, it can be used to convince the child to cooperate with further sexual acts by threatening to show the photo to others, such as parents, clergy, or schoolmates. The photos are often traded or sold to other adults.[22]

The child experiences a great loss of control because the photographs can be reproduced an infinite number of times and can be distributed literally throughout the world. He never knows when one of these photographs will come back to haunt him, even years later as an adult.

SEXUALIZED TALK

Talking to a child about sexual matters for legitimate educational purposes is very appropriate. In fact, *not* talking to children about sexuality is a form of sexual neglect. Here again, the dynamic that must be present to make the process abusive is for the adult to be taking part in the activity for his or her own sexual excitement. Examples of this form of abuse include sexualized talk, suggestive language, flirtations, or propositioning. In many ways this can be a form of verbal exhibitionism. Often the talk is more romantic than sexual in nature. However, the effect is very similar since the child is being used to meet the adult's needs and is not in a position to give consent. The child is treated as an equal when in fact he is not. He is treated as a lover rather than as a child. The relationship takes on the dynamic of a marriage. In some cases this "surrogate spouse" relationship can be set up even if there is no overt sexual contact. The emotional relationship is sexualized and romanticized. There may be flirting, pet names, and cards or gifts exchanged which are appropriate to a lovers' relationship. The child has access to information about the parent that is not age- or role-appropriate, such as details of the parent's sex life. Men who have had this type of relationship with their mother may feel guilty leaving her and coupling with another woman. They feel guilty, as if they are being unfaithful. The mother may do all she can to reinforce this guilt, such as saying that there isn't a woman good enough for her son, being hypercritical of women he dates, complaining of how lonely she is without him, how poorly he is treating her after all she did for him, and how ungrateful he is.

VERBAL AND EMOTIONAL ABUSE OF A SEXUAL NATURE

This is a form of verbal abuse in which the adult uses sexual terms to describe the child. Examples include "motherfucker," "faggot," "prick," "cocksucker." This is not commonly seen as sexual abuse. When Finkelhor interviewed 521 parents, he found that respondents as a whole did not consider calling a child a faggot or whore to be sexual abuse.[23]

I believe this behavior is abusive sexually because it pairs one's gender, sexual orientation, or body with shame. As adults, people who have been subjected to this type of abuse frequently refer to themselves with the disrespectful terms that they were called as children.

MAKING FUN OF THE CHILD'S SEXUAL DEVELOPMENT, PREFERENCES, OR ORGANS

This is another form of sexual talk. It is more overtly abusive because the attention is more clearly critical, and it is particularly humiliating when done in front of friends, other family members, or in public. Often the child is told that he is not allowed to get angry or hurt about the comments because they were meant "only as a joke." An example of ridiculing a child's sexual development and organs is a parent comparing one child's penis to another child's or to an adult's.

SHOWING THE CHILD PORNOGRAPHIC MATERIALS OR MAKING THEM AVAILABLE TO THE CHILD

This is often done under the guise of "educating the child." These materials may be auditory or visual in nature. When the behavior is abusive, the child's welfare is not the primary goal—the sexual gratification of the adult is. Showing a child sexually explicit materials, for the purpose of teaching anatomy or to explain childbirth, may be very appropriate. Again, there are some who will disagree with me. For example, Walters has written:

> Recently some professionals have asked whether exposure to pornographic films constitutes "sexual abuse" of children or "emotional abuse" of children in the area of sexuality. Much has been said on both sides of this question, and some professionals are even including literature with obscene words in this category.
>
> These are areas in which specialists in child abuse should not get involved. Calling the viewing of a pornographic movie or the reading of a book containing profanity or obscenities "sexual abuse of children" is a perversion and corruption not only of the terms, but also of professional roles.[24]

People who show a child pornography often do it in order to encourage the child to copy the behavior he or she sees or to convince the child that sexual contact between adults and children is appropriate.[25] Pornographic written and visual materials often have an incest theme.

THE ADULT EXPOSING HER OR HIS GENITALS TO THE CHILD FOR SEXUAL GRATIFICATION

Nudity does not equal exhibitionism. As before, the intent of the nudity is central to determining whether the behavior is abusive or not. The stereotypic form of exhibitionism is a man in a coat who jumps out of the bushes and exhibits his penis to shock the viewer; he may also masturbate. Sexual phrases, often spoken with an angry tone, may also be a part of the ritual. When this occurs, it can be very frightening to a child.

Many other forms of exhibitionism also exist. A parent may perform a "striptease," complete with music, in front of the children. Sometimes an adult will indirectly expose her- or himself by showing or making available to the child photographs or her- or himself. My clients have given me many examples of covert exhibitionism. For example, the adult will ask the child's assistance in getting dressed, often requesting that the child perform some task that the adult is quite capable of performing. In one case, a mother regularly asked her son to help her put on and fasten her front-hook bra and to pull up her stockings. She did not have any physical handicaps and had no difficulty dressing herself when he was not at home. In another case, a mother frequently asked her son to examine and touch her genitals under the guise of having him check for signs of cancer. A father would "accidentally" walk through the living room naked when his children had friends over. And a mother who always wore a robe, unless she was home alone with her son, at which time she wore only a see-through night-gown, repeatedly came into his room to make sure he was doing his homework.

Many people who expose themselves for sexual gratification are never labeled exhibitionists. One reason is that the act is performed in a covert manner. Another reason is because the diagnostic manual of the American Psychiatric Association states that the criteria for exhibitionism consist of "recurrent, intense, sexual urges and sexually arousing fantasies, of at least six months' duration, *involving the exposure of one's genitals to a stranger.*" It also states that "the condition apparently occurs only in males, and the victims are almost entirely female (children or adults)."[26]

An excellent example of a mother exposing herself to her son is found in *Portnoy's Complaint*. The mother began this "game" when her son was a child, and it continues into his adulthood:

"Feel."
"*What?*"—even as she takes my hand in hers and draws it towards her body—"Mother—"

"I haven't gained five pounds," she says, "since you were born, feel," she says, and holds my stiff fingers against the swell of her hips, which aren't bad . . .

And the stockings. More than twenty-five years have passed (the game is supposed to be over!), but Mommy still hitches up the stockings in front of her little boy. Now, however, he takes it upon himself to look the other way when the flag goes fluttering up the pole—and out of concern not just for his own mental health. That's the truth, I look away not for me, but for the sake of that poor man, my father! Yet what preference does Father really have? If there in the living room their grown-up little boy were to tumble all at once onto the rug with his mommy, what would Daddy do? Pour a bucket of boiling water on the raging, maddened couple? Would he draw *his* knife—or would he go off to the other room and watch television until they were finished? "What are you looking away?" asks my mother, amused in the midst of straightening her seams, "You'd think I was a twenty-one-year-old girl; you'd think I hadn't wiped your backside and kissed your little tushy for you all those years. Look at him"—this to my father, in case he hasn't been giving a hundred percent of his attention to the little floor show now being performed—"look, acting like his own mother is some sixty-year-old beauty queen."[27]

MASTURBATING OR OTHERWISE BEING SEXUAL IN FRONT OF THE CHILD

This is another form of exhibitionism. I am not talking here about when a child accidentally walks in on parents who are being sexual. I am referring to adults who get sexually high by risking being seen by children or setting up situations where there is a likelihood that they will be discovered being sexual, such as leaving a bedroom door open during sex while children are in the next room. Victims of this type of exposure frequently think they are to blame for having seen the adult and feel guilty or ashamed about what they have done "wrong" or for being "bad." Some people who have been subjected to exhibitionism as children go on to become voyeuristic and compulsively seek opportunities to view others being sexual.

Sometimes the adult will mask the abuse by telling the child that he or she is merely educating the child by showing him what sex or masturbating is like. A client of mine had parents who would be sexual in front of him, and he would then be quizzed on what they were doing. In a therapy session he and his brother described one such incident they recalled from their childhood:

"Son, what is this?"
"Your penis."
"Now what is your mother doing?"
"Sucking it."
"What is that called?"
"A blow job."

This interaction continued while the parents had intercourse and orgasm. At first my client was very resistant to believing that his parents were being inappropriate. Although he stated that he did not teach his own children about sex in this manner, nor would he encourage others to do so, he still thought of it as an educational experience and thought his parents' intentions were honorable. He began to change his view of the situation when his brother pointed out that even after they could correctly answer all the questions asked by the parents and could correctly identify all the various parts of the body, their parents continued to insist that they watch them be sexual until the two boys left home immediately after high school. He began to see that his viewing of his parents' sex acts were for their benefit and not his own.

VOYEURISM

The stereotype of voyeurism involves a man who hides in some bushes, looking in someone's window hoping to see people undressing or being sexual. Household voyeurism is very similar in that the voyeuristic person's goal is to obtain sexual gratification by viewing someone else in a sexual manner. The viewer frequently masturbates as he or she is watching or uses the memory of what is seen to masturbate later. Adult voyeurism can appear as a preoccupation with the child's body and development. The adult makes repeated observations about how the child is or is not physically maturing. For example, one father nightly asked his children at the dinner table if they had developed any pubic hair yet. If they had, he insisted on checking, to "make sure it was forming properly."

Overt examples of household voyeurism include hiding in someone's closet to watch that person undress or masturbate, boring peepholes in bedroom or bathroom walls, and watching teenagers "making out." I worked with one client whose father kept a two-story ladder next to the house and would nightly climb it so that he could see in his children's bedroom and watch them undress.

More covert examples of voyeurism include walking in on people bathing or dressing without their permission, and staring or leering at someone's sexual organs. Sometimes children awaken to find a family member standing over their bed staring at them for no apparent reason. One of my clients told me how embarrassed he was as a teenager because he was forced to share a closet with his mother. When he first told me the story, I imagined that he lived in a small house and that space was scarce. In fact, he was an only child and lived with his parents in a fifteen-room house! Each morning as he dressed, his mother would enter his room without knocking, go to the closet they shared and remove one piece of her clothing. As she left the room, she would make some comment about his body, such as "Why are you trying to cover yourself? Have you grown something I haven't seen before?" Seconds later she would return "to obtain another piece of clothing" and to make another statement, such as "I remember when I used to rub baby powder on that cute butt of yours." This went on until she had, item by item, gotten all of her clothing or until he was fully dressed. When he complained to his mother, he was told that the human body is beautiful and that he had nothing to be ashamed of. When he complained to his father, he was accused of "being a pervert for thinking dirty thoughts" about his mother and for "implying that she was up to something." The overt message was accurate. The human body is beautiful and he didn't have anything to be ashamed of, because he was not the person who was being inappropriate. Unfortunately, he did feel ashamed because he was being treated in a disrespectful manner and then was further mistreated by being told that what he believed was happening was not really happening. The covert message was that since the human body is beautiful, nothing bad can be happening, and so your perceptions are inaccurate and your feelings are inappropriate.

People who have been victimized repeatedly by a voyeuristic parent or others have a very difficult time describing their history to therapists or in group settings. They fear that the listener is getting sexually excited by the description of the sexual abuse. Unfortunately, there are people who have a morbid curiosity about sexual abuse or who find it sexually stimulating. When a therapist focuses excessively on the sexual details of the abuse, this is referred to as privileged voyeurism.[28] The therapist is using the power of her or his position of authority to meet her or his sexual needs at the expense, both emotionally and financially, of the client. This is a reenactment of the dynamic of the original sexual abuse and ought not to be tolerated. If you think that you are being mistreated by a helping professional, consult the agency that licenses that type of professional for the procedure to file a complaint. You had no power as a child to stop your abuse, but you do as an adult.

FORCING OVERLY RIGID RULES ON DRESS OR OVERLY REVEALING DRESS

If forced to dress in an extreme manner, a person may begin to feel ashamed of his or her body. Sexually compulsive adults or others who believe that sexual urges are so easily triggered and powerful that they are nearly impossible to control may attempt to lessen the perceived risk of sexual contact between family members by trying to eliminate all sexual clues in the environment. They mistakenly believe that if people keep their bodies covered this will prevent sexual arousal and therefore sexual activity. They do not understand that most sexual abuse is based more on a power dynamic than on a sexual urge.

People who were sexually abused will frequently take responsibility for the abuse by saying that it was their fault because they exposed "too much of their bodies" and those who abused them "couldn't help themselves." People who sexually abuse others will often reinforce this belief by blaming the victim and saying that the fault lies in the victim's behavior.

Those who come from families that rigidly required inappropriately revealing dress may then raise their own children in the opposite but equally rigid manner and require their children to remain completely covered, regardless of social norms or weather conditions.

STRIPPING TO HIT OR SPANK, OR GETTING SEXUAL EXCITEMENT OUT OF HITTING

This category overlaps with physical abuse. The adult claims to be disciplining the child but is actually using his misbehavior, real or imagined, as an excuse to be sexual. The adult will often impose rigid and extreme rules on the child in such a way that he will be unable to avoid violating them, so that the "discipline" will be justified.[29] Many of my clients recall the sensation of their fathers' erect penises against the front of their bodies as they held them over their knees and spanked them.

In other cases the "discipline" has sexual overtones because it is done on the parents' bed. The child is told to strip, or the adult undresses him, and then strikes the child as he lies across the parents' bed. In some cases the child is stripped in front of other family members or in a place where others, such as neighbors or the boy's friends, are likely to see the punishment. The public nature of the event adds to the sense of powerlessness and increases the level of humiliation and shame. The adult may also call the child sexual names or accuse him of sexual crimes while "punishing" him. For example, the adult may call the boy "motherfucker," "faggot," "prick," or "cocksucker," or insist that the boy was thinking about sex, masturbating, or wanting to have sex with someone and is being punished for these "sins." Some of the adults who take part in these acts are diagnosed as having the sexual disorder of sadism. People with this disorder find it sexually exciting to inflict psychological or physical suffering and humiliation on their victims.[30] I have worked with men who have experienced this type of abuse as boys and who become sexually excited by being beaten and verbally humiliated. They would also use "phone sex" services and pay to have someone insult or degrade them over the phone.

HAVING THE CHILD BE SEXUAL WITH ANIMALS

In this case, an adult instructs the child in fondling or licking the animal's genitals or has the animal lick the child's genitals. Part of the trauma of this type of abuse is that in severely dysfunctional families the relationship with the pet may be the only safe relationship that the child has, and then even this relationship is sexualized. Victims of this type of abuse may go on to seek out other animals to be sexual with, as children and as adults.

ENGAGING THE CHILD IN PROSTITUTION

This can be done in three ways. The most passive type of involvement occurs when the adult is prostituting her- or himself or pimping others, and the child is openly exposed to these actions and is led to believe that it is normal, desirable behavior. A more active type of abuse is to use the child to solicit customers for a prostitute. This is done to reduce the chance of arrest for the adult. The third and most intrusive type is when the child's body is actually rented out to an adult for sexual reasons. It is estimated that 300,000 American children are involved in prostitution and pornography.[31] Because of the frequency and number of different adults being sexual, the child is put at a very high risk of contracting venereal diseases and AIDS.

People sometimes justify these acts in economic terms, saying that the family is impoverished and that prostitution is a way for the child to help support himself and contribute to the family. However, most poverty-stricken parents would never even think of using their children in this fashion.[32] Others argue that the child is taking part in the activity for his own personal gain. Although some children who are cast out by their families or who have run away to avoid gross mistreatment at home engage in sex for money to buy food, most child prostitutes are merely tools of adults who receive the profits.

Focusing on the financial aspects of prostitution avoids looking at the psychological cost to the victim. Having one's body rented out for use by another is extremely dehumanizing. The child is being treated as an object. Many people who have been mistreated this way begin to think of themselves as subhuman or nonhuman. They go on as teenagers and adults to be sexual with others for money or for other forms of payment.

WITNESSING OTHERS BEING SEXUALLY ABUSED

Even if a child is not actually touched in a sexual way, viewing or hearing others being sexually abused can be extremely traumatic. The knowledge that sexual abuse is not only possible but likely in one's own family is a frightening thought to have to live with on a daily basis. If one child is being actively sexually abused and another child in the same family is not, the child who is not being touched will seek to understand the reason he is not being treated in the same way. He may become extremely self-conscious, wondering, "If I do this, will it happen to me too?" or "What if I stop doing this; will that cause it to happen?" In some cases the child who is not touched suffers more than the child who is actually being touched. The symptoms of a person responding to the knowledge that another member of the family is being sexually abused is labeled "incest envy" by some authors.[33] In some families the only attention available is sexual; what the child craves is parental attention, not sex.

Some children feel guilty that another child in the family is being mistreated and will attempt to provoke or otherwise get the parent to abuse them as well as a way to protect the sibling. As one client put it, "If I'm getting it, that means my brother was getting it half as often."

Common Misconceptions about Child Sexual Abuse

MYTH: Children are most likely to be sexually assaulted by a stranger.

FACT: 75–95 percent of offenders are known and may be related to the child.

MYTH: Children lie or fantasize about sexual activities with adults.

FACT: In developmental terms, young children cannot make up explicit sexual information—they must be exposed to it; they speak from their own experiences. Sometimes a parent will try to get a child to report sexual abuse falsely. Primary indi-

cators of such a report are the child's inability to describe explicitly or illustrate the act, or a grossly inconsistent account.

MYTH: The sexual abuse of a child is an isolated, one-time incident.

FACT: Child sexual abuse is usually a situation that develops gradually over a period of time, and the sexual abuse occurs repeatedly.

MYTH: Nonviolent sexual behavior between a child and adult is not emotionally damaging to the child.

FACT: Although child sexual abuse may involve subtle rather than extreme force, nearly all victims will experience confusion, shame, guilt, anger, and a lowered sense of self-esteem, though they may reveal no obvious outward signs.

MYTH: Child molesters are all "dirty old men."

FACT: In a recent study of convicted child molesters, 80 percent were found to have committed their first offense before the age of thirty.

MYTH: Children provoke sexual abuse by their seductive behavior.

FACT: Seductive behavior may be the result but is never the cause of sexual abuse. The responsibility lies with the adult offender.

MYTH: If children did not want it, they could say "stop."

FACT: Children generally do not question the behavior of adults. They are often coerced by bribes, threats, and use of authority.[34]

MYTH: When a boy is sexually abused, the act is perpetrated by male homosexuals.

FACT: Most child sexual abuse is perpetrated by men who are heterosexual and do not find sex with other men at all attractive. Many child molesters abuse both boys and girls.

MYTH: When a boy and a woman have sex, it is the boy's idea, and he is not being abused.

FACT: Child abuse is an act of power by which an adult uses a child. Abuse is abuse; a woman abusing a male child is still a child abuser.

MYTH: Males who were sexually abused as boys all grow up to abuse children sexually.

FACT: Only a portion of abused boys go on to abuse children.

Questions to help identify your thoughts and emotions:

What emotions did you experience while reading about the various types of sexual abuse?

Has your definition of sexual abuse changed after reading this material? If so, how?

How common do you think sexual abuse is? How common in your gender?

2

Frequency of Sexual Abuse

I T is frightening to realize how widespread sexual abuse is in our society and yet how strong the denial of it is[1]. Many people believe that because there are biblical injunctions and governmental laws prohibiting sexual abuse it is rare. However, people engage in many illegal behaviors of various levels of severity, such as driving over the posted speed limit, lying on tax returns, distributing and using cocaine or marijuana, writing bad checks, and so on. As Bixler has pointed out, just because there is incest taboo doesn't mean that incest doesn't happen.[2]

The topic of incest and other forms of sexual abuse have only begun to receive attention in both the popular and scientific press in the last ten to fifteen years.[3] Until recently the literature on people who have been sexually abused has been relatively scarce. In 1955 Weinberg was reporting that the incidence of incest was one or two cases per million.[4] Over twenty years later Meiselman reported that incest was "a relatively rare event" and placed the incidence at one or two per hundred.[5] Bixler wrote that if Meiselman's data was accurate then less than .006 percent or 1 out of 18,000 boys had experienced mother-son incest.[6]

The women's movement led to more study of the sexual abuse of females. Most of the writing concerned individual case histories rather than the results of large-scale research projects. Most of the writing about sexual abuse has been about females, perhaps because of the widely held assumptions that boys often initiate the sexual contact they have with adults and that these contacts (regardless of the origins) do not negatively affect boys.[7] Our society mistakenly believes that "girls get raped and hate it, but boys are seduced and love it."

It is common for a person who has been abused to think in extremes: all or nothing. Therefore, when asked about the frequency of sexual abuse the victim often assumes either that *everyone* has been sexually abused and just doesn't talk about it, or just the opposite—that he is unique, the *only* one who has had such an experience. Many victims are surprised to learn that other males have been abused. They did not hear male sports figures, actors, or other celebrities talk about their childhood abuse. Until very recently, articles, television programs, and books did no more than make passing references to nonoffending male victims or female offenders. Male victims were left to think that either the sexual abuse of males didn't happen or that it was too disgusting to be talked about.[8] The idea that large numbers of males are sexually victimized is actually fairly new. Sarrel and Masters report, for instance, that the original investigators for the monumental and often-quoted Kinsey report, which surveyed large numbers of men throughout the United States about their sexual experiences, never asked the subjects whether there was any history of sexual assault in their backgrounds.[9]

The advent of the men's movement brought "grass roots" pressure from men for information on sexual abuse and its treatment. With an increase in the awareness of sexual abuse came an increase in the reporting rate. In the state of Minnesota, reports in the year 1986 of male and female sexual abuse were up 77 percent from 1984, and up 133 percent from 1982.[10] In Minnesota one of every twenty-five male high school students and one of every fourteen male college students reports that he is a victim of sexual abuse.[11] A review of several national studies puts the prevalence of sexual abuse in males at between 2.5 percent and 16 percent.[12] If the rate of abuse is constant from year to year, then *at least* 46,000– 92,000 boys under the age of thirteen are sexually abused *each year in the United States alone*.[13] A study done by the Canadian government and by the Canadian Gallup Polls interviewed two thousand people of various ages and found that one-third of the males had experienced some type of sexual abuse as a child.[14]

As staggering as these estimates are, we should remember that most sexual abuse of children of both sexes goes unreported and that male victims are particularly underidentified. One study found that two-thirds of the suspected child abuse cases that were known to professional helpers were not reported, despite the mandatory reporting laws that require filing a report. This figure included 87 percent of the cases known to teachers and other school personnel.[15] Physicians make only 14 percent of the child abuse reports in the United States. Another factor contributing to the inaccurate picture of the problem is that there is no accepted definition of what constitutes sexual abuse, so it is difficult to gather data and to compare the results of different studies.[16] Let us next examine some of the specific reasons why male sexual abuse victims are underidentified.

Reasons Male Sexual Abuse Victims Are Underidentified

↣One reason many sexual abuse victims are not identified is because the counselors or therapists they meet with do not give them permission to talk about sexual issues. If the professional never brings up the subject, the client can get the message that it is taboo. A second common dynamic is that the topic may be only superficially discussed, because of the therapist's denial or lack of awareness of the client's behavioral and emotional clues; since the therapist is unable to discuss it in a confident manner, the client then drops the subject, much to the relief of both. A third reason why victims go unidentified is that the professional's definition of sexual abuse may not include what was done to the particular client. The experience may be discussed in detail, but the label of abuse is never applied to it.

↢ Some sexual abuse victims are told that their memories are merely fantasies or wishes and did not actually happen. They are told that even violent sexual thoughts involving one's family are normal. Much of the belief that clients make up stories of incest experiences comes from the work of Sigmund Freud, who at the turn of the century was attributing neurosis, at least in females, to childhood incest. However, this theory was so unacceptable to Freud's colleagues and, in many ways, to Freud himself that Freud later wrote that his patients were merely reporting fantasies and not memories.[17] Not all helping professionals agree with Freud today. As one author put it, "Ascribing these events (sexual abuse) to psychological fantasy may be easier and more interesting for the therapist, but it may also be counterproductive for the most efficient resolution of symptoms. I am not discounting the role of fantasy in psychic development. It is important, however, to distinguish between fantasy and the fact of child molestation."[18]

A variation on the fantasy theme can be found in the current legal system. Children who report sexual abuse and then become involved in litigation are frequently accused of imagining or lying about the abuse. As Gardner wrote in *The Parental Alienation Syndrome and the Differentiation between Fabricated and Genuine Child Sex Abuse,* "My experience with children who have genuinely been abused sexually is less than that with children who have fabricated sex abuse. This relates to my deep involvement in custody litigation in which the vast majority of children who profess sexual abuse are fabricators."[19]

In her research, Meiselman reported that some of the therapists she was using to gather data on sexual abuse had clients who described incest but the "therapist considered it unwise to disrupt the course of ongoing therapy by further probing what might cause the client to focus on incest."[20] But these therapists did not reveal how the course of therapy would be negatively affected by focusing on incest. Since so many adult problems can be traced to childhood sexual abuse, it seems to me that the course of therapy would be disrupted by *not* focusing on the incest.

I have found that clients who are not ready to deal with sexual abuse will merely deny or repress information that is too threatening for them to be aware of. In addition, in my experience, I have found that it is extremely rare for clients to prefer to focus on sexual abuse in order to avoid "dealing with problems in their present life situation." Usually, if anything, it is the other way around—the client would rather talk about anything but sexual abuse.

Frequently, counselors and therapists will not ask about incest and other sexual abuse because they are afraid of the answer. Sexual abuse is a difficult issue to deal with personally and professionally, and until very recently, most helping professionals did not receive any significant training in how to deal with sexual abuse victims. In a survey of protection workers in state departments of social services, 76 percent of these workers reported that their education on incest was deficient, and 95 percent stated that they needed additional training.[21] Since treatment professionals often do not know what to do with the problem, they avoid, consciously or unconsciously, knowing the problem exists in their clients.[22] For example, when I was providing some training to a chemical dependency treatment program, I asked one of the counselors how many of his clients had been sexually abused. He told me that he asked about sexual abuse during the assessment interview but "didn't see much evidence of sexual abuse" in his clients and thought it "was a pretty rare occurrence." When I sat in on one of his assessment interviews, I noticed that he asked open-ended questions, such as "How often do you use alcohol?" until he came to the topic of sexual abuse, and then he asked, "You weren't sexually abused, were you?" Not surprisingly, he did not hear about sexual abuse from his clients very often.

Some treatment professionals claim they do not bring up the subject of incest, because they don't want to insult the client by implying that he might have come from "that kind of family," or because it might encourage the client to make up false incest experiences. Following this kind of logic, counselors ought not to ask about drug use to prevent the client from making up phoney histories of alcoholism. When I was employed as a chemical dependency counselor, I was never once tempted when someone told me their drug use history to say, "Now, how are you going to prove that? How do I know that those things really happened? Perhaps you just wish you were a drug addict. This could all be just a fantasy, something you wish would happen." This sounds shocking, yet many of my clients were told similar things when they disclosed their sexual abuse histories to other professionals.

Some helping professionals choose their career as a way to deal with their own traumatic histories. If the counselor or therapist is an untreated sexual abuse victim or perpetrator, these unresolved issues can interfere with his or her ability to work effectively with clients. As a part of my early training I served as an intern at a chemical dependency treatment program and worked with a very sensitive and caring counselor in a group setting. I watched him work with several of the women in the group while they talked

and cried about sexual abuse that they had endured at the hands
of their fathers. He was quite gentle and supportive of these female
clients. A few days later, a male client began to describe how he
too had been victimized sexually as a child by his father. The counselor suddenly began yelling, "You're just saying that to get attention. Stop crying and act like a man. Even if it did happen, that
was a long time ago. How long are you going to hold on to your
resentments? You'll never get sober at this rate." Needless to say,
everyone in the group was shocked at this outburst from the counselor and at how differently he treated male and female victims.
Following the group session I asked the counselor in private what
his thinking was, why he responded that way. He began yelling at
me, saying that I was trying to undermine his authority, that "alcoholics would rather talk about anything other than their drug
use," and that this was just an attempt on the client's part to avoid
the "real" issue. As a result of this incident, the male client left
treatment prematurely, and the remaining clients no longer brought
up sexual abuse issues. Several years later I learned that this counselor had wisely sought out therapy to focus on his own sexual
abuse experiences with his father.

Some victims do not receive treatment for their sexual abuse
histories because they come to therapy seeking help with other
problems and they never get to the core issue. Very few of my
clients come into my office directly stating that they are seeking
help because of childhood sexual abuse.[23] Usually other issues are
discussed first. These issues may involve difficulty in relating to
others or a general sense of worthlessness or fear. Many of my
clients who were sexually abused as children have many self-
defeating behaviors as adults, such as chemical misuse, over- or
undereating, suicide attempts, self-mutilation, not completing tasks
or otherwise failing. While these are clearly serious problems, it is
important that the underlying causes of these behaviors, which may
include sexual abuse, also be addressed. Many people wrongly believe that just because a person's overt self-defeating behaviors have
been stopped all the effects of sexual abuse have been healed. I
often have clients who have completed chemical dependency treatment, have stopped their drug use, regularly attend Alcoholics
Anonymous, and yet are very unhappy. They continue to have sexuality and intimacy struggles. In some cases well-meaning chemical

dependency counselors or sponsors promise them that if they just stay sober long enough these problems will "take care of themselves." Unfortunately, even after years of sobriety these people find that the problems don't disappear—in fact, they often get worse. Some people return to chemical use in an attempt to cope with the pain they experience around their low self-worth and sexuality issues. Whenever I am referred a client who has a long history of repeated chemical dependency treatments (or another addictive disorder) and an equally long history of relapses, I begin to search for clues suggesting sexual abuse.

The Individual's Definition of Sexual Abuse

Even when helping professionals do ask about sexual abuse, many clients who were victimized as children will not report it. This is not because of dishonesty or even lack of trust; instead, the individual often has a definition of sexual abuse that does not include what was done to him. Such clients do not acknowledge that they were abused because they do not think they were. Therefore, it is not enough to ask a client whether he was abused; a therapist must ask about specific behaviors and feelings. I learned this lesson from a woman I was working with in a halfway house. I asked her in a session if she had ever been sexually abused, and she said she hadn't. Later on in the session, somehow she started talking about how she used to suck on her grandfather's penis. I said, "I thought you said you hadn't ever been sexually abused." "That's right, I haven't been," she responded. "Well, what do you call your grandfather sticking his penis in your mouth?" I asked. "It was just a game. Sexual abuse is when someone has sex with you when they are mad at you," she answered. Clearly, this woman's definition of abuse conveniently did not fit what had been done to her. The definition did, however, protect her from the sense of betrayal she had. After further discussion she became aware that she had in fact been sexually abused by several of her relatives.

Another example of a person with a definition of sexual abuse that did not fit what happened to him is a client of mine who described how his mother would come into his room uninvited and make sexual comments about his teenage body as he dressed. She would also call him into the bathroom as she bathed and would soap her genitals as she talked to him about dinner or school. Although he felt very uncomfortable during these events, he did not see them as sexual abuse since his mother never actually *touched* him. His definition of sexual abuse required that physical contact take place between the people involved. I then described the situation with the genders reversed and asked him if a father watching his teenage daughter dress and rubbing his genitals in front of her would be abusive; the client at this point began to have a different view of the events he experienced.

Another difficulty in helping people identify that they were sexually abused is that the abuse may have taken place before the individual developed the ability to speak.[24] Preverbal infants are unable to "encode" the abuse memory as words. Then as adults the victims recall the abuse only as images, often flashes, "blips," or as emotions or sensations. Evidence suggests that infants have a memory capacity from birth.[25] An example of recall coming in the form of sensations is my client who had trouble breathing and began gagging when another client was talking about sexual abuse. As time went on, he began to experience a sensation that he described as being "dirty, having something on my face." He reported that he was driven to try to wash his face off but that no amount of washing brought him relief. Later, he was, in some respects, relieved to learn from his mother and other family members that his father had a history of putting his penis in his children's mouths and ejaculating on their faces when they were infants. This helped him to understand why he would become enraged if his partner attempted to have oral sex with him. When confronted by the adult children, the father stated that it was obvious that they were making the whole thing up because infants couldn't remember what happened to them. But his wife reluctantly stated that she had seen him do it on several occasions; he then retorted, "The children were too young for it to have hurt them."

Since there is a stereotype that all males who were sexually abused as children become child molesters themselves, many nonoffending victims will not disclose that they were sexually abused. They fear that therapists will think of them as perverts, or will not believe that they have never abused any children, or will be required to report them to some agency. They also fear that they will be at risk for legal problems, having their children taken away, or losing their jobs.

When a boy is abused by another male significantly older but yet not legally an adult, the younger boy is seldom seen as having been victimized. People view this sexual contact as merely "playing doctor," or "inappropriate sex play," or as a sign that at least one of the boys is homosexual. The older boy's larger size, greater strength, and greater knowledge are ignored, and the two are mistakenly viewed as peers. When a teenage boy is sexual with a female youngster, it is more likely to be viewed as sexual abuse.[26]

The issue of sexual orientation can also cause a client not to be identified as a sexual abuse victim. In some cases an adult client who is homosexual will report that when he was a young boy an older male was sexual with him. The client often does not see this as sexual abuse—quite the opposite: he sees the man as "doing him a favor" by helping him "get in touch with his gayness." The client overlooks the power difference between himself and the older, experienced man and how he is being exploited. Since gay men are still not widely accepted and are in fact an oppressed minority, this topic is a highly charged political issue. When I seek to point out the abusiveness of the situation, the client may think that I am attacking homosexuality in general, rather than condeming the sexual abuse of children by adults. Being a member of an oppressed group does not give anyone license to abuse others.[27] Some gay men who seek to discuss their histories of sexual sexual abuse are told by both heterosexuals and other homosexuals that such abusive treatment is common in our society, implying that since it is common there are no real negative effects from it. They are told that sexual assault and childhood "seduction" are experiences that "go with the territory" and are part of "the price you pay for being different."[28]

People often wrongly assume that same-sex contact is the same thing as homosexuality. For example, Walters writes, "Many female children are approached for sexual gratification by adult males, and many male children are approached by adult male homosexuals. . . . Most approaches made by adults to boys are of a homosexual nature, while those made to girls are usually heterosexual."[29] Although it may appear that these men are homosexual because they are being sexual with someone of their own sex, it is important to remember that most men who sexually abuse children have a *hetero*sexual (other sex) orientation when it comes to adults. Many of these men who approach boys and are therefore labeled homosexual also approach girls. It is important not to confuse child molesting with sexual orientation, for this confusion leads to much of the homophobia (the fear of homosexuals) that is widespread in our society. Sexual abuse is more a power orientation than a sexual orientation.

When an adult male gives "gifts" or money to a female child with whom he is having sexual contact, most people can see that it is merely as a ploy to buy the girl's silence or to hide the abusive nature of the contact from the child, himself, and others. When the child is male, people have a more difficult time applying the same standard. The boy is often seen merely as a young homosexual, or worse, as a "hustler" who is using his youth to gain materially from an old homosexual.[30]

The Female Offender

Another reason why many men have difficulty identifying themselves as sexual abuse victims is that the offending adult in their cases was a woman.[31] Women who sexually abuse boys can be family members (aunts, older sisters, mothers, grandmothers), trusted non-kin (stepmothers, teachers, child care workers, physicians), or strangers. When the sexual contact is between mother and son, society traditionally sees the male as the one responsible. Take, for example, this Bible verse: "Cursed is the man who sleeps with his father's wife, for he dishonors his father's bed" (Deuteronomy 27:20). In more recent times, a case occurred involving a mother and a nineteen-year-old.[32] The son "compelled his mother to have intercourse with him and then threatened to kill her." He was treated for nine years and at first was seen three times a week, but he was never considered a highly motivated patient by the therapist and was diagnosed as having a borderline personality disorder. At no time in the published article does the therapist refer to the client as having been a sexual abuse victim. In fact, as a child the boy was beaten by his father and he witnessed his mother being beaten and strangled. She lost a pregnancy as a result of one of these assaults. The boy's parents had sex at night with their bedroom door open. The mother bathed with the boy, soaping his body as he sat between her legs. He reported "being sexually aroused by looking at her breasts and genitals." She would also sleep with the boy, and "he would caress her and become sexually aroused. When he touched her genitals she would 'awaken' and stop him." When the boy was high school age, his mother "regularly dressed and undressed in his presence." He began to masturbate to fantasies of his mother and to "speak openly of his sexual interests to his mother" who "reluctantly succumbed." For the next three years there was intercourse, up until he was arrested. The sexual contact often took place after the mother had been drinking, and she would "caress him while dressed in sheer 'shortie' nightgowns" and making statements such as "I bet you want to have intercourse with me. As long as you're going to have it anyway, you might as well go ahead and get it over with." This was not a pleasurable experience for the boy; instead, he "felt doomed to remain with his mother, as he felt helplessly trapped by his sexual preoccupation with her."

Another case with similar dynamics that clearly involves a boy, rather than a young man, is that of an eight-year-old boy who "sexually assaulted" his mother.[33] According to a study of the case, when he was seven years old, Bobby climbed into his mother's bed and began to squeeze her breasts. Five months later he fondled her and attempted to "insert his erect penis into her anus." At age six he "unsucessfully attempted sexual intercourse with an adolescent babysitter." In these examples, Bobby is presented as the offender. From the information in the published article, I draw a different conclusion. I do not see Bobby as the offender and his mother as the victim. I see the boy as having a long history of abuse and neglect. I believe that the baby-sitter was sexual with him, not he with her, and that his being "forced to perform fellatio" on a playmate was also sexual abuse. I think that Bobby's behavior is a logical result of the dynamics in his dysfunctional family: his "mother lost custody of her first two children because of neglect," and she "attempted suicide by overdosing after her husband learned of her sexual affair with her brother-in-law." In addition, Bobby's father had a "history of extramarital affairs" and a collection of pornography that was "accessible" to Bobby. I view this case study as an example of victim blaming. I think it demonstrates a lack of understanding of the dynamics of victimization.

Many of my clients were told by friends or family when they talked about a woman being sexual with them when they were boys that they ought to feel happy, because they were lucky to have had the opportunity to be sexual at such a young age. In addition to being told that they were fortunate to have had the opportunity to be sexual by the perpetrator(s) of the sexual abuse, friends, or family, these men also got this message from the media. Films often portray women being sexual with boys as harmless and glamorous. *Private Lessons* and *Homework* are two examples of this glamorization.[34] These films are rated R and are widely available on videotape, in the comedy section of video rental stores. The cover of *Private Lessons* shows an illustration of a boy standing on three schoolbooks in order to become tall enough to reach the lips of the adult maid who is entrusted with his care. Even more graphic is the cover for *Homework,* which reads, "Every young man needs a teacher. In *Homework,* Joan Collins proves the perfect teacher for young Tommy, but her classes are conducted after school and definitely do not include the three *R's*. But who's complaining? Not Tommy. Meanwhile, back in the schoolyard, Tommy's buddy Ralph has his own private tutor, Ms. Jackson, who teaches him those tricky French conjugations."

In both of these films, the women are significantly older than the boys and they are in positions of authority. Here again, sex is related to power differences. These films are *not* about young men having an opportunity to learn about sex with their peers. They are about women using their positions of power to abuse those in their care sexually. These films are widely available and are classified as comedies. They teach males who were abused that they should have enjoyed the sexual contact and that mistreatment of boys by women is humorous.

Since sex between women and boys is supposed to be glamorous, boys who do not enjoy it are likely to question their masculinity or sexual orientation. I often hear clients wonder if they are gay because they did not enjoy their first sexual contact with a female. It turns out that their discomfort was not due to their sexual orientation but rather to the exploitative nature of the experience.

When I first began working in a mental health clinic, I would contact child protection workers as required by law when I suspected child abuse in a family. After several cases I began to notice a disturbing pattern. When I reported a case that involved a girl or a boy being abused by an adult male, there was rapid and efficient action. However, when I reported a boy being abused by an adult female, very little was done; in many cases nothing was done. My clients saw the agency's lack of concern as a sign that what had been done to them was acceptable and that they had no business calling it abuse; this only added to the trauma they had experienced. In anger I began calling the agency, saying, "I have a case here where it appears that a twenty-three-year-old male is having intercourse with a thirteen-year-old female. Do you think a child abuse investigation is in order?" Only after I was told "Absolutely, this clearly is a case of abuse" would I say that I must have "misspoken," that I meant to say that it was a twenty-three-year-old *female* having sex with a thirteen-year-old *male*. I found then that my clients began to get better attention. Fortunately, people's awareness of male sexual abuse is increasing, and I no longer find this tactic necessary.[35]

One widely held myth about the sexual abuse of males is that it is not possible for a male, boy or man, to obtain or maintain an erection when threatened or attacked. For example, Walters writes, "A daughter may be physically receptive to the adult male (or at least capable of sexual relations), while the male must have an erection and maintain it [in order to have sex with a female]. Perhaps because of cultural bias and values, the male child would be guilt-ridden and unable to produce an erection."[36] Many people, including victims, falsely believe that an erection means enjoyment and willing participation. However, research shows that just as women who are being sexually assaulted sometimes lubricate and even are orgasmic, men who are forced to have humiliating and frightening sexual experiences can and do maintain erections.[37]

Boys are often viewed as "willing victims" when it comes to the topic of sexual abuse. Walters writes, "Adult women do seduce adolescent boys who are 'willing victims,' just as adult men seduce women who are 'willing victims.' If we were to label this behavior as sexual abuse, we would be on very shaky ground."[38] I disagree with him for two reasons. First, by definition one cannot willingly be a victim; the term is contradictory. Second, when an adult is sexual with a child it is not a peer relationship: there is a power difference that must be taken into account.

An example of how society tends to view boys as willing sexual partners for women is found in this "Dear Abby" column:

> Boy's early sex life disturbing to mother
> Dear Abby: When my son was 12 years old a 19-year-old college girl had sex with him. (She was a "sitter" we hired to stay at our house over a weekend when we went out of town.) When he was 14, a 27-year-old married woman had sex with him all summer. I didn't know about these experiences while they were going on. He is 16 now and he just told me about these sex experiences, and I was very much upset. Lately he has been spending a lot of time at the home of a 38-year-old divorced woman. He denies that there is any sex going on, but I don't believe him. I told his father, and he just said, "Boys will be boys; don't worry about it." I feel as though my son was molested even though he was a willing partner. Is my husband right? What is your opinion?—Upset Mother[39]

The mother appears confused when she writes, "I feel as though my son was molested even though he was a willing partner." The word *molest* means "to trouble, annoy, interfere with or meddle with so as to trouble or harm,"[40] yet the mother sees her son as willing. This seems like a contradiction. Abby treats this case as a legal and educational issue rather than a sexual abuse issue. She responds, "Even though your son was probably a willing partner, the women with whom he had sex are guilty of having sex with a minor, which is statutory rape." She concludes by saying, "A father-and-son talk is long overdue, but at this stage of the game it would be like giving a fish a bath." For me, this is an example of how sex role stereotypes work against males who have been sexually abused and make their recovery more difficult than it needs to be. I do not think Abby would have taken this situation so lightly if the letter had concerned a sixteen-year-old *girl* and a thirty-eight-year-old *man*. It is unfortunate that Abby did not use her influence to challenge the myths surrounding male sexual abuse.

Because of the stereotypes we have about gender and sexuality, female offenders are generally thought to be rare. As Sagarin wrote, "Mother-son relationships are probably the rarest of all true incest, to such an extent that anthropologists have been unable to uncover a single society in which they have been permitted."[41] He goes on to say, "There are almost no women child molesters; in fact, there is no instance that has come to my attention of a legal charge of such a nature." Female offenders do not fit the "dirty old man offering candy to the little girl" stereotype that society has of offenders, and therefore they do not get identified. Twenty years ago many treatment professionals thought there were very few women alcoholics because females did not show up in court records for driving-while-intoxicated charges or in detox units. However, it was later discovered that women who were stopped by police officers (who were usually male at that time) were not charged or put into detox but were taken home because it would have been "unladylike and too embarrassing for her" to be taken to the police station. In addition, fewer women worked outside the home and therefore could drink "on the job"; they would not then be fired as they might have been if they had been employed outside the house. Once treatment professionals broadened their criteria for identifying what constituted chemical abuse, many more women were able to receive help. Similarly, as more men are speaking up about their childhood abuse, the criteria for identifying what constitutes sexual abuse will be changed. It will become clear that although the style of female offenders is different from that of male offenders, it is just as damaging, and it happens with much greater frequency than is currently believed.

Society tends to view the sexual offenses of women as relatively insignificant. When 521 parents were asked about the seriousness of different types of sexual abuse, they rated adult female perpetrators' actions with both male and female victims as less abusive than those of adult male perpetrators with male or female victims.[42] In discussing the severity of the effects of sexual abuse Courtois wrote, "Abuse perpetrated by a male is believed to be more damaging than that by a woman."[43] These attitudes are important because they affect who gets identified and treated. As Finkelhor has written, "What people think is abusive may also affect how they react towards the participants. If people think having an encounter with an exhibitionist is extremely abusive they will react with more alarm when a child reports such an encounter, even if the child is not upset. If they think that a sexual encounter between a 12-year-old boy and a 27-year-old woman is not very abusive, they may laugh about it even though the child feels exploited."[44] The trauma of sexual abuse is only increased when it is compounded by prejudice and misunderstanding.

An example of the minimization of women's being sexual with boys appears in an article titled "Children Not Severely Damaged by Incest with a Parent."[45] The authors report on two children who were in incestuous relationships with a parent. One case was that of father-daughter incest, and other mother-son. The boy was thirteen years old. The contact involved his performing oral sex and sucking on his mother's breasts as well as intercourse. Although both children are described as having "prolonged sexual contact with the parent without being at least manifestly seriously disturbed emotionally" and as "relatively unaffected by the incest," the authors go on to report that the boy was aggressive, stole, set a fire, broke windows, ran away, and exhibited himself to younger boys. The boy also experienced an ongoing fear that "something awful might happen to him," that "terrible things happen" to innocent bystanders, and that "each day brought with it the possibility of calamity." My impression is that as a child he was seriously affected by the sexual contact and that additional symptoms will become apparent when he becomes an adult.[46]

It is estimated that women make up 5 percent of the perpetrators in all cases of abuse of girls and 20 percent in the abuse of boys.[47] Even when female perpetrators are identified, society has difficulty holding them responsible for their actions. Finkelhor has written, "When women appear as abusers, it is most often as accomplices to men, not as abusers themselves. It is rather infrequent for women on their own to turn to children for direct sexual gratification."[48] Ruth Mathews has found in her work that females who are coerced by a male into sexually abusing children usually have a history of being physically abused by that male adult.[49] They are also extremely dependent, socially isolated, and they have a very low sense of self-worth.

Because of the belief that women merely abuse children because they are forced to by males, treatment providers, when faced with a family in which both parents have sexually abused a child, will often view both the child and the woman as victims of the male. The woman's offender mentality and behavior will go unchallenged and untreated. Not asking female clients about their possible of-fending behaviors in their past or ignoring the existence of female offenders is a disservice to them and to the society. The more abu-sers who get treatment, the fewer victims we will have in the future, and the healthier our society will be.

When women are identified as the sole abuser, the behavior is explained in terms of gross pathology.[50] For example, as Judith Lewis Herman wrote, "Apparently the taboo against mother-son incest is breached only in bizarre circumstances."[51] On the other hand, men who abuse children are often referred to as "normal in all aspects other than having been sexual with a child," as if it were normal for men to abuse children. One researcher offered an ex-planation for why women abusers may be underidentified and viewed too often as extremely disturbed:

> ✘ The socially accepted physical intimacy between a mother and her child may serve to mask incidents of sexual exploitation and abuse on the part of a mother. It may be that only sexually abusive moth-ers who are handicapped by serious mental illness or intellectual deficiency are detected since, by reason of their psychological im-pairment, they lack the skills to conceal successfully this behavior.
>
> In the limited contact we have had with cases of mother-child incest, the same dynamics and motivations found in regard to the incestuous father are evident in regard to the incestuous mother.[52]

Thus, in the same way that people used to think that mastur-bation caused mental retardation and mental illness because the only people who publicly masturbated were those in insane asy-lums, we have a skewed view of women who abuse children. I believe that as we become more open to the idea that women can and do abuse children, we will begin to ask more questions and discover more cases and learn, as some researchers have suggested, that women who abuse are very similar to men who abuse.

Mathews has also identified several types of female offenders apart from those who are accomplices with male abusers.[53] She describes the "experimenter/exploiter." This category is made up usually of adolescent females who sexually experiment with a much younger child. The abuse is frequently of short duration and takes place in baby-sitting situations. The second type is called the "pre-disposed offender" and is made up of adolescents and adults who have themselves been sexually abused. The abuse tends to last much longer and is highly ritualized. The third category Mathews calls the "teacher/lover," and it is made up of adults who think of their abusive behavior with a young teenage boy as a "love affair." Mathews's last type of female offender is the "psychologically disturbed." These women have severe psychological disorders and commit violent abuse when in an unstable condition, often in the company of other adults.

Mathews is not alone in identifying female offenders. Sarrel and Masters identified three categories of boyhood sexual abuse by females:

1. Forced assault: sexual approach marked by the use of physical restraints or believable threats of physical violence, or both

2. "Baby-sitter" abuse: the seduction of a young boy by an older woman or girl who is not a relative which may involve direct or implied threats if the incident is reported to parents (if the victim were female, this would constitute statutory rape)

3. Incestuous abuse: sexual seduction of a male minor by a female relative[54]

The thought of an adult violating a child is repulsive to most of us, and therefore child abusers are often thought of as monsters or less than human. This stereotype/bias makes it very difficult for many people to think of women, particularly mothers, as sexual perpetrators. Many people like to view the mother-child relationship as pure, sacred, and immune to the possibility of abuse. Therefore, when sexual contact takes place between a mother and son, the boy is very likely to see himself as the offender. As Nasjleti has written, Boys often fear that having sex with the mother is indicative of their having a mental illness. Because mothers are viewed as nonsexual beings in this culture, incapable of sexually abusing their own children, boys molested by their mothers often assume responsibility for their own molestation."[55]

Ignoring, denying, rationalizing, and minimizing will not protect the children in American society. Once we are open to the fact that adults, both female and male, are sexually abusing large numbers of children every year, we will be better able to provide comfort and treatment to the victims and offenders who so desperately need it. We can never significantly modify the way some men view and treat women as long as we ignore the way some women treat boys. Likewise, we can not expect to have a society of gentle men who turn to other men for support and nurturance as long as we tolerate men abusing and neglecting boys.[56]

Questions to help identify your thoughts and emotions:

If you (your loved one) were (was) abused by a man, how did this affect your view of your (your loved one's) manhood? How did it affect your view of homosexuality?

If you (your loved one) were (was) abused by a female, using Mathew's categories what type of offender was she?

What effect did experiencing abuse from a female offender have on your view of your (your loved one's) sexual abuse?

When you first told someone about your (your loved one's) sexual abuse, how did that person respond to the information that the offender was female? What impact did that person's reaction have on your view of the abuse?

3

Factors Affecting the Impact of Childhood Sexual Abuse

T HE effects of childhood sexual abuse are frequently lifelong and severe.[1] The effects of sexual abuse are so profound not only because sexuality is so personal but also because there is more than a sexual aspect to the abuse. Sexual abuse is also physical, mental, emotional, and spiritual abuse. It affects all areas of life. In addition, sexual abuse is not naturally occurring or accidental.[2] It is the result of purposeful human behavior. It is not something that *happens to you,* like getting struck by lightening; it is something that is *done to you,* by someone, on purpose. Although the offender may not have intended to hurt you, he or she did intend to be sexual with you and thereby did you harm.

Many authors have pointed out that several factors influence how powerfully the victimized person will be negatively affected.[3] Naturally, each person is unique and will react to his victimization in his own way, based on the personality and personal resources he had prior to the onset of the abuse. The following factors, however, will influence an individual's response:

How coercive, threatening, intrusive, deviant, and violent the abuse was

The age at which the abuse began

How long it lasted

How frequent it was

How many adults took part in the abuse

What the child's relationship with the offending adult(s) was

How adults (other than the abuser or abusers) in the victim's life responded to the abuse

How Coercive, Threatening, Intrusive, and Violent the Abuse Was

Violent or life-threatening sexual assault tends to be more traumatic than abuse in which tricks or coercion is used.[4] Sixty percent of the sexually abused children in one study had been threatened or had force used on them.[5] In addition, the more intrusive an act, the more disruptive it is. For example, being exposed to is usually less upsetting than being touched, which in turn is less intrusive than being penetrated anally or orally. The use of bondage or other physical restraint also adds to the trauma. In most cases the more deviant the sexual act, the greater the negative impact. A child who is publicly sexually abused as part of a ritual that includes animal sacrifice and the drinking of blood is likely to suffer greater effects than one who is sexually abused without the ritual and violence.

The Age at Which the Abuse Began

In the cases I have worked on I have found that the earlier the abuse takes place in a person's life the more severe is its impact. Incest between mothers and their sons that involves intercourse usually occurs between ages 10 and 18.[6] However, studies report that 41 percent of sexual abuse starts before age 6.[7] Unfortunately, reports of sexual abuse to even younger children, age 2 and under, are not unusual.[8] One study that looked at the emergency room records of boys admitted due to sexual abuse found that their ages ranged from 3 years to 16 years, with an average age of 9.7 years.[9] Another study of a similar group of boys found boys as young as six months being admitted for medical treatment as the result of sexual abuse.[10]

Some people romanticize the sexual abuse of boys, particularly when the offender is a female. The widely accepted myth is that a young man falls in love with an older woman who gently assists him into manhood. However, table 3A–1 (see the chapter appendix) shows the ages of children who were victims of actual or attempted sexual abuse. As you can see, the majority of the abuse (81 percent) took place against prepubescent children, which shows that sexual abuse is more a power dynamic than a sexual encounter. Finkelhor reports that the greater the age difference between the victim and the offender, the more negative the experience. When one looks at the abuse perpetrated by parents, it is again clear that for both female and male offenders their victims are children, not young adults capable of free choice. The median (most common) age of the child involved in father-son sexual abuse is approximately nine. The median age of the child involved in mother-son incest is even younger, at approximately seven years.[11]

When a child is sexually abused at an early age, it tends to set him up to be vulnerable to repeated abuse from others, both within and outside the family. Many victims of childhood abuse report long histories of sexual harassment and unwanted sexual advances by teachers, employers, and other authority figures.[12]

How Long the Abuse Lasted

The more prolonged the abuse history, the more profound the effect. This is because the more frequently a child is subjected to sexual abuse, the more stages of development that can be interfered with. Russell found in her study that the average duration for abuse among the female child sexual abuse victims she studied was four years.[13]

How Frequently the Abuse Took Place

Even one episode of sexual abuse can be very damaging, but the more frequent the abuse, the more impact it has. People whose abuse pattern was one of many incidents of abuse spaced closely together never had time to stabilize between each occurrence. In her study of female child sexual abuse victims, Russell found that in 48 percent of her cases the child had been abused between two and twenty times, while in 10 percent of the cases the abuse had taken place more than twenty times.[14] I have worked with men who were abused on a daily basis, at least once a day, for the entire time they lived in their parents' home. This means that they were abused literally hundreds of times.

How Many Adults Took Part in the Abuse

The greater the number of adults who take part in the actual abuse, the more likely the child is to form a view of the world as inhabited only by dangerous people.[15] The more offenders, the greater the child's sense of powerlessness and the fewer places he has to turn to for help and protection. If the abuse is restricted to only one or even a few adults, the child has more of an opportunity to believe that safe adults exist.

What the Child's Relationship with the Offending Adult(s) Was

The more closely related the abuser was to the child, the more upsetting the abuse.[16] This factor, as with the others, can be conceived of as a continuum. At one end of the continuum are people completely unknown to the child. Next along the continuum are people known only because of their proximity to the child's home: people known to be neighbors but without even a casual relationship. Next are people known through casual or business relationships, such as mail carriers or neighborhood merchants, people whose names may or may not be known but polite interaction takes place. These people are followed by people from trusted groups, such as church members or distant relatives. Then come trusted care givers, such as scoutmasters, clergy, teachers, babysitters, and closer relatives. At the extreme end of the continuum are close kin, such as grandparents, siblings, aunts, uncles, stepparents, and parents themselves.

One of the commonly held myths about sexual abuse is that it is perpetrated by strangers who lure children away from school playgrounds by offering them candy. Although child molesting by strangers does occur, the majority of sexual offenses toward children are committed by someone the child knows and trusts. Summit puts it this way: "A child is three times more likely to be molested by a recognized, trusted adult than by a stranger."[17] Nevertheless, despite evidence to the contrary, many people hold on to the idea that strangers are responsible for sexual abuse. I once saw an ad in a newspaper which was placed by a group of people who were seeking passage of a law that would require the death penalty for anyone convicted of child molesting. I thought such a law would put children in a very difficult position. Since most child abuse takes place within the family, the child would be forced to remain silent about the abuse, for speaking up about it would lead to their parent or stepparent being put to death. It seemed to me that the law would not have any effect on reducing the frequency of sexual abuse, merely on the reporting of it and therefore on the treatment of adults and victims.

Table 3A–2 (see chapter appendix) shows that for both males and females, strangers are much less likely to be the assailant than are parents or other family members. These figures are particularly powerful when you take into consideration how much more difficult it is for a child to accuse a family member of sexual abuse than it is to accuse an outsider; consequently, these figures are probably low. Often there are multiple offenders in a family. Meiselman reported that approximately a third of the people in her study were being sexually abused by more than one family member or knew that other members were also being abused.[18]

How Adults, Other Than the Abuser(s), Respond to the Abuse

The most significant factor in determining how powerfully a child will be affected by abuse is how he is treated by those around him following the abuse experience. Those children who are fortunate enough to have supportive people available to them will have less difficulty than will those who are left to their own resources. However, many children are neglected by the adults around them who, for various reasons, do not notice the abuse or do not take any action to stop it. Symonds termed this lack of response the "second injury" to the victim.[19] Some parents and other care providers will ignore clues that point to a child's being victimized, such as the following: blood in the child's underwear, extreme loss of appetite, great difficulty sleeping or recurrent nightmares, children who scream, cry, and beg not to be left with a certain relative or baby-sitter, unusual awareness of sexual matters, publicly masturbating, sudden changes in eating, clinging behavior, self-destructive acts, aggression/violence toward others, attempts to initiate sexual contact with adults, hypervigilance, drawing pictures of sexual acts or of people with detailed genitals, depression, high anxiety, restricted emotions, suicidal gestures, profound change in school performance, radical loss of interest in previously enjoyed activities, truancy, vandalism, running away, "booby-trapping" or putting barriers in front of the bedroom door, use of protective rituals prior to going to bed, wearing many layers of clothes to bed, sleeping with bats, knives, or other weapons, bed-wetting after being toilet trained, being very still or having a rigid posture while being dressed or undressed, sleeping or hiding in protected areas such as under beds or in closets, sleep walking, and expressions related to being physically deformed or damaged.[20]

For many reasons, victims have a difficult time verbally telling others about the abuse. To begin with, children have a limited vocabulary—they may not have words for the events and emotions they are experiencing. Even if the child can describe what is happening, he may be afraid to tell anyone because he has been warned, overtly or covertly, to keep silent. The abuser may threaten to end the relationship or commit suicide, which, if the abuser is a parent, is a fairly significant threat. Other threats include: withholding privileges, break-up of the family, leading to the child's being sent to an orphanage and to family poverty, public humiliation for the child or the adult, the abuser or the child being sent to jail or a mental hospital, destruction of the child's personal property or pet, and mutilation or death of the child's loved ones or the child himself.[21] I worked with one man who as a child was forced to watch his father beat to death not one but several of the child's dogs when the child attempted to tell someone outside the family of the incest.

In fear for his own life the child wisely chose to remain silent until he was an adult and had moved to another state.

Threats that sound unbelievable to an adult sound very plausible to children. Because of the adult's greater size and knowledge, he or she appears godlike or superhuman to the child. For example, one offender told his victims that he had paid people in blue cars to drive past their houses to ensure that the children were "keeping our game secret," and that if the children weren't being good the people in the blue cars would bomb their houses and kill the children's families. Naturally, by chance someone in a blue car did eventually drive past every one of the children's houses, making it appear to the children that the offender could indeed kill their families. Adults who were threatened in this manner as children often mentally "beat up" on themselves for "believing such nonsense," forgetting that a child's mind and an adult's mind are very different.

If the offender is a family member or someone else who has easy access to the child, that child has a great deal to lose if he discloses the abuse. If he is ignored and nothing is done, his action will anger the abuser(s) and put him at risk for greater abuse. Physical abuse is often present in sexually abusive families.[22] So the child is in a double bind: if he protests the sexual abuse, there is likely to be an increase in the physical abuse. In many cases the sexual abuse is the lesser of two evils. Physical abuse was present in 32 percent of the cases of father-son incest and in 50 percent of the mother-son cases.[23] Awad reported on a child who told his mother he was being sexually abused by his father, but she did not believe him because she thought he was just trying to retaliate for the beatings his father had been giving him.[24]

Some offenders make an overt or covert agreement with their victims that if the child cooperates the offender will not abuse other children in the family. The child then keeps quiet in order to protect the other children. Unfortunately the offender(s) may have this same agreement with several children in the family. I worked with one family in which each of the five children thought that he or she was the only one being abused.

Offenders talk to their victims in terms of what *"we* are doing" rather than of what *"I* am doing." The child sees himself as an accomplice in the act, rather than as a victim. If a child has accepted a bribe or favor, the offender(s) can hold this over him to ensure continued silence. It is common to hear a victim state, "I didn't tell anyone because I was afraid I would get punished."

Another reason why children do not report sexual abuse is that it may be the only attention they are getting.[25] The attention the adult is showing the child may seem worth the cost of being used sexually. The child may find the physical sensations pleasurable as well. However, this physical pleasure does not eliminate the abusive nature of the contact, and in fact may make it more abusive because the child is more likely to feel guilty and responsible later on when he learns that sexual contact is not acceptable between children and adults.

Some children don't report sexual abuse because they don't realize there is anything worthy of reporting.[26] If most of the neighborhood kids are being treated the same way, particularly if there is no violence associated with the sexual contact, or other family members are being sexual with one another, then there doesn't seem to be anything abnormal going on.

Even when children are able to verbalize what is going on, some adults will accuse them of making it up, exaggerating, or seeking revenge, or they will say it was a dream or something the children saw on television. Often the focus of the adults' response to the child's disclosure will not be on what the offender did wrong but on what the child was doing wrong: "Why was he in that place? Why did he wait so long to tell? What did he do to invite the sexual contact?" Courtois reports that nearly half of all incest victims attempted to disclose the abuse and were met with disapproving responses.[27] Regardless of whether the disclosure is made to family members or to strangers, the result is often the same: the adult does not respond in a helpful way. If the child tells a family member and is ignored, what is the use of going to a stranger? If the child does tell a nonfamily member and this adult won't accept what the child is saying, what hope does the child have?

People who disclose sexual abuse are often placed in a catch-22, or double bind. If the victim has shown no overt negative effects, the disclosure will be discounted: "If it did happen, it doesn't seem to have caused you any problems. Why worry about it now?" On the other hand, if the victim has shown numerous effects following the abuse, particularly such symptoms as being defiant, running

away, vandalism, or sexual acting out, the disclosure will be discounted as an attempt to blame someone else for the negative behavior.[28] "Who are you to point the finger at someone else's behavior after all the trouble you have caused?"

It is more difficult for a victim, child or adult, to be believed when the offender is a well-respected member of the community, such as a teacher, coach, clergyperson, therapist, physician, or law enforcement professional. It is not unusual to read descriptions of men who molest children like this: "The offender was a forty-year-old successful salesman, a faithful husband, and a good provider."[29] This image helps to protect the adult, for the parent must be very strong and self-assured to stand by her or his child and publicly accuse a visible and potentially powerful adult member of the community. It is much easier for the parent to believe that the child is at fault or lying than to take on the task of confronting the offending adult.

A parent may wish to deny that any abuse took place because of guilt. When the sexual abuse is revealed, the parent realizes that the child has been showing signs that something was wrong which the parent overlooked or minimized. The parent may be aware of some way that he or she contributed to the abuse, such as repeatedly hiring a baby-sitter whom the child begged not to be left with. As Rogers and Terry have pointed out, parental denial can range from refusing to believe that anything took place, refusing to accept the details of the abuse, or refusing to think that the abuse had any impact on the child.[30]

With a history of generations of sexual abuse in a family, abuse can be the norm, and family members think, "That's what being a kid is. It happens to everybody. It's no big deal." In some cases, the parent wants to deny or ignore the abuse because the offender is a family member, perhaps his or her own parent, the child's grandparent. The parent was abused by the same offender as a child, and noticing the current abuse is too painful because of the memories and emotions it triggers. So, in order to suppress their own pain, these parents ignore the abuse of their children.

Some parents or guardians will not blame the child or will not deny that the abuse took place. Table 3A–3 in the chapter appendix shows the results of a study that reported the reactions of forty-eight parents who discovered that their child had been sexually

abused.[31] As you can see, the majority of the parents were angry, upset, and/or frightened, all of which are appropriate responses. Only a small percentage of the parents reported being annoyed with the child (10 percent) or thought the child was inventing the abuse story (4 percent).

However, in some families, although the abuse is talked about, no action is taken. The abuse is talked about once or twice and then no longer discussed. The adults' hope is that there was no negative impact or that the effects of the abuse will go away if the topic isn't mentioned again. The child is left with the message that his pain isn't important enough to do anything about and that therefore he as a person isn't important either. Another similar response is just to tell the child to avoid the abuser(s): "Everybody knows he is just a dirty old man. He can't hurt anyone. Just don't stay alone in a room with him anymore." The child is expected to cope with the abuse and the abuser alone, and the community's resources are not made available to him. Table 3A–4 in the appendix shows the reasons why twenty of the parents did not report the abuse. Half of them seemed to be more concerned about the abuser than their child. Half stated that they felt sorry for the abuser or did not want to get the abuser in trouble. Nearly half (45 percent) did not believe that the situation was serious. One might assume that the more serious the offense, the more likely a child is to report it to the parents. One researcher, however, found just the opposite, that the more serious the abuse, the *less* likely the child was to report it, because of fear of the parents' reaction.[32]

Adults may ignore the child's being abused for many of the same reasons that children keep quiet in the first place. Often, an offending parent or other abusive family member will threaten a dependent adult family member with divorce, violence, public humiliation, and loss of financial support if the sexual abuse is interfered with. I once worked with a family in which the father would withhold child support payments from the mother unless she left the children with him one night a month. He used this night to abuse them sexually. The mother knew what was happening but saw no choice, since she could not support her children on her income. In a society in which women have been dependent on men for social status and economic support, it is sad but not surprising that many women have had to choose between protecting

their children and protecting themselves. One hopes that as women gain more power and status in our society, fewer of them will be placed in this horrible situation.

When abuse within a family is uncovered, the family members will frequently continue to keep it a secret, to avoid embarrassment and possible legal consequences. The offender may agree to stop drinking or using other drugs, change jobs, get religion, move to a new town and "start a new life," recommit to the marriage, or simply promise that "it will never happen again."[33] In too many cases, superficial promises are made and the system continues as before, with perhaps a period during which there is no further abuse or the offender merely becomes more careful or the child is pressured into silence again. Offenders would have others believe that they made a one-time error, had a bit too much to drink, or will offer some other excuse. Unfortunately, this is seldom the case; in one survey child molesters admitted to an average of sixty-eight offenses.[34]

When sexual abuse is discovered in a family by an outside party, society usually responds to it as a legal problem rather than as a therapeutic issue. The offender obtains legal counsel rather than psychological counseling.[35] The child and the adult enter an adversarial arena in which the adult seeks to discredit the child. Frequently, no member of the family is provided with treatment. If the adult is found guilty, the result may be incarceration or some other punishment, and in most cases there will be no treatment, so the offender will be released from prison or jail and will reoffend. If the offender is given treatment, this is usually viewed as another form of punishment.

With all the possible consequences that a child can face as a result of disclosing sexual abuse, it is amazing that any child speaks up and no surprise that many who do, later deny or withdraw their earlier statements. Although this brings great relief to those around the child, it does nothing helpful for the child and only adds to the myth that child sexual abuse is merely in the imagination of children who carelessly accuse innocent adults. I am often asked if children lie about sexual abuse. My answer is, "Yes, children lie about sexual abuse in the same way adults lie about it. They all are dishonest about how often it happens, to whom, and how much it hurts."

Thinking about the Factors
as a Continuum

Using the factors I have discussed earlier as a guide for imagining a continuum, the sexual abuse pattern that would probably have the least negative impact on a victim's life would be this one: a single, nonviolent encounter at a later stage of childhood, with a complete stranger, combined with a family and a society that noticed that something undesirable had been done to the child, believed the victim, and provided him with support and guidance. At the other end of the continuum would be a pattern of ongoing, frequent, violent abuse that started at a young age and was perpetrated by numerous close family members, combined with a hostile attitude toward the child from society when he attempted to gain assistance.

Questions to help identify your thoughts and emotions:

At what age did your (or your loved one's) sexual abuse begin? You may want to get out old photographs of yourself at that age so you can see what you (he) looked like and what size you were (he was) then.

Who do you know who is currently that age (a niece, nephew, your own child, someone in a friend's family)?

How do you feel when you think about somebody that age being sexually mistreated in the ways you (or your loved one) were?

How long were you (or your loved one) sexually abused?

How frequent was the abuse?

How many people sexually abused you (your loved one)? Was the person (or persons) who abused you (your loved one) a stranger, friend of the family, baby-sitter, relative, parent, older sibling, teacher, or clergyperson?

What did you (your loved one) do to let people know that the abuse was taking place?

How did other people react to the sexual abuse? (Did they ignore it, deny it, accuse you of wrongdoing, make excuses, overlook clues, punish you, believe you, or protect you?)

Appendix

Table 3A–1
AGE OF CHILD AT THE TIME OF ABUSE OR ATTEMPTED ABUSE

Age in Years	Percent of Children
0–6	37
7–12	44
13–16	19

Source: David Finkelhor, *Child Sexual Abuse: New Theory and Research* (New York: Free Press, 1984). Reprinted with permission of The Free Press, a division of Macmillan, Inc., from *Child Sexual Abuse: New Theory and Research* by David Finkelhor. Copyright, 1984 by David Finkelhor.
Note: $N = 52$

Table 3A–2
GENDER OF ASSAILANT AND VICTIM IN CASES REPORTED TO THE SEXUAL ASSAULT PROGRAMS

Relationship	Female Assailant/ Male Victim	Male Assailant/ Male Victim
Parent	19	50
Stepparent	2	13
Other cohabitating adult	1	15
Sibling	4	23
Other relative	3	20
Authority figure	9	35
Friend/acquaintance	6	58
Stranger	0	12

Source: Minnesota Program for Victims of Sexual Assault, *Biennial Report: Fiscal Year 1985–1986* (St. Paul: Minnesota Department of Corrections, 1987).

Table 3A–3

PARENTS' REACTIONS TO DISCOVERY OF ACTUAL SEXUAL ABUSE

Reaction	Percent of Parents
Angry at perpetrator	90
Emotionally upset	88
Frightened	81
Guilt (felt bad for not protecting child)	77
Embarrassed that others might know	10
Annoyed with child	10
Thought child might be inventing story	4

Source: David Finkelhor, *Child Sexual Abuse: New Theory and Research* (New York: Free Press, 1984). Reprinted with permission of The Free Press, a division of Macmillan, Inc., from *Child Sexual Abuse: New Theory and Research* by David Finkelhor. Copyright, 1984 by David Finkelhor.

Note: $N = 48$

Table 3A–4

PARENTS' REASONS FOR NOT REPORTING SEXUAL ABUSE OF THEIR CHILD

Reason	Percent of Parents
Wanted to handle situation by self	90
No one else's business	75
Felt sorry for abuser	50
Did not wish to get abuser into trouble	50
Wished to forget incident	50
Didn't want neighbors and friends to find out	45
Incident was not serious	45
Child may have been at fault	15
Fear of retaliation by abuser	15
Police or social workers might frighten child	15
Agencies rarely do anything	11

Source: David Finkelhor, *Child Sexual Abuse: New Theory and Research* (New York: Free Press, 1984). Reprinted with permission of The Free Press, a division of Macmillan, Inc., from *Child Sexual Abuse: New Theory and Research* by David Finkelhor. Copyright, 1984 by David Finkelhor.

Note: $N = 20$

4

Life Areas Affected by Childhood Sexual Abuse

✻ But the surest way of all to deny a child time and space to discover his capacity for self-love and self-admiration is to abuse him physically, sexually or emotionally.[1]

A S I have stated earlier, childhood sexual abuse is more than a sexual act—it affects all aspects of the victim's life. Although there is overlap among the different life areas, I will describe them separately so as to make the effects of abuse easier to understand. Some of the effects of sexual abuse do not become apparent until the victim is an adult and a major life event, such as a marriage or birth of a child, takes place. Therefore, a child who seemed unharmed by childhood abuse can develop crippling symptoms years later and can have a difficult time connecting his adulthood problems with his past.

The Physical Aspects

When someone is sexually assaulted, the physical nature of sexual abuse is clear. An assault can leave the person's body injured or maimed. Studies of emergency room records show that half the cases of sexual assault that involve boys are violent and that boys are more likely to be physically injured than are girls.[2] Other physical consequences of sexual abuse include gonorrhea, herpes, syphilis, pubic lice, scabies, AIDS, and tearing of the anal structures. In addition, the child may be injured by being beaten or held down. A sexual assault can kill a child. In New York City the primary cause of death for sexually abused infants and children is rectal hemorrhage.[3]

In addition to suffering the physical trauma, the victimized person may question his ability to defend himself and may not trust his body to function in times of crisis. He may question what it is about his body that "invited" the physical contact. He may begin to hate his body since it is a reminder of the humiliating experience. He may shut himself off from his body, seeing it as a hateful, ugly thing. He may dress in a manner that hides his body or that makes him unattractive. Some victims have a paradoxical view of their bodies: they view them as misshapen, ugly, or disgusting, yet possessing some power or ability that causes people to be driven to be sexual with them.[4] They see their bodies as both distasteful and dangerous. I worked with one client who assumed that at some point in the therapy we would eventually be sexual and was shocked to find that I had no intention of being sexual and was having no difficulty at all maintaining that boundary. He believed that he had driven his father and other male authority figures to be sexual with him and that the same thing would happen to me. He was somewhat disappointed to learn that he did not have the power he thought he possessed and yet relieved that he could have a nonsexual relationship with a man.

A victim may be labeled "accident prone," meaning that he does not pay attention to his body in relation to his surroundings and tends to bump into things or injure himself by walking in front of moving objects. In most cases he is not trying to injure himself; he is merely unaware of where his body is in respect to the rest of the world. (Some victims do purposely injure themselves, by cutting or burning their bodies. See the "Behavioral Aspects" section of this chapter.) As an adult, a victim often continues to mistreat his body by over- or undereating, smoking, or abusing drugs. Several of the authors of the personal recovery stories in this book mention their misuse of drugs and food.[5]

Many abuse victims don't trust their bodies because of the bizarre sensations they experience when they are having a profound dissociative response. Frequently a victimized person will report that he will "leave" his body or "check out" so that the abuse happens "only to my body and not to me."[6] Some of my clients reported that while the abuse was taking place they thought, "You can touch my body but you can't hurt *the real me*." Dissociative responses are very common in people who have experienced any kind of trauma. Dissociation is a method of coping with an experience that would otherwise be overwhelming; it is a process through which the person compartmentalizes various parts of his personality, emotions, or body, and sees them as separate from his "true" self.[7] Some common signs of dissociation are "freezing," getting tunnel vision, "spacing out," difficulty with concentration, forgetting what was recently said, staring at some detail in a room, and experiencing a sense of emotional numbness or unreality.[8] Other symptoms frequently reported include experiencing a sense of shrinking or of having various parts of one's body grow, tickle, burn, or seem as if they are unattached. These sensations are frightening and appear to be out of the individual's control, so he seems to be at war with his own body.[9] People who are in a dissociative state will make statements like these:

"If I were here I'd be really mad."

"I feel like my arms aren't connected to my body."

"If I were here my butt would really hurt."

"I feel like my mouth doesn't belong to me."

"My hands feel huge, bigger than the rest of my body."

"It seems like the real me is over to one side of my body."

Another factor that contributes to the victim's sense of his body as separate from himself or out of his control occurs when his body experiences erection, ejaculations, pleasure, or arousal during some aspect of the sexual contact.[10] Many times sexual abuse is not violent or assaultive, and the victim's body will respond with enjoyable sensations even though the victim's mind is confused, terrified, or horrified. Even if the sexual contact is assaultive or violent the victim may experience erection and even ejaculation. The victim may then wonder if he is abnormal, a pervert, or "kinky," equating his body's physical response with pleasure. He may have the sense that his body has betrayed him.[11] Offenders, victims, and society in general use erection, ejaculation, and orgasm as proof that the victims must have wanted or enjoyed the sexual contact, so no actual abuse took place and therefore no treatment is needed. However, even if the child enjoyed all aspects of the relationship, physical and emotional, abuse still took place. The child's pleasure is incidental, a by-product. The goal of the relationship was the gratification of the adult, regardless of the impact on or cost to the child.

The physical aspects of sexually abusive touch, whether violent or not, teach the victim that he is not in charge of his body, that others can and will touch him without his consent. I agree with other authors who believe that children are not in a position to give consent to any sexual contact with an adult.[12] This is because of the power structure that is inherent in a child/adult relationship. As one report put it, "A mature heterosexual love relationship is one in which two adults share a mutual passion and a mutual reliance. The strength of the relationship is directly proportional to the equity and balance of the reciprocal interrelationship. An incestuous relationship is essentially one that has mutually exclusive aims."[13] In other words, the relationship between a child and an adult is never a peer relationship. Children are dependent on adults for food, shelter, nuturance, attention, protection, and for modeling appropriate behavior. A child's definition and understanding of the world is based on what his family, particularly his parents, teach him by their words and actions. The adult always has more information and power. Therefore, the child is never in a position freely to give or withhold consent. He will do whatever necessary to maintain the relationship with the parent.[14] When Sandfort interviewed boys ages ten to sixteen who were in sexual relationships with adult male members of a pedophile support group, he stated that the sexual contact had no negative impact on the boys.[15] Yet he also reported that in at least one case it was difficult to interview the boy because he "had only a vague idea of sexuality as a concept." A child who does not understand the concept of an act can not give informed consent to take part in it. A child can only submit (comply, yield, surrender), he cannot consent (give approval, grant permission).

Children are uninformed about sexual matters and are taught that adults are authority figures to be obeyed. I once saw an associate of mine teaching her daughter this lesson. I drove the woman to her home after a business meeting, and she introduced me to her young daughter. The woman showed me around her farm and then, as I was about to leave, she told her daughter to give me a goodbye kiss. Both the daughter and I were uncomfortable with this since we had just met and really had no relationship. I was glad to hear the daughter protest and refuse to kiss me. The woman insisted, and I politely refused as well. The woman began to yell at her daughter, saying that she was embarrassing her and demanding that she kiss me. Right before my eyes I was seeing this girl being trained not to be in charge of her body.

For an adult it is sometimes hard to imagine how difficult it would be for a child to say no to an adult. Try kneeling on the floor, facing someone who is standing on a chair, and you will get some idea of how big adults look to children. Adults who wonder why a child doesn't question the appropriateness of the offender's desire for sex or "fight back more" are viewing the boy as a miniature adult, rather than as a child. Children are actively discouraged from questioning the directives of adults; those who do are called impolite, defiant, and disrespectful. It is unreasonable to expect that a young child will challenge an adult, particularly if that adult is a family member. Children are not taught to be suspicious of their family members. Remember, most sexual abuse is of very young children, not teenagers, and the offender is an adult known to the child. The responsibility for the relationship's appropriateness rests with the adult, not the child.[16] To focus on why children don't resist more or speak up sooner is to endorse a victim-blaming model of sexual abuse.

Questions to help identify your thoughts and emotions:

What do you think about your body?

How much do you trust it?

How do you (your loved one) treat your (his) body (drug use/misuse, proper food, exercise)?

In what ways were you (your loved one) taught that your (his) body is not your (his) own?

How does the issue of consent affect your ability to see yourself (your loved one) as having been victimized?

The Mental Aspects

Although 50 percent of the boys who are admitted to hospital emergency rooms because of sexual abuse do not demonstrate physical evidence of it, they are still "scarred" by the experience.[17] Many abuse victims will report that the actual physical sexual abuse was not the worst aspect of the experience; rather, it was carrying such a powerful secret that must be protected. In many ways this makes sense. The sexual touch only happens periodically and only in a limited number of situations, but the knowledge of the abuse is with the person at all times and everywhere he goes. He must bear the burden of deciding what, if anything, to do with the information he has, information that could lead to his being taken away from his family, causing an adult, perhaps even a parent, to go to prison, or leading to the break-up of the family. This is a great hardship on a young mind.

As the child's physical boundaries are being violated by the sexual touch, his mind is also being violated. As has already been discussed, the child begins to think of his body as something that others are in control of. In addition, the adults doing the abusing often tell the victim that what he thinks is happening is really not.[18] In some families, abuse is just ignored or denied. Anyone who brings the topic up will be told that he or she is crazy or that what he or she is saying never happened. Another method is to blame the victimized person by saying that he wanted the sexual contact and enjoyed it. A third method is to rename the abuse. Sometimes the person abusing will call the abuse a game and lead the victimized person to think that he is special because he "gets" to play. A common justification is that the adult is merely teaching the child about sex, not really abusing him. I once worked with a woman who was told by her father as he had sex with her, "I'm doing this so you will know what sex is and so you will know how to keep people from abusing you. I'm doing this because I'm your father and love you." The double message was very confusing for her: "How does being abused help me to keep others from abusing me?" She assumed that she must be stupid or crazy because she could not see the "logic" in her father's behavior. When she asked her sister about it, her sister said that the same thing had happened to her and that it did not make any sense to her either. When she asked her mother about it, she was told, "It's your father's duty to teach you about sex. I'm sure he wouldn't do anything to hurt you. You'll understand when you're older and thank him." Regardless of which technique is employed, the effect is the same: the child learns to distrust his or her view of reality.

Another reason a victim may not trust his memory of the abuse is because it may have taken place at night in the dark. In some cases the child is actually asleep when the sexual contact starts. Some children will lie still and act as if they are asleep, hoping the offender will leave. Others will cry out. Often the offender will then act as if the child was having a bad dream and he or she merely came in to wake the child.[19] The child goes to breakfast the next morning and has to face the person who, only hours before, was sexually abusing him or her and now acts as if nothing happened. The child will have a difficult time trusting his thoughts and memory. He will wonder whether what he thinks happened actually did, or was it only a dream?

Covert contact is particularly powerful in teaching the victimized person not to trust his thoughts and perceptions of the world. When the abuser is the child's parent, the situation is particularly disruptive since the person who taught the child about reality is now denying reality. Covert abuse is camouflaged. The person doing it is saying one thing is happening when in fact something else is taking place. For example, one client told me that when he was a boy his mother would always insist on washing him, even after he was old enough to do it himself. She would soap up her hand and then rub it all over his body, focusing for several minutes at a time on his penis. If he protested, she said, "I'm just making sure that you don't get any venereal diseases. You act like I enjoy doing this. I'm doing my duty as a mother. You're so ungrateful!" He was in a double bind; if he did not protest, he was pretending that what she was doing was acceptable; if he did protest, he was being "ungrateful" and "paranoid."

In an attempt to make sense out of the nonsense of a sexually abusive family, victims will make seemingly irrational connections between events. They develop many superstitions, just as early humans did, in an effort to explain and gain the appearance of control over the world around them. They develop rituals to protect themselves. For example, I knew a man who could sleep in a bed only if the foot of it was facing south. He had shared a bedroom with his brother when he was young. His uncle, who also lived in the house, periodically came into the room at night and sexually abused my client's brother. My client was never touched by his uncle, and as a child he decided that this was due to the placement of his bed. As an adult, he knew that his childhood explanation was not valid, yet he was unable to sleep in any bed that was not in the proper position. He traveled a great deal and went to great lengths to obtain a hotel room in which the bed was placed correctly. He was embarrassed about asking which direction the beds faced, but he did it anyway.

DISSOCIATION

In order to cope while the abuse is taking place, many victimized persons will dissociate. Unfortunately, the response of dissociating tends to continue into adulthood, and many people find themselves dissociating even in situations that are not abusive. This response keeps them emotionally distant and unable to achieve a high level of intimacy with others.[20] As adults, many victims continue to dissociate whenever they are exposed to something that reminds them of their childhood abuse or to anything that triggers a shame response, including intimacy. A mild form of dissociation or depersonalization is to refer to oneself in the third person, saying, for example, "A lot of guys would be angry about getting abused," rather than "I am angry about being abused"; or "You know it hurts to be abused," instead of "I know it hurts to be abused." Since many people, particularly men, have been taught to ignore their feelings, many of my clients think that this kind of lack of emotion is not unusual or that it is merely part of being a man.

Others think that their inability to concentrate because of dissociation means that they are stupid or "going crazy." Ironically, the dissociation response that is so common in trauma victims and is misinterpreted as a symptom of insanity can be embraced by survivors as a sign of their sanity and evidence that the abuse took place. Instead of viewing the dissociation as an enemy, one can view it as an ally, validating that the abuse took place. In sessions when my client dissociates, it triggers a dissociation response in me, and I will then ask my client, "Where did you just go?" Usually he had been dissociated. I have found that once my client is educated on what dissociation is he will begin to notice when it happens and learn from it. Having a name for the experience is comforting for many people.

There is a diagnostic category for people with persistent severe dissociative responses: the depersonalization disorder. The *Diagnostic and Statistical Manual of Mental Disorders* describes it in this way: "An alteration in the perception or experience of the self in which the usual sense of one's own reality is temporarily lost or changed. This is manifested by feelings of detachment from and of being an outside observer of one's mental processes or body, or feeling like an automaton or as if in a dream. Various types of sensory anesthesia and a sensation of not being in complete control of one's actions, including speech, are often present."[21]

To overcome the tendency to dissociate or "space out" while reading about sexual abuse, several of my clients found it helpful, although painful, to read aloud alone or with a trusted person. The sound of their own voices kept them present and aware of their emotions.

Since there is a likelihood that the victim was in a dissociative state during the time of the abuse and shortly after, a dreamlike quality or a sense of unreality is attached to any memories that he has of it. This quality makes the memory hard to trust. In addition, many of the memories are only in "blips," flashes of memory, or are recalled from impossible vantage points, such as seeing one's self hovering at ceiling level. Many victims have large blocks of time in their childhood that they cannot recall, or they will have difficulty remembering what just took place when they are under stress. Frequently victims report having sudden and intrusive thoughts of being violent or of sexually abusing a passerby or loved ones, including their children. Often these thoughts seem to come from outside one's true self and are accompanied by a fear of loss of control. All of these experiences combine to convince the victim that his mind is somehow faulty and not to be trusted. Many victims report that they had no conscious memory of the abuse until suddenly a word, a smell, a place, a bodily sensation or position triggered something and a flood of memories came back. Since the person lacked any awareness of the abuse prior to this triggering experience, he has a very difficult time trusting these seemingly new memories (or are they fantasies, he wonders).[22]

Multiple personality is the most extreme example of a dissociative response. People with this condition have two or more distinct personalities within them that take full control of their behavior.[23] Research has shown that a majority of people with Multiple Personality Disorder (MPD) had a history of sexual abuse in their childhood.[24] MPD is common enough that one of the mutual-help groups, VOICES in Action, has a special interest group for people who have it as a result of having been sexually abused (see chapter 20). Saltman and Solomon identified these clues to MPD: a history of family members or friends saying the individual is acting "out of character" or "not like himself"; a reputation for lying or pretending; distinct and repeated changes in

Speaking, including rate, volume, and accent

Style of facial expressions

Beliefs, attitudes, or interests

Eating patterns

Dress style

Penmanship[25]

Questions to help you identify your thoughts and emotions:

As a child, what methods of dissociation did you use?

How were they helpful in coping with the abuse?

As an adult, what methods of dissociation do you (your loved one) use?

In what ways are they helpful? In what ways are they causing problems in your life?

THE VICTIM MENTALITY

One of the most crippling aspects of sexual abuse is the development of a victim mentality. Most people have been mistreated to one degree or another in their lives, but the experience of being mistreated alone does not cause someone to develop a victim's outlook on life. It is only when a person is abused and then left to cope with it on his own that the victim mentality begins to form. The abused child begins to organize his world around his wound. The victim mentality is a view of the self and the world. The world is seen not as safe and predictable, but as dangerous, unpredictable, and uncontrollable.[26] The victim has learned from being abused that what he does, wants, feels, or thinks makes no difference.[27] Even after the abuse stops, he continues to think of himself as ineffective, powerless, and worthless. Everything that happens is seen through the filter of his victim viewpoint. This view of the world becomes habitual and forms a belief, which prevents the victim from being aware of evidence that contradicts the belief. An example of this is the generalizing of the characteristic of the abuser(s) to everyone on the planet or to everyone of the gender of the abuser(s). Most of these victims' beliefs are self-defeating in adulthood. Thoughts such as "Men aren't to be trusted," "Anyone who shows any interest in a child is a molester," or "All women want to do is hurt me" lead to further isolation and prevent healing. If the abuser was a family member, the victim may believe that everyone in the world is like his abusive/neglectful family members. As one client commented, "If the people who are supposed to love me sexually exploit me, what would strangers do to me?"

A person with a victim mentality will constantly be asking "why" questions: "Why did this happen to me?" "Why didn't anyone stop it?" "Why didn't I tell someone?" Underneath all these questions is the belief that somehow the abuse is really the victim's fault and that he asked for it or deserved it. Combined with the "why" questions are endless "shoulds": "I should have punched him and run," "I should never have been in that room at that time," "I should have known this was going to happen," "I should have enjoyed it." The whys and shoulds combine to reinforce the mistaken belief that the child had a choice. By definition, however, victims don't have a choice; the abuse is something inflicted on them. People confuse submission with willingness.

Often those around the victim reinforce his belief that he is somehow responsible for the abuse. When he reveals the abuse, as a child or as an adult, he is likely to hear others ask the why questions and state the shoulds: "Why didn't you tell me sooner?" "You should have told someone," "Why did you go back to church if that was happening there?" "You should have realized what he was doing," "You should have done something about it before it got worse," "Why did you keep it a secret?"

Some researchers believe that most people have several basic assumptions, or beliefs about the world, that are challenged when they are victimized.[28] These assumptions basically are: I am invulnerable, I can't be or won't be hurt; I have worth; and the world is understandable and has meaning. The experience of victimization clearly demonstrates that the child is not safe, perhaps not even in his own home, forcing a rethinking of the first assumption. The second assumption must also be questioned, since what kind of sense does it make that worthwhile people are mistreated? This brings into play the third assumption: since the world is an orderly place that is based on logic, how does the boy make sense out of bad things happening to him? He must be a bad or worthless person. Once the victim determines that the abuse is a result of his badness, his world is a little less out of balance. What is happening makes sense after all. If the abuse is a result of his badness, then if he can just stop being bad, the abuse will stop. So the victim mentality begins as a defense mechanism in childhood.

As a way to cope with the abuse the child believes that he has a choice and therefore some power in the situation. I describe this situation this way to those of my clients who are resisting seeing their helplessness as children and are resisting letting go of their victim belief system: Imagine a small boy sitting watching TV. His parent walks in and without a word burns the boy's hand with a cigarette. The parent then returns to the kitchen as if nothing had happened. One way the child can understand this experience is to believe that it was his fault. Obviously, he has been bad and his parent is merely trying to help him. If he determines how he has been bad and corrects it, his parent will never be forced to burn him again. He is in control of whether he gets burned again or not. A second interpretation the boy may have is that he is the child of a rageful, violent parent, who, at any time, without warning, for no apparent reason, will burn him and that there is nothing he can do to stop it. The abuse has nothing to do with his behavior, he is merely the most convenient target; he is powerless. Which explanation is more comforting to the child? The first one. Which explanation is more accurate? The second. In sexual abuse there is a reversal of roles and identities. The offender will think of her- or himself as not having had a choice about what happened and will hold the child responsible for what did take place. He or she may even be angry at the child for "what he did." The child will think of himself as responsible for the abuse, that he should have stopped it, and will feel guilty and ashamed.

Society can reinforce the victim's self-blame in several ways. When sexual abuse is discovered in a family, the child is often removed from the household. Although this may be the best way to protect the boy from further abuse or from being pressured by family members to deny that abuse has taken place, he may view the situation as further proof that the abuse was his fault. The offender is not uprooted from her or his home, but the child is. It may appear to him that he is being punished and that therefore he must have done something wrong.

Another example of the reinforcement of the victim mentality can be seen in cases where child protection services or law enforcement personnel are alerted to the possibility that a girl may have been sexually abused by a family member. The investigators will interview the girl and her parents and may even remove the girl from the home. Unfortunately, in many cases the boys in the family will not be viewed as likely victims too. The investigators will fail to look for clues that the boys may also have been sexually victimized. Although the daughter may be protected and given treatment, the boys will be ignored. The boys will assume that the abuse they experienced is unimportant and that in fact they are unimportant.

Although the victim mentality begins as a useful childhood coping mechanism, when it continues into adulthood, it becomes obsolete. The victimized person has become an adult, with the choices and power of a man, but he continues to think of himself as little, helpless, and at fault for all the mistreatment he receives. He goes through his adult life training others to treat him poorly by being passive and not standing up for himself. He settles for what he can get and assumes that he is to blame for his mistreatment. Whatever misfortune befalls him he has learned to sit and take it, that complaining will only make it worse, and that to object is meaningless, just as it was when he was being abused. The abuse was a normal part of his childhood and nobody did anything to stop it, so he thinks that abuse is a normal, acceptable part of life. He may be harassed on the job and afraid of employers and other authority figures.

On the other hand, he may do just the opposite and become aggressive, treating others poorly before he can be hurt. He may view the world as being made up of victims and victimizers, and may decide that it is his turn to do some abusing. He may try to be perfect, thinking that is the way to avoid mistreatment and to gain attention. Unfortunately, nothing he does will be good enough for himself, so he won't enjoy his accomplishments. Since he lacked control over himself as a child, he may become obsessed with control as an adult. He will be preoccupied with attempting to control himself and others, while fearing that he will suddenly lose control.[29]

Often, when a person seeks out therapy for the symptoms resulting from childhood sexual abuse, the professional views his victim mentality as a symptom of a personality disorder. The professional may correctly identify the pattern, so the diagnosis fits, but it does not address the reasons for it. The sexual abuse never gets addressed, and the client's victim mentality remains unchanged.

There are several diagnostic categories that child sexual abuse may predispose someone to:[30]

Histrionic Personality Disorder: Constantly seeks reassurance or approval, is inappropriately seductive, preoccupied with appearance, shows exaggerated emotional expression and/or shallow expression of emotions, constantly seeks to be the center of attention, and has no tolerance for frustration.

Borderline Personality Disorder: Impulsiveness in a manner that is self-damaging in life areas such as sex, spending, drug use, shopping; a pattern of unstable and intense interpersonal relationships; inappropriate intense anger or lack of control of temper; identity disturbances, with uncertainty about self-image, gender identity, goals, and so on; marked shifts in mood, from normal to depressed to irritable; intolerance of being alone; self-mutilation or suicide attempts; and a chronic sense of emptiness.

Avoidant Personality Disorder: Easily hurt when criticized; few friends or one close friend; does not get involved with others without certainty of being accepted; avoids situations where embarrassment or appearing foolish might be possible; exaggerates the dangers in everyday tasks or situations.

Dependent Personality Disorder: Inability to make routine decisions without excessive reassurance; lets others make major decisions for him; agrees to do distasteful tasks and agrees with people in order not to be rejected; uncomfortable being alone or avoids being alone; preoccupied with abandonment; easily hurt by disapproval.[31]

The diagnostic categories I most often use when treating sexual abuse victims are these:

Dysthymia: A chronic depressed mood for most of the last two years, including over- or undereating, difficulty sleeping or oversleeping, low energy, poor sense of self-worth, difficulty concentrating or making choices, and a sense of hopelessness.[32] Herman found in the victims she studied that 60 percent had symptoms of major depression, which is even more severe than dysthymia.[33]

Post-traumatic Stress Disorder: Recurrent, intrusive, and distressing thoughts or dreams of the abuse; flashbacks; intense distress when in the presence of situations that remind the victim of the abuse; efforts to avoid thoughts, feelings, or situations similar to those associated with the abuse; inability to recall important aspects of the abusive events; a sense of detachment from others; restricted expression of emotions; sleep disturbances; outbursts; exaggerated startle response; and overly vigilant for signs of danger.[34]

In order to change your victim mentality, you must first become aware of it. You may find that this way of thinking is so habitual that you are unable to notice when you are thinking in a victim manner. Talk with others who understand the victim mentality and encourage them to point out examples of the victim mentality at work in your life.

Questions to help you identify your thoughts and emotions:

As you read about the victim mentality, how did you feel?

As a child, how did your victim view of the world help you to cope?

Complete the following sentences with the first thing that comes into your awareness:

The world is . . .

Men are . . .

Men never . . .

Men always . . .

Women are . . .

Women never . . .

Women always . . .

Because of my past . . .

If only . . .

I always . . .

I never . . .

My thoughts . . .

My body . . .

My emotions . . .

Look over your responses. What do they tell you about yourself and your view of the world?

Are there aspects of the way you think and view the world that you dislike? If so, what changes would you like to make?

Give some examples of your (your loved one's) victim beliefs.

How has your (your loved one's) victim view of the world negatively affected you?

THE OFFENDER MENTALITY

While the victim mentality is one of self-blame, the offender mentality is one of other-blame. This is the mentality that leads people to say such things as "The child seduced me. I couldn't help myself." As you can see, the victim and offender mentalities fit well together. The victim blames himself for the abuse, and the offender agrees with that explanation. If the offender does not blame other people for the abuse, he or she may blame circumstances for it. For example, some parents will cite overcrowding as the reason they have a child sleep with them.[35] However, one researcher found that in most cases where children were "forced" to sleep with a parent and ended up being sexually abused, there were other alternatives available and space limitation was merely an excuse to justify the behavior.[36]

A person with an offender mentality can continue to abuse others and not be overwhelmed with guilt. Without guilt, however, there will not be remorse and emotional pain, so there will be no internal motivation to stop the abusive behavior. When confronted, offenders deny that the abuse took place and say that even if it did take place the other person was at fault. This is one reason why it is so important to determine carefully if and when it is therapeutically correct for a victimized person to confront his abuser(s). If the victimized person is relying on the offender(s) to validate that the abuse happened and to take responsibility for it, he is setting himself up for disappointment.

Someone with an offender mentality will often paint her- or himself as the misunderstood victim of a "hung-up" society that won't tolerate her or his "broad-minded" approach to sex, which includes sex with children. He or she can usually find someone else who will agree with her or his views.

There are organizations and publications that promote adult/child sex and seek to eliminate all laws related to incest, child pornography, statutory rape, and age or consent. They see themselves as championing the rights of children to have sexual freedom. Although such people have existed in many societies, they are always a small minority.[37]

Many times people will explain incidents of sexual abuse by pointing out that the offending person had been using chemicals, such as alcohol, at the time of the abuse. The belief that alcohol causes sexual abuse is a useful one: the offending adult, her or his spouse, the court system, the victim, and in some cases the therapist can all believe that as long as the offending adult doesn't drink then everything is taken care of. In fact some offenders will purposely ingest alcohol prior to abusing a child as a way of excusing the behavior. I have worked with several clients who sexually abused their children while drinking. They were sent to chemical dependency (CD) treatment and told that if they stayed sober they would stop abusing their children. To some degree it was true. Each time they abused their children they got drunk or high first. Then they would go back to CD treatment, where their chemical use would be focused on and their sexual issues ignored. It was not until they got treatment for the sexual problems that they were able to stay sober and stop abusing their children.

Depending on the study, the rate of problem drinking or alcoholism in fathers who sexually abused their children is anywhere from 15 percent to 73 percent.[38] One study reported that nearly 25 percent of the imprisoned fathers drank a fifth or more per day or drank in a way that caused difficulties with employment.[39] The percentage of alcoholics decreased as the age of the child increased. This data does *not* mean that alcoholism causes sexual abuse to take place. The presence of drugs only makes it more likely that sexual abuse will take place because of the lowering of inhibitions and the lessening of impulse control.

There is no single cause of sexual abuse—this is a much more complex issue. Meiselman classified and described incestuous fathers in seven ways.[40]

1. *Endogamic* (68 percent of the total). These men were seen as heavily dependent on their families for emotional and sexual needs, and were unwilling or unable to satisfy sexual needs outside of the family, such as by having an affair or using prostitutes. This group was further broken down into two

subgroups: personality disorder and subcultural variety. The men in the personality disorder group were often shy and ineffectual in social relationships, had a tendency to think in a paranoid manner, were overcontrolling, preoccupied with sex, and often sexually involved with a prepubescent daughter. The subcultural variety were men from isolated rural areas that were semitolerant of incest and were moralistic.

2. *Psychopathic* (16 percent). These men tended to have criminal records and were generally sexually promiscuous, with little emotional attachment to their victims. *Psychopath* is a term that has become infrequently used. Generally speaking, it refers to a person with a personality disorder that causes them to behave in socially unacceptable ways, without having regrets or feeling guilt.[41]

3. *Psychotic* (5 percent). These men are described as having severe ego disorganization. When people are diagnosed as having a psychotic disorder, they commonly experience difficulty with reality testing, have delusions, hallucinations, and inappropriate moods.[42]

4. *Drunken* (5 percent). In these cases the incest took place when the father was "extremely intoxicated."

5. *Pedophilic*. These men were generally attracted to young children as sex partners and therefore may have lost interest when the child developed secondary sex characteristics. The American Psychiatric Association defines pedophilia as a sexual disorder, with the essential feature being "recurrent intense sexual urges and sexually arousing fantasies involving sexual activity with a prepubescent child (usually 13 years old or younger)."[43]

6. *Mentally defective*. This group is made up of men with such low intelligence that there was a reduction in ego controls.

7. *Situational* (5 percent). This category was used when the incest occurred only during times of high stress for the father.

Questions to help identify your thoughts and emotions:

How did the person or persons who abused you (your loved one) explain or justify what they were doing?

Using Meiselman's categories, what type of person(s) abused you (your loved one)?

The Emotional Aspects

I find that trusting emotions is more powerful than trusting thoughts when dealing with sexual abuse, for emotions will provide clarity even when thoughts are clouded and confused. Sexual abuse has an important emotional component, because the victimized person is often told what to feel or what not to feel. Once again he is taught not to trust the information that his body is giving him. He is often taught that he has no right to feel afraid or angry about what has been done to him. He has been victimized and cannot trust others—they have hurt him. He cannot trust himself—he has been told that his views are faulty. He has learned that the world is a dangerous place, and there is nobody to trust. His fear of others will make it difficult for him to open up and get support.

Some people respond to trauma by shutting down their awareness of their emotions. They frequently will believe that their emotions are bad and that they need to be in control of them at all times, or else they will be overwhelmed and may "go crazy" or become violent. This emotional numbness makes it very difficult for them to be intimate with others. This flattened affect is often misinterpreted as a sign that the child, and later the adult, was not negatively affected by the sexual contact. The lack of affect is not seen as a clear symptom of trauma; rather, it is seen as a sign of lack of trauma. As one client told me, "I must not have been hurt by it, I have never cried about it." But then he added, "In fact, I haven't cried about anything since it happened."

In order to be unaware of emotions one must become unaware of one's body. Some victims are so shut down and unaware of their bodies that when they are injured they don't notice it. They continue to take part in sports even after they have been injured and do not give their bodies time to mend and heal. Another response to abuse is to become hyperaware of one's emotions, preoccupied, or overwhelmed by them. The slightest disappointment is experienced as a tragedy, any new situation becomes terrifying, the most minor indiscretion is met with outrage.

FEAR

One emotion that abuse victims have difficulty with is fear. A milder form of fear is mistrust. Often, abused people will constantly question the motives of others. Since they have been mistreated in the past, they fear that everyone is somehow out to take advantage of them again. More extreme examples are recurring nightmares, fear of abusing one's own children, fear that they are going to be abused by others, and vague, unexplained fears that "something bad is going to happen." Sometimes abuse victims will develop rituals in order to try to prevent the impending disaster they fear. These rituals lead to obsessive thought patterns and compulsive behaviors. One client I worked with had a compulsive need to have the last word in a telephone conversation. She thought that this would somehow ensure her safety and the safety of the person she had been talking to. She had developed this behavior as a child and continued it into her adulthood. Since the sexual abuse often takes place in the child's bedroom, many sexually abused people have conditions that must be met for them to be able to sleep. Some will wear numerous layers of clothing in order to hide and protect their bodies. Others need the bedroom door locked to ensure that nobody can sneak in. Some want the door left open because their abuser used to come into their room at night, lock the door, and touch them.

For a child in a sexually abusive family there is much to fear. The fear of discovery is constant. Victims are afraid that they will be blamed for what happened (and they often are). They fear that they will be not only blamed but punished as well. Often the offending person threatens the victim with being beaten or killed if anyone learns about the abuse. If the secret of the abuse gets out to the community, the family members may be separated because of a divorce or because the offending family member is jailed. Another common fear of victims is of being kicked out of the family. Sometimes when abuse is discovered the victim is removed from the household, not the offending adult. To the child it appears that he is being removed from his home because he is at fault. Family members may reinforce this view of the situation by saying, "If you hadn't opened your mouth, none of this trouble would have happened."

As adults, sexual abuse victims carry with them many fears. Often they will have phobias, fear of authority figures, or fear that if they are near children they will be abusive or that someone will think they are going to be abusive. I knew a man from a sexually abusive family who refused to tuck his children into bed at night for fear that a neighbor might be able to see him through the childrens' bedroom window and would call the child protection services, thinking that he was in there being sexual with his children.

Some victims suffer from panic attacks during which they suddenly and unpredictably experience a severe sense of dread, accompanied by sweating, shaking, and a rapid, pounding heartbeat.[44] People with this condition have an extremely difficult time recovering from sexual abuse because they are so handicapped by the panic. Often the use of medication under the guidance of a psychiatrist is required to bring the panic down to a level where psychotherapy can be effective.

GUILT

Many sexual abuse victims have an inappropriately high level of guilt. They believe that they have done something wrong, when in fact it was they who were wronged. This excess guilt may show up in a tendency to be overly apologetic. Victimized persons often experience guilt about what they did or didn't do in order to cope with the abuse. For example, people who pretend to be asleep when the abuse is taking place may later tell themselves that they ought to have screamed or fought off the abusing person. Others report feeling guilty about liking the attention they were getting or enjoying some of the physical sensations during the physical contact. This guilt reinforces their belief that they were a consenting party to the sexual act and just as responsible as the adult. This self-blame is sometimes reinforced by clergy in giving absolution to sexual abuse victims. When the victim is assigned penance, he is being told that he is a sinner, rather than someone who was sinned against.

SHAME

Shame is a sense that one's personhood is damaged, inadequate, or worthless.[45] I view shame as the most powerful and damaging emotional effect of sexual abuse. The paradox is that the person who has been violated is the one who has a sense that there is something wrong with him. Sometimes the victimized person is told this directly ("You should be ashamed of yourself!"), but most of the time the message is covert. Since shame is related to a person's "self" and not merely to an experience, the shame becomes part of the victim's identity, and it follows him into adulthood affecting his view of himself and everything he does. He does not look on himself as someone who *had something horrible done to him* but rather as *someone horrible*. The shame becomes personalized so that it is a part of his identity. The experience of shame includes a sense of being transparent, that one's badness or worthlessness is visible or somehow apparent to others. Therefore, the victim often assumes that everyone somehow knows that he has been abused, is dirty, or is a "pervert."

Shame can inadvertently be reinforced by therapists. Consider, for example, the use of the word *confession* in this sentence from Meiselman: "The first issue, which has been raised several times in this book, is that of belief or disbelief of the patient's confession of incestuous experience."[46] The definition of *confess* is "to admit or acknowledge one's faults or crimes; own up to one's guilt."[47] One need not confess to being victimized; one only confesses when one has done wrong.

People with an excess of shame tend to have unrealistic expectations of themselves. They believe that they need to compensate for something, even if they don't know what it is; but they are sure something is basically wrong with them and with most of what they do. They think either that they can do nothing well or that they have to do everything perfectly—that they are the worst or the best. This is sometimes referred to as "victim grandiosity."[48] Highly ashamed people avoid eye contact with others and may even avoid mirrors so that they don't have to see themselves. They will often have a never-ending monologue in their heads about what useless or unacceptable people they are. They have difficulty accepting even constructive criticism since they hear it as a personal attack.

Shameful people frequently lash out in rage at those around them. Some become violent toward others, picking fistfights, hurting or torturing animals, or, in more socially acceptable ways, participating in violent sports such as boxing, rugby, or football. They attempt to hurt others as a way of coping with the intense emotional pain they are experiencing.

LONELINESS

People who have a great deal of shame will be very lonely, because they think of themselves as being unworthy and incapable of having intimate relationships. The isolation and self-hatred that many sexual abuse victims suffer lead many of them to become depressed and suicidal.

Often, sexual abuse victims have difficulty relating to other children because their worlds are so different. It is hard to be spontaneous and playful when one has been sexually abused the night before by one's own parent. This further adds to the victim's isolation.

ANGER

An abused person usually has a lot of anger. He commonly has three main targets for his anger: the person who abused him, the people who did not protect him from the abuse, and himself. He may have difficulty expressing this anger. The shame he feels will tell him that he doesn't deserve to be angry, that he wasn't entitled to better treatment. He may also confuse feeling angry with being abusive and may strive to be different from the person who abused him by "never getting angry." In some cases the only time a victim will allow himself to experience his anger is when he is hearing stories of someone else being abused or when fighting for a cause.

Questions to help identify your thoughts and emotions:

In what ways do you feel ashamed? How is this related to being sexually abused?

How were you treated by the person(s) who abused you if you showed your anger? Your hurt? Your fear?

In what ways are you afraid of people? What kind of trust issues do you have?

What emotional issues do you (your loved one) have as a result of being sexually abused?

The Behavioral Aspects

One particularly frightening behavioral effect of childhood sexual abuse is self-mutilation.[49] The victim will cut, burn, pick at, hit, bite, or scratch himself. Although the victim and those around him may attempt to explain the injuries as the result of accidents, the self-mutilation is deliberate. Several authors have offered explanations for self-mutilation,[50] suggesting it is:

An act of rage. The victim has intense anger and rage about the abuse but is in a position where he is unable to express it in a less self-defeating manner. Some victims will fantasize that they are inflicting on their abuser(s) what they are actually doing to their own bodies.

An act of self-punishment. The victim blames himself for the abuse and seeks to punish himself. As one client put it, "When I have been punished enough, the bad things will stop."

An act of punishment for the victim's body. This explanation is often given by victims who experience arousal or ejaculation during the sexual contact.

An attempt to make oneself unappealing. Victims who believe the sexual contact is a result of their appearance may attempt to disfigure themselves in order to stop the abuse.

A distraction from emotional pain. Focusing on the physical pain caused by the self-injury can serve to distract the victim from his emotional pain and from memories of the abuse.

A method of dissociation termination. Victims who are in a profound dissociative state following an episode of sexual abuse may bring themselves back to reality through the use of pain. As one client put it, "It is better to feel pain than to feel nothing at all."

A method of proving one's existence. The sense of unreality, emptiness, and depersonalization of a dissociative state can be so overwhelming that the victim seeks to assure himself of his existence by inflicting pain. In the words of one client, "I hurt, I bleed, therefore I am."

A sign of ownership of one's body. The victim's body is being treated like an object by the abuser(s). The victim reclaims his right to his body by the self-abuse. His self-inflicted injury is an act of defiance. One client explained it this way: "As I burned myself I thought, I will decide how much pain I am in, not you."

A sign of strength. The victim is in a helpless situation. The pain he inflicts is reassurance that he can withstand whatever is done to him. Put another way, "If I can stand what I am doing to myself, I can survive whatever they do to me."

A cry for help. The injury is a signal to others that there is something wrong in the victim's life. Since families with sexual abuse have power taboos against talking about the abuse, the wounds serve as a silent cry for assistance from those outside the family. Unfortunately, the self-mutilation is merely viewed as a sign that the victim is insane and not to be believed. If the victim ever does verbalize that sexual abuse is taking place, it is likely to be viewed as the delusion or lie of a mentally ill person. One client reported, "I carved the word *pain* in my arm with a razor blade and wore short-sleeved shirts to school and church. But everyone acted like it wasn't there."

Suicidal attempts are frequently made by sexual abuse victims.[51] Herman found that 38 percent of the victims in her study were so depressed that they had attempted suicide.[52] Briere and Runtz found that sexual abuse victims were twice as likely as nonabuse victims to attempt suicide.[53] The greater the number of abusers, the greater the inclination toward suicide. They also found that victims tended to think about killing themselves with greater frequency than did others.

I have had many clients talk about how, as they drove to and from work each day, they were thinking to themselves, "It sure would be easy just to steer into that oncoming traffic or drive into that tree. It would be all over. Everyone would think it was an accident. My family would get my insurance money. Everyone would be better off." Others have described having to struggle to keep from throwing themselves in front of trains.

Sometimes the suicidal acts are more covert. I worked with one client who would drive very fast without his seatbelt, hoping that he would go off the road or that his car would be struck and he would be killed. Whenever people commented on how his smoking three packs of cigarettes a day and being massively overweight was going to kill him, he would reply, "Let's hope so." Everyone responded as if he were joking.

If you have had suicidal thoughts, write them down. Killing yourself is agreeing that keeping the sexual abuse secret is more important than keeping yourself alive. It is the ultimate loyalty to the abuser and the ultimate in self-betrayal. Write down all the reasons you have decided to choose life and recovery. Ask someone who cares about you to write down the reasons they want you to remain living. Write an agreement with that person that for the next twenty-four hours you will not harm yourself. Renew this agreement tomorrow.

ADDICTIVE DISORDERS

It is not surprising considering all the pain victims experience that they often turn to alcohol and other drugs to medicate their emotions and to repress their memories. One researcher reported that 20 percent of the victims in her study stated that they had abused alcohol or other drugs in an attempt to deal with depression and loneliness.[54] Others reported that 60 percent of the men in residential substance abuse treatment programs had been sexually abused as children.[55] Being chemically dependent as an adult makes you vulnerable to further physical or sexual abuse and reinforces the idea that you wanted it or deserved it.

If a person is physically or psychologically addicted to drugs, it is usually necessary for him to detoxify, receive treatment for this disorder, and experience a period of sobriety before he will be able to benefit from sexual abuse therapy. Of course, not everyone who uses drugs, even abusively, is addicted. The signs of psychological addiction include preoccupation with using and a loss of control, such as being unable to limit drug intake. A diagnosis of physical addiction requires withdrawal symptoms, such as having the "shakes" in the morning.

ABUSIVE RELATIONSHIPS

Abusive relationships, whether emotionally, physically, or sexually abusive, are familiar to victims. They grew up being mistreated, so to be in an abusive relationship as adults seems normal to them. Many have watched their parents mistreat each other and assume that isolation, bitterness, and violence are elements of all relationships. The abused child may become the man who is victim or abuser or both. He may be a victim in one relationship and the victimizer in another. Some victimized persons become hyperresponsible, thinking that if they achieve enough or do enough for others they will not be mistreated and no one will notice that they are unlovable. As one client put it, "My outsides look great. But my insides feel horrible."

SEX

In addition to teaching the victim not to trust his view of reality, mentally or emotionally, sexual abuse also teaches him a powerful message about what sex is. Those who have been sexually abused learn that touch and sex are related to power, fear, shame, anger, confusion, secrecy, and, often, physical pain. The victim does not see touch/sex as something done *with* another person, but something done *to* another person. Often this association is so powerful that the victim becomes physically nauseated even when someone initiates respectful, mutual, consensual sex with him. This symptom is often what brings men to therapy, wanting to know what is wrong that they become ill when in a sexual situation. Silver, Boon, and Stones wrote that more than 80 percent of the victims in their study reported that having sex brought back memories of childhood incest.[56] Many of my clients report that when they are in a sexual situation, even when they are with someone they love and trust, they will be very frightened. Often they will have bodily sensations, memories, or emotions that remind them of being abused. When this happens, they will often dissociate. Sometimes these experiences are triggered by a certain word being said or by certain acts, such as oral sex or having intercourse in a particular position.

One survey found that 25 percent of the victimized males studied reported sexual dysfunctions, including inhibited sex drive, premature ejaculation, difficulty with erection, and inability to ejaculate.[57] Only 5 percent of the nonvictimized males in the study described these symptoms. Many sexual dysfunctions and disorders exist which in some cases have their roots in childhood sexual abuse:

Premature ejaculation: This is the inability to control ejaculation or "coming." For sexual abuse victims this can serve as a way to end sex when it becomes frightening or otherwise uncomfortable.

Erectile dysfunction: Also called *impotence,* this is difficulty in getting or keeping an erection or "hard-on." Again, in some cases, this is a way of avoiding a sexual situation.

Retarded ejaculation: Not being able to ejaculate or "come."

Exhibitionism: Exposing one's penis to nonconsenting people to obtain sexual excitement.

Fetishism: Sexual excitement from nonliving objects, for example, shoes.

Sexual masochism: Getting sexual pleasure from being beaten, humiliated, or having pain or injury inflicted to one's self.

Sexual sadism: Sexual pleasure from causing another person to suffer physically, mentally, or emotionally.

Frotteurism: Going into crowded places in order to get sexually excited by rubbing against or touching strangers.[58]

Some of these responses do not become apparent until the victim enters into marriage or another committed relationship. Prior to this the victim may report few or no sexual difficulties. However, when the victim's sexual partner has become "family," sex suddenly becomes frightening or distasteful for it is too similar to the incest experience.[59] Some victims report that they are able to function while masturbating, when having an affair or one-night stand, or with a prostitute, yet are unable to function with someone with whom they have a strong emotional relationship. Many victims will report that they are sexually attracted to people on the street yet cannot imagine being sexual with the partner they live with or are married to. One client believed that sex was something disgusting that was inflicted on one person by another. He was able to obtain an erection with prostitutes but not with his wife: "I couldn't possibly dirty my wife by having sex with her; I love her too much to put her through that." Regardless of how his wife asked for sex, he still believed that she really didn't want it and that if they were sexual it would destroy their marriage.

Some sexual abuse victims' experiences taught them that sex was always for the other person's pleasure and that the victim was there only to give and never to receive. He may only be comfortable focusing on the wants of his partner. Other abuse victims become sexually excited by situations or objects that prevent them from forming intimate sexual relationships with other people: for example, sex with animals or sexual excitement over enemas, urine, or feces.

Often sexual abuse victims have the view that the world is made up entirely of people who are victims or victimizers. They have a difficult time separating sex and abuse, tending to think of them as one and the same. They worry that they are being used by their spouse or sex partner. They may feel guilty or become anxious when they enjoy sex. They often are preoccupied with their partner's pleasure and ignore their own desires. This view leads to difficulty enjoying sex. As one client put it, "If I ask for sex and enjoy it, I must be using my partner. Or if my partner is enjoying it, I am being used." He had a problem seeing that sexual intercourse could be a mutually rewarding experience in which no one was being mistreated.

In some cases, but certainly not all, people who were abused as children grow up to reenact the abuse they suffered by becoming sex offenders themselves.[60] Sometimes patterns of abuse are seen generation after generation. A person is sexually abused at age seven, grows up, and abuses seven-year-old children who grow up to abuse still more seven-year-old children.

Another response often seen in people who have been sexually abused is promiscuous or compulsive sexual behavior. When I studied the membership of the self-help group Sex Addicts Anonymous, which exists to help people stop self-abuse and other abusive sexual behaviors, I found that 37.1 percent of the male members identified themselves as having been sexually abused as children.[61] This behavioral pattern is often used as evidence that the victims are hypersexed individuals who desired sexual contact even as children. Others conclude that the victim must not have been negatively affected by the childhood sexual abuse because they view the promiscuous or compulsive sexual behavior as a sign that the victim really enjoys sex. Often just the opposite is true: the more compulsive the act, the less pleasurable it is.

One explanation for why children who have been sexually abused go on to initiate further sexual contact with adults and then to become adults who are promiscuous or compulsive about sex is offered by Mary de Young.[62] She views this behavior as a counterphobic response. A phobia is an intense fear of an object, person, place, or act that is so great that the person panics and wants to flee. *Phobia* comes from the Greek word for *dread*.[63] A counterphobic response is one in which the person compulsively and repeatedly puts himself in the presence of the anxiety-producing situation in order to have a sense of mastering the fear. Unfortunately, this seeking out of sexual situations makes it appear that the victim is a willing participant.

Many sexual abuse victims report being confused as to their sexual orientation. Boys who were abused by males often question their masculinity, fearing that they "appear" or are homosexual.[64] Some become homophobic and even violent toward those they perceive as homosexual in an effort to "prove" their own masculinity. If the boy is gay and is abused by a male, he may confuse abusive sexuality with his sexual orientation. Many of my clients who are gay mistakenly regard childhood sexual experiences with much older males not as child molesting but as acts whereby the man helps the boy "come out." It is a politically sensitive issue to confront this dynamic in a gay client and to break the code of denial and secrecy that surrounds sexual abuse: I run the risk of being seen as unaware or even hostile to gay concerns. It is important that neither the client nor I become distracted by the political issues, remaining instead focused on the therapeutic issues.

One response to all the confusion, shame, and fear about sex is for the victim to shut down sexually. This can be done by not thinking about sex, dressing in a way to appear unattractive, not masturbating, or avoiding sexual contact with another. When diagnosed, this is called sexual aversion disorder.[65]

Questions to help identify your thoughts and emotions:

What is your view of sex?

What are your values concerning sex?

How has having been sexually abused affected your sex life? (Or how has being in a relationship with someone who was sexually abused affected your sex life?)

In what ways have you been sexually abusive/disrespectful to others?

What sexual issues need addressing in your life?

The Spiritual Aspects

I believe that sexual abuse is also spiritual abuse. In my work with abused persons I have found that unless this dynamic is addressed, the healing is incomplete. To a young child, adults seem to be gods. They are able to make light appear and disappear, provide food and shelter, cause pain, and are huge in size. If spirituality is the belief in a superior being, and a child learns that her or his "gods" are abusive, he or she will unconsciously take this view into adulthood and apply it to other forms of God.[66] Burdened with this belief, the victim may shun religion and have no use for God. He may be angry at God for not protecting him from the abuse. One of my clients was terrified of dying for fear that there was an afterlife and that his abuser would be there and the incest would continue. He said, "God didn't protect me when I was alive. What makes you think he will protect me when I'm dead?"

Another response is to be terrified of God, perhaps fanatically focusing on religious matters in an attempt to be safe. Many of my clients who were abused by men report hating to say the "Our Father" prayer and not knowing why. At the same time it does them no good to think of God as a woman; since the abuse was overlooked by their mothers, they do not trust female figures either.

Some victimized persons will attempt to explain the sexual abuse using a spiritual or religious framework, saying, for example, "The abuse is God's way of teaching me a lesson or punishing me for my sins. Once I learn the lesson or have been punished enough the abuse will stop." One drawback to this explanation is that when the abuse does not stop, the victimized person continues to blame himself and his lack of goodness. Some victims are driven by their shame into religious communities or orders in an attempt to atone for their "sins" or "evilness" related to their sexual abuse.[67] Others seek out rigid and punitive churches that teach that any and all sexual acts or thoughts are bad, which, rather than helping the victim to heal, further reinforces his sense of being unacceptable. Still others find themselves in groups whose leader, by virture of his "holiness," has sexual access to any and all members of the group.[68] Those who resist the sexual contact are labeled as having a loss of faith and are threatened with exclusion from the group or punishment in an afterlife. This dynamic is an echo of the incest family system from childhood, so it does not seem that unusual to the victim.

Questions to help identify your thoughts and emotions:

What are your current spiritual beliefs?

What is your concept of God/Higher Power?

What are the advantages of having a God/Higher Power? How is your concept of God/Higher Power affected by having been sexually abused?

Are there any aspects of your current religious/spiritual practices that are a reenactment of your sexual abuse?

Up until this point you have been working to gain an understanding of what sexual abuse is and how it is harmful. You are now ready to focus your attention on the healing process and apply what you have learned. This is where your work begins to pay off.

5

Recovery Issues

As a victim, you already know, all too well, the harm that sexual abuse causes. What you may not know is that you can be healed. You can be free of the shame, fear, and loneliness that has plagued you for so long. Many victimized people never hear this message of hope.[1] They read an article or see a program which discusses sexual abuse but focuses only on the negative consequences. Some people get the impression that sexual abuse victims must remain damaged forever. When people learn that many of my clients are sexual abuse victims they often exclaim, "How can you stand to work with those people? It must be terribly depressing!" My response is always, "On the contrary, working with people recovering from sexual abuse is very rewarding as I am witness to profound courage, strength, and growth. I am very fortunate to be a part of people transforming their lives."

You have already shown your resolve to recover by reading this book. The remainder of the text will focus on how you can reclaim those things that were taken from you when you were abused.

The Terms *Victim* and *Survivor*

Words are powerful things. Therefore, we need to pay attention to the words we use to describe ourselves. Some people, particularly women, need to call themselves incest or sexual abuse *survivors.* Most women need to be affirmed concerning the power and strength they do have, since traditionally they have been (wrongly) viewed as passive and weak. On the other hand, American society teaches men that they are the strong ones and are responsible for every-thing that happens to them, which gives men little permission to see themselves as having been victimized.[2] At first, therefore, it is very important for men to use the term *victim* when talking about themselves and their experiences. I often have men consult a dictionary for the meaning of the words *victim* and *abuse*. It is a powerful experience for a man to think of himself as "anyone who suffers as a result of ruthless design or incidentally or accidentally";[3] as someone destroyed, injured, or otherwise harmed by, or suffering from, some act or circumstance, a person who suffers a loss;[4] as someone who suffers "from any destructive, injurious or adverse action"; as someone who is "wrongly or improperly misuse[d], . . . deceive[d]," a victim of "a corrupt practice."[5] Men who resist using the words *victim* and *victimization* often don't believe in their own innocence and still think of themselves as somehow responsible for the abuse.

I do not think it is inconsistent simultaneously to refer to someone as a victim and also reinforce that whatever action, or lack of action, he took was an acceptable response to the abuse. As a child he had no choice whether to be abused or not. He did have a limited number of alternatives on how to respond to this situation. It is important to make this distinction: that the child was power-less to stop the abuse—that is the definition of victimization—but that he made the best attempts to cope possible under the circumstances. His efforts at self-preservation may have included dissociation, running away, trying to tell another adult, and other attempts. This demonstrated ability to make self-protective decisions can be drawn on during the course of therapy when difficult adult decisions must be made. As several authors have pointed out, powerlessness and lack of responsibility for the victimization does not mean that the victimized person is also powerless or helpless when it comes to taking action to recover from the effects of the abuse.[6]

One reason why men frequently have difficulty thinking of themselves as victims is that in recalling the abuse they mentally picture themselves as men rather than as boys. Therefore, I ask my clients to bring in photographs of themselves and, if possible, of the offending person(s) to help them recall more accurately the body size and build differences that existed. This helps to put the power differential in perspective as well.

Once a man has gained an intellectual and emotional acceptance of the impact of his sexual victimization, I then encourage him to begin to think of himself as a survivor. Although the term *survivor* is viewed by many people as a positive label, I think that eventually it too needs to be dropped so that the individual doesn't think of himself as a victim or a survivor but merely as a person. A lifelong embracing of either term keeps the man focused on and bonded to the abuse experience and prevents complete healing.

Questions to help identify your thoughts and emotions:

> What thoughts and emotions does the term *victim* trigger when you apply it to yourself (your loved one)?

> What thoughts and emotions does the term *survivor* trigger when you apply it to yourself (your loved one)?

Groups

There are various types of groups that may aid a person in recovering from sexual abuse. Some groups are ongoing, meaning you can join at any time and stay as long as you need to. Other groups are time-limited and meet for a specified number of times.

Mutual-help groups. These are peer groups in which nobody has the right to tell another person what to do or not do. No money changes hands (other than to pay rent for the meeting room), since everyone is there to help and be helped. Many of these groups have adapted the Twelve-Step Program of Alcoholics Anonymous to fit the issue of sexual abuse (see chapter 20). Some authors believe that the Twelve-Step approach may be fraught with problems for sexual abuse survivors[7] since the First Step uses the term *powerless* and because Twelve-Step groups traditionally encourage members to take responsibility for their lives and to forgive others.[8] I find the goals and methods of the Twelve Steps to be highly consistent with my treatment goals for my clients. I do *not* encourage my clients to take responsibility for what was done to them when they were children and were powerless. However, as adult survivors they are no longer powerless and can take responsibility for how they lead their lives from here on. As for the steps related to forgiveness, AA's wording is clear: "Made a list of people we have harmed and became willing to make amends to them all."[9] Nowhere does this program say anything about how to relate to the people who have harmed you. The Twelve-Step program is one of self-healing and self-forgiveness. Therefore, I see no need to modify the Twelve-Step program when applying it to sexual abuse survivors.

The purpose of these groups is to provide a safe, supportive environment in which the members can heal at whatever pace they choose. The advantage of these groups is that they are low cost, and a person may attend for as long as he needs to. A disadvantage is that most of these groups are open to anyone on a drop-in basis, which means that nobody screens members, and people with offender mentalities or with severe mental disorders can join and become disruptive.

Education groups. These groups are often a part of a workshop and are designed to provide information on sexual abuse and its effects. The advantage of these groups is that members can gain useful information without having to discuss their own personal issues.

Treatment groups. A group of this type may be a part of a formal treatment program. It combines the components of peer support and education, and is facilitated by a counselor or therapist. These groups often follow a predetermined plan and are time-limited, meaning that they meet for a specified number of sessions. They tend to focus on insight into problem areas, some emotional expression, and behavior change. The advantage of this type of group is having a professional guide and more structure than mutual-help groups.

Therapy groups. These groups are similar to treatment groups in that they are run by a professional helper, but they differ in that the focus tends to be broader. In addition to addressing insight, appropriate emotional expression, and behavior change, these groups often explore the members' core beliefs and values and seek to bring unconscious and subconscious material to conscious awareness.

Regardless of the type of group you attend there are several benefits to be gained. First, being in the presence of others who have also been sexually abused helps to reduce the sense of isolation that is common in abused people. A group is a place where you can stop keeping the abuse secret. Listening to others will "normalize" some of what you have experienced. You will learn that you are not the only one to have the reactions you struggle with. Being a member of a supportive nurturing group will be helpful in healing your shame.[10]

In addition, groups can help dissolve denial and repression. As you listen to others' stories, you will find yourself thinking, "He's saying what happened to him was sexual abuse, and the other members are believing him. A similar thing happened to me, so that must mean I was abused too." Or, "I don't think he deserved to be treated abusively, so that must mean I didn't deserve to be abused either." You will begin to have access to memories and emotions that were unavailable prior to hearing other people's stories. You will also have an opportunity to notice your family rules and your beliefs about yourself and your place in the world. You may find that your victim mentality is very apparent to others while you are blind to it and to the effect it has on your life.

In some groups you will have members who are further along in the grief/recovery process. These people can act as role models, offering hope and describing what to expect. Groups provide a setting in which to experiment with new behaviors. If you have been passive in the past, you can practice being assertive. If you have always taken care of others, you can see what it is like to be taken care of.

For those who come from a family where it was not safe to work on recovery or to think in ways other than that conditioned by a victim mentality, it may be necessary, at least for a while, to stop having contact with the family of origin. Swink and Leveille called this process "orphanization."[11] In order to have a sense of community and tradition, many survivors bond together to recognize important events (birthdays, weddings, deaths, graduations, holidays), to create a new "family."

No matter which type of group you attend, along with your sense of relief you will likely experience some fear. As one client humorously said at his first group session, after listening to the other members tell their histories, "I'm very glad to be here. I'd rather be anyplace else. I like you guys already, go away." He knew that his discomfort was telling him that he was overcoming his denial. He was doing something important and needed to be careful. Even a safe group will be frightening at first. In fact, in some ways, if you come from a very abusive family, the healthier the group, the more unfamiliar it will seem and the more frightening because you won't understand the "rules." The honesty, openness, acceptance, and nurturing will seem scary at first. A safe group will be respectful of your need to go at your own pace. If you find yourself in a group that reminds you a lot of how your family was, with secrets, "special" relationships, or a lot of covert rules, you need to find another group.

Questions to help you identify your thoughts and emotions:

When you think about being in a group and talking about your sexual abuse history, how do you feel?

If you are not currently in a group, what keeps you from joining one? How do you think you could benefit from becoming a member of a group?

If you are a member of a group, what are you gaining from attending your group?

Grief—A Natural Response to Sexual Abuse

Symonds described four phases of response to being violated.[12] The first reaction consists of shock and disbelief. This is followed by what he called "frozen fright," which is a detached pseudo calm during which the victim is compliant and appeasing. (It is this appearance of cooperation that will be confused with consent when the victim looks back on the experience.) The third phase is a delayed but chronic traumatic depression combined with "bouts of apathy, anger, resignation, resentment, constipated rage, insomnia," and repeated replaying of the events. The final phase is characterized by resolving the traumatic experience and integrating it into the victimized person's behavior and life-style.

However, before this fourth phase can occur, a grief process must take place. Whenever something is taken away from a person, he will experience a grief response. When someone is sexually abused, there is a great deal to grieve. Each person grieves in his own way, but grief responses tend to follow a pattern made up of five stages: denial, bargaining, anger, sadness, and acceptance/forgiveness (see figure 5–1).[13] People move back and forth among the stages, can be experiencing more than one stage at a time, and move from stage to stage at varying rates. Recovery is more a process than an event. At any time during the process men who are recovering from addictive/compulsive disorders may find that they return to these behaviors/thoughts as a way to cope with the grief. This may be a sign that they are suppressing some emotions, moving too rapidly, or expecting too much of themselves. Recovery ought to be a self-respecting process, as opposed to another form of abuse. It is important that you be gentle with yourself.

DENIAL

Denial takes many forms. In its strongest form it is called repression: the person has no conscious recall of the event.[14] The memory stays in the victim's unconscious mind and has an effect on him, but he does not realize it. Often, when I have information that leads me to believe that a client has been sexually abused, I will ask him, "If you had been sexually abused, would you want to

Denial
"Nothing happened."

Bargaining
"Something happened, but . . ."

Anger
"Something bad happened, and I don't like it!"

Sadness
"Something happened, and it cost me a lot."

Acceptance/Forgiveness
"Something happened, and I have healed from it."

Figure 5–1. THE STAGES OF RECOVERY

remember that?" Sometimes my client will say, "No, I would prefer never to know that." A person who responds in this way may be using repression to keep from recalling something that he believes is too painful to be aware of. He will become aware of the abuse when he is ready and not before. In these cases it is disrespectful and fruitless to try to convince him to look at the information that suggests that he was sexually abused. However, I will discuss with him what it would mean to him if he had been abused. In some cases the answer is, "If one of my family had sexually abused me, it would mean that I could never be around them again and that would be too painful to bear."

A less powerful form of denial is suppression: the person has clues that he was abused but seeks to ignore the meaning of the information. Thoughts concerning the abuse are available to him, but through a conscious effort he tries to "block the thoughts" and their meaning. The thoughts become subconscious but then periodically intrude into the person's consciousness, only to be suppressed again. See, for example, in Greg's story (chapter 7), where Greg thinks to himself, "Grandpa could not have done that to me!" Greg has information that logically points to his being abused, yet it is so painful he wishes to deny it. Even as the memories about the abuse become more and more conscious, denial will continue to play a role until the person believes it is safe enough for him to begin to believe his memories. The therapeutic task in the denial stage is to begin to believe that the abuse actually took place.

Staying in the denial stage is costly. It stifles creativity: the victim cannot think spontaneously because he is censoring himself to avoid recalling the abuse memories. Keeping a secret from others requires a great deal of energy; even more energy is required to keep something secret from oneself. The energy used to suppress the abuse memories is energy that is not available for other efforts. Recovery frees this energy for other uses.

Other costs of denial include vague loss of control fears; specific but irrational loss of control fears, such as suddenly vomiting in public or wetting your pants; a decreased ability to be empathic with adults, babies, or pets that are in pain; or a desire to punish or hurt those who are vulnerable. In order to deny your own experience you will probably want to avoid seeing others' pain and vulnerability.

A helpful technique throughout all stages of the grief/recovery process is writing letters that you never send.[15] Writing helps you to slow down your thoughts and thereby become more aware of your emotions. Once you have written a letter, you may want to read it to your therapist and your group. This can be even more powerful than the writing.

For some people writing letters is too cognitive and prevents them from freeing up emotions. The use of art, however, bypasses the need for language and therefore can trigger memories and emotions from very early childhood. Many of my clients have had powerful responses to drawing or working with clay. Some have done picturebooks of their lives made up of drawings or photographs of themselves or pictures cut from magazines. People having trouble feeling an emotion may benefit from drawing or somehow creating an image of that emotion. For example, drawing a picture of anger, shame, or sadness can help.

A question to help you identify your thoughts and emotions:

In what ways have you denied your (or your loved one's) sexual abuse? How has this denial been helpful? How has it hurt you?

BARGAINING

A client once told me, "I began the bargaining stage when the pain of my denial became too massive to ignore." The defenses of denial and bargaining often overlap. When a person is in the bargaining stage, he will acknowledge that something happened but will attempt to convince himself and others that there was no trauma associated with the experience. This is the "Yes but" stage of recovery. The therapeutic task in this stage is to overcome the family myths and social stereotypes and misinformation that allow sexual abuse to take place in the first place, preventing victims from talking about it and about the impact it has had on them.

Clients and other therapists often ask me how I can tell the difference between someone who is bargaining and someone who actually experienced something that was not traumatic. They want to know if an adult can have sexual contact with a child and not have it negatively affect the child. Personally, I do not spend a great deal of time debating this issue, since, if they do exist, I do not come in contact with these people. People do not seek out therapy if they aren't struggling with something painful. I have found that people who were not abused do not have the severe symptoms that abuse victims have, and they do not have to work very hard to convince themselves or me that they do not have any pain concerning the event in question. People in the bargaining stage often go to great lengths to explain how, although it may appear that they were abused, in fact they were not. This is one reason group therapy and support groups are so valuable for a man who has been sexually abused: the other group members can see how illogical and transparent his rationalizations are as he attempts to explain away the abuse.

Here are some common phrases that sexually abused men use early in recovery:

"I remember what happened, but *that* isn't sexual abuse."

"I recall what happened, and I asked for it, so it wasn't abuse."

"I know what she did, and I wanted it."

"I can't deny it happened, but it's my fault it happened."

"Even if it was abuse, it didn't affect me seriously."

"He had a terrible childhood. He can't be blamed for what he did to me."

"He is sick. He couldn't help himself."

"It didn't happen enough for it to matter."

"I always got paid or got a gift, so it wasn't abuse."

"My imagination tends to be overly active. Now that I think seriously about it, I'm sure it never actually happened. I think it was just a fantasy."

"Even if I was hurt by it, I should be over it by now."

"I'm overly sensitive. I tend to exaggerate and get dramatic over little things."

"He was just trying to help me get in touch with my gayness."

"She was just teaching me about sex."

"My baby-sitter didn't *abuse* me. If anyone was being used, it was her. I just got lucky."

"It only happened once, so it didn't hurt me."

"It was a long time ago. It's time to forgive and forget."

"It is better to be sexually abused than to get killed. It could have been worse."

"I can't do anything about it now. There's no sense in even talking about it."

When a person is in the bargaining stage his ability to doubt is very powerful. An example of the strength of the denial that remains in the bargaining stage can be seen in the case of one client of mine who worked in the same factory as the man who abused him as a child. Although the other group members and I strongly advised against it, this client sought out the man over their lunch break and asked him, "Do you remember sexually abusing me when I was a kid?" "No," was the man's answer. "You don't remember taking me in your garage and putting your cock in my mouth when I was a kid?" "Sure, I remember that," the man replied. My client's response was, "Are you sure? You're not just saying that to make me happy, are you? Maybe it wasn't me." In spite of this information from the man who abused him, my client still was not convinced for several months that the events he recalled had actually taken place.

One form of bargaining is pseudoforgiveness. This occurs when the victimized person attempts to move from denial straight into forgiveness without experiencing any of the emotions associated with the abuse. I sometimes see this in a client from one session to the next. One week he is denying that there was any abuse, but the next week he has decided that yes, indeed there was abuse but he has forgiven his abuser(s) and is ready to move on to other issues. As Mike Lew in *Victims No Longer* has written, "True forgiveness does not arise from denial. It can only occur when there has been a complete understanding of what has happened, including the nature of the wrongs and where the responsibility lies."[16]

Serenity and peace are associated with actual forgiveness; pseudoforgiveness is merely intellectual, and the person's emotional response is flat. The focus is on avoiding the victimized person's emotions. It is a very empty, unsatisfying state. Sometimes a man will rush into pseudoforgiveness because those around him—his partner, family, or therapist—are uncomfortable and tense about his having powerful emotions. In order to put everyone at ease, he acts as if he has done his grieving—then everyone, except him, feels better. If the victimized person has regular contact with the person(s) who abused him, he may be tempted to move into pseudoforgiveness in order to protect the abusive person(s) from feeling guilty or ashamed. This is a replication of the childhood abuse: the older person's wants are given a high priority while the younger person's needs are ignored. It can also be a covert contract between the victim and the offender. The victim is afraid that he is still at the mercy of the offender, and so he offers up his pseudoforgiveness in hopes of being safe from further abuse.

Another form of bargaining comes after a man talks about his sexual abuse to a therapist or in a group for the first time. When he is met with acceptance and support, he feels a great sense of relief, even a high.[17] The bargaining aspect of this experience comes in when he says, "I feel so great now that the secret is out. It is as if a huge weight has been lifted from my shoulders. That's all I really needed. I don't need to come back for any more therapy. Everything is all right now."

Still another form of bargaining takes place in group settings when a client says, "What happened to me is different from what happened to the rest of you guys." Some people will imply that what happened to them was so horrible and disgusting that recovery is not possible and that they cannot even describe what took place. This is sometimes referred to as victim grandiosity. On the other end of the range, some men will minimize their own abuse, seeing it as "not as bad as what the others had to endure." A third version is: "Since I'm such a worthless person, I don't deserve to be a member of this kind and supportive group." When one of my clients said to his group, "I don't deserve to be here," another member agreed with him, adding, "None of us deserved to suffer what it takes to qualify to be a member of a sexual abuse survivors' group. But since you were abused, you deserve the same healing that the rest of us do."

A sign of someone's being in the bargaining stage is his use of the phrase "willing victim." This is an oxymoron: the words contradict one another. The definition of willing is "accepted of choice or without reluctance; given, offered voluntarily; acting, giving readily and cheerfully; of the power of choice."[18] Even if you agreed to the sexual act, either by words or by actions, you didn't really have a choice because you were a child. A "yes" from a dependent, powerless person who can't say no and have it mean anything is worthless.

When in the bargaining stage, many people find that a constant argument or civil war goes on in their heads: "It really happened." "No, it didn't." "Yes, it did." This goes back and forth, seemingly forever. If you find this happening, you may find it useful to choose a side and write a letter to yourself or someone else arguing that point, making no attempt to be objective or to see both sides. Once that is done, write another letter arguing the opposite side. Pay attention to your body during the writing of each letter and listen to what your emotions are telling you.

Regardless of the stage of recovery a person is in, I encourage him to talk to others and to wait at least a couple of weeks before actually mailing any letters to anyone as a part of the recovery. If you want the satisfaction of sending a letter without any risks, you can put the letter in an envelope, seal it, and drop it into a mailbox without addressing it. There is something very rewarding about the sound of a mailbox clanking shut.[19]

Another form of bargaining is not trusting your emotions and memories by believing you require outside "proof" that the abuse happened. It is very unlikely that you will find that kind of evidence. Sexual abuse is usually done in secret. The only traces left are the emotional and behavioral scars left on the victims. Most people who abuse children will not admit it, so the "proof" must come from within, in the form of emotions, sensations, or memories. An example of looking for external evidence of abuse can be seen in the case of a client of mine who had been repeatedly anally sexually assaulted. He doubted his memories, thinking that if it had actually happened, someone would have noticed and put a stop

to it, or at least said something. He believed in his family more
than he believed in himself. In his memory (which he called a recurring dream) he saw himself looking down into the toilet and
seeing the blood from his injured rectum. He also had an image of
himself in a car on the way to a hospital, holding himself up off
the seat because sitting was too painful. In his bargaining he told
himself that he would send for copies of his hospital records, and
if these documented that he had been sexually abused, he would
believe it. When he received the records, they stated that he had
been admitted to the emergency room and had been treated for
anal wounds. But the cause of the injury was listed as accidental.
He was outraged. He began yelling, "How could they ignore the
obvious fact that I had been raped? How dare they ignore an injured child?" He had begun to believe his internal evidence and to
move into the anger stage.

Questions to help you identify your thoughts and emotions:

What bargaining techniques have you (your loved one) used?

Draw yourself and the person(s) who abused you. What does
this tell you about yourself?

ANGER

The third stage of grief in men is commonly anger.[20] Anger begins
to come when a person acknowledges not only that something happened but that it was abusive and harmed him. It is the beginning
of believing that what was done to him matters because he matters.
For many victimized men this stage is a welcome relief. They have
been going through their lives, passive and afraid. When they begin
to become aware of their anger, it gives them a sense of power and
energy to make changes. Becoming angry is the beginning of acceptance and of moving from the view of self as a victim to the
view of self as survivor. You cannot get angry about the abuse and
still blame yourself for it. Bass and Davis call anger "the backbone
of healing."[21]

When a client has trouble becoming aware of his anger, I encourage him to think of someone he cares about who is the age at

which he himself was abused, such as his son or nephew, and to imagine that child being sexually abused. In groups, a man who is having trouble getting angry about his own abuse will begin to find his anger when he hears another group member's story. Often people can begin to get angry about someone else's mistreatment before their own. Sometimes just saying "I am angry" over and over again, louder and louder, will help in the process of finding the anger.

Once a man experiences being angry and learns that nobody, including himself, is hurt, he finds it easier to identify and express anger in the future. Sometimes, after working with someone on anger in a group, he will say, "That's anger? That wasn't so bad. In fact, I kind of liked it." Other men, rather than being relieved, are very frightened of finding their anger. They are afraid that they are so angry they will harm themselves or others. When moving into the anger stage, some people experience sudden and intrusive violent thoughts, images, or urges. Examples I have heard include these: while driving, having the urge to swerve into a crowd of people on the sidewalk; imagining strangling one's pet or throwing it from a window; thinking that when the kitchen cabinet is opened there might be someone's severed head on the shelf; without apparent reason suddenly wanting to begin screaming in public. Naturally, these urges can be very frightening, and many people think they are going insane when they experience them. I encourage my clients to focus the anger on the person(s) who abused them, rather than walk around with this vague, generalized fury. It is important for people who are having these violent thoughts to have a safe place in which to talk about them. When these thoughts are kept secret, their power and frequency increase.

If you are having trouble becoming aware of your anger, letter writing can assist you as well. Write a letter to yourself or someone else stating what you have to be angry about, how you have been mistreated, and the effects it has had on you. Write about how angry you are that you have trouble finding and expressing your anger. Letter writing is a way to get those "unspeakable" thoughts out of your head by putting them down on paper. If you have a revenge fantasy, rather than deny it or act on it, write it down. You will get relief, and nobody will be hurt or frightened by your anger and thoughts.

Along with the anger often comes a desire to "get even" with the abusing person(s). This desire is, of course, natural, while also impossible to act on. You can never do to the person who violated you what he or she did to you. You were a child; he or she was an adult. That person is still an adult, so even if you assaulted her or him, it would not be the same as what happened to you—it would be adult to adult, not adult to child. However, as Martin Symonds has pointed out, there is a paradoxical way in which you can "get even" with the person(s) who mistreated you: continue to live and live well.[22] Every day that you choose to live, you destroy the power of abuse to destroy you.

At the anger stage of recovery, men often have revenge dreams in which they seek out the offending person in order to rape, physically or verbally attack, or kill her or him. Some men find these dreams satisfying and healing. Others find them very disturbing and fear that such dreams are a sign that the dreamer is "just as sick/bad/evil/and so on" as the person(s) who abused him. Having violent dreams is not a sign that the dreamer is planning actually to carry out the action. It is merely a safe way for your subconscious mind to let you know how very angry you are.

The only times I have been afraid of clients is when they attempt to suppress their anger, not when they have expressed it in appropriate ways. Sometimes I help clients practice screaming in my office as a way to reduce the tension they are experiencing and to get the thoughts out in the open. I sometimes suggest that clients buy some safety goggles at the hardware store, go into their basement, and throw plates or bottles against the wall while yelling. In order to reduce the cost of this, I suggest that they go to garage sales or recycling centers to get the glassware. Another version of the same technique is to go to a large body of water where there are no swimmers and to throw rocks while making some vocal sounds. Another popular technique is to get a length of rubber hose, like the type used on automobile radiators, and use it to strike pillows or the floor. It makes a very satisfying noise and can drain off a great deal of energy. I encourage you, when using any of these techniques, to use your voice. If you don't know what words to use, make some sound. The vocalization will be most effective if it comes from deep in your body. You will be able to feel your stomach and abdomen tighten. I strongly suggest that people who are hitting pillows view it as a physical act designed to expend energy rather than as an act of violence. Therefore, I *never* ask my client to imagine that the pillow he is hitting is the person who abused him. I have found that people who imagine they are beating up on someone feel guilty later, and this greatly lessens the healing aspects of the experience.

While in the anger stage, some men find themselves getting very angry at people or things other than the person(s) responsible for the abuse. They begin to notice little things about their partner, friends, group members, and therapist that really grate on their nerves. It is important to sort out how much of this anger is reasonably about the person it is being directed at and how much of it is more appropriately aimed at the abuser(s). For example, when I have a client a who tells me I cheated him out of one minute in the previous session, I suspect that he is trying out his anger and that our interaction is more about his learning to stand up for himself than about whether we actually ended sixty seconds early. Therapy ought to be a safe place in which to practice being angry with an authority figure in a respectful way. A therapist who is afraid of your appropriately expressed anger, or one who allows you to mistreat her or him, is setting a poor example for you.

Sometimes the target for the anger is anything weak or helpless. The victim may become outraged at the sight of a puppy, kitten, or human baby because on some level it reminds him of his childhood vulnerability and of how he was taken advantage of. As he learns to be gentle with others, he learns to be gentle with himself.

Although some authors think that it is easier and less threatening for abuse victims to be angry at people other than the offender(s),[23] I have found just the opposite. In many more cases I find that my clients have a much easier time being angry at the person who actively or more overtly abused them than at the people who mistreated them by lack of attention, not noticing, or not providing protection.

It is in the anger stage that many men begin to exercise. They find that the anger gives them the energy to run or lift weights or play active sports and to take better care of their bodies. These activities further add to their sense of strength.

A question to help you identify your thoughts and emotions:

Draw yourself and the person(s) who abused you. Are these drawings different from the ones you drew earlier? What does this tell you about yourself?

SADNESS

Sadness comes when a man realizes that he was wronged and that he has lost something that he can never retrieve. It is a very unpleasant realization, so many men seek to avoid the sadness stage. They prefer to remain angry, thinking that if they become aware of their sadness they will lose their sense of power forever, become too vulnerable, and get mistreated again. I refer to these people as professional victims. They hold on to their resentments, become self-rightous, and may even become verbally abusive to others who do not hold the same views they do, particularly when it comes to the topic of child sexual abuse. They accuse people who disagree with them of "not being sensitive to survivor issues" or of being "pro-offender." They react to a difference of opinion as if it were a personal attack and become enraged. Ann Meissner uses the term "destructive entitlement" to describe those people who believe that because they were injured they are entitled to hurt others.[24] They hurt themselves and others in the name of their past victimization. They have learned that they were not responsible for their childhood abuse but act as if they are not responsible for any of their actions. They blame others for anything they dislike. If these people are employed as professional helpers, they are likely to impose their views on their clients and to discourage, overtly or covertly, their clients from moving into sadness and then to acceptance/forgiveness.

There is great loss because of childhood sexual abuse and much to be sad about. In workshops I have done on sexual abuse, I have asked people to list what they lost as a result of being abused. Here are some of the losses they identified: innocence, self-worth, virginity, trust of others, sense of safety, and time, because of the effects of the abuse.

During the sadness stage people often become very sensitive. They have suppressed their pain and sadness for so long that now they tend to cry "without reason" or at the slightest provocation. For example, a client came to his appointment crying because a butterfly had been killed by his car windshield as he drove to my office.

He reported that whenever his dog sought him out to play or be stroked, he would be overwhelmed by sadness and would weep. Any innocent or vulnerable living thing reminded him of his childhood abuse and triggered tears. He was relieved to learn that this was only a temporary state and would pass.

As a person moves through the sadness stage, he will notice how his tears change. At first, crying will be very difficult and painful. He may fight back the tears by holding his breath, not making any sound, trying to think of something pleasant, or shaming himself for needing to cry. Later in this stage, the tears will seem to come from somewhere very deep and often are accompanied by a sense of being a small child. There is often a sense of great loss and loneliness. This is a time when being held may be a very comforting experience, but only by someone who is comfortable with men crying and knows how to touch in a nonsexual manner. Still later in the recovery process the tears are followed by a sense of healing, coming together, wholeness.

When faced with the sadness stage, you can gain a great deal by writing goodbye letters to the things you have lost because of the abuse you experienced—for example, the relationships you never had because of your shame and fear of intimacy, or the type of parents you never had, or the loss of your spontaneity. Victimized children have difficulty being spontaneous and playing because they have to take life so seriously. It is difficult to focus on having fun when the night before you were forced to have oral sex with an adult family member.

Another way of acknowledging your sadness and loss is to go to a card shop, buy yourself a sympathy card, and send it to yourself through the mail. Ask others who care about you to do the same. Notice what thoughts and emotions are triggered as you open and read these cards. Try reading them out loud to yourself and to others.

Questions to help identify your thoughts and emotions:

What are some significant things that you have lost because of your (your loved one's) sexual abuse?

What can you do as an adult to begin to experience some of those things now?

What have you lost that you can never regain?

What can you do in order to learn to relax and play more?

Write a letter to yourself at the age you were when you were being abused. Tell that little boy that he is blameless for what is happening to him and that he will survive it. Describe to him the man he will grow up to be. Read the letter aloud. What thoughts and emotions do you have as you do this?

Draw yourself and the person(s) who abused you. Are these drawings different from the ones you drew earlier? What does this tell you about yourself?

ACCEPTANCE/FORGIVENESS—THE DESIRED OUTCOME OF THERAPY AND RECOVERY

When contracting with my clients for therapeutic services, I clearly state that in my opinion the task of therapy for the sexual abuse victim is for him to gain a sense of personal worth and strength and to forgive his offender(s). This empowering is accomplished in several ways. First, through the corrective experience of the therapy relationship, the client learns to trust and interact with the therapist, who teaches and models new behaviors and attitudes. Second, the client generalizes these new skills in other relationships. Clients may choose to confront the person(s) responsible for the sexual abuse, but often the process of preparing for this event does the necessary healing. At this point the client can begin to forgive those who abused him so that he is not bonded to them by hatred. As the client acts in a new, more self-enhancing manner, the victim mentality with which he has been viewing the world begins to dissolve. The final stage of grieving begins to take place when the person who was wronged has acknowledged the abuse, felt as well as expressed the emotions he has about it, and begins to put it in its proper perspective. He no longer blames himself for the abuse or punishes himself for what he did or didn't do in order to cope with it. He becomes less and less likely to see himself as helpless, hopeless, and defective. This will make him less vulnerable to further exploitation. He will begin to accept himself and to treat himself with respect and affection. Although he will never forget what was done to him, he will be able to stop organizing his life and personhood around it. He will have a scar rather than an open wound.

Many men have difficulty with the concept of forgiveness, for they mistakenly believe that it means they are saying that the abusive behavior is acceptable or didn't really hurt them. Fitzgibbons offers this thought: "Some have been hurt so deeply that they cannot use the word forgiveness because it implies that those who have injured them will never be accountable for their misdeeds. These people are more comfortable stating that they are willing to let go of their desire for revenge, because it will ease their pain and help them forget."[25] Abuse is *always* wrong and *always* hurtful. Forgiveness does not mean that you condone the abuser's actions. Forgiveness allows the hurt to be in the past and not to continue into the future. The emotional energy that was being used to maintain resentments is made available to be used in other, respectful relationships. Fitzgibbons describes four benefits of forgiveness: (1) freedom from the "subtle control of individuals and events of the past"; (2) a decreased likelihood that the anger will be misdirected toward others who were not responsible for the hurt; (3) a lessening of the fear of violent impulses; (4) a facilitation of the "reconciliation of relationships," if so desired.[26]

Forgiveness and grief are processes, not events. You will find that you will be in one stage about one aspect of your abuse and at the same time in a different stage in relation to another aspect of it. Perhaps you have reached the sadness stage about what the abuse cost you as a child, while you are in the bargaining stage about what you have lost as an adult.

It is during the forgiveness stage that many men have dreams in which they replicate the abuse experience, except they are saved by someone or there is some other happy ending, such as the offending person accepting responsibility for his or her wrongdoing and requesting forgiveness.

When you find yourself in acceptance and forgiveness, you may want to write a letter to the person(s) who abused you, offering forgiveness. In most cases people do not send such letters because they are not interested in having contact with these people. Remember that you forgive others because it helps you, not because it helps them. You can also write yourself a letter forgiving yourself for things you did or didn't do in order to survive the abuse. Another area of self-forgiveness is the things you did to others as a result of your shame. Twelve-Step programs encourage the making of amends as a part of self-forgiveness for wrongs done.

With forgiveness and acceptance comes a sense of serenity. Unlike the pseudoforgiveness I discussed in the bargaining stage, true forgiveness does not require great effort to maintain. The healing is deep and broad. One question that haunts sexual abuse victims is "Will I ever be normal?" I think what is really being asked is "Will I ever be acceptable or healthy?" When a man has stopped thinking of himself as unworthy or abnormal and views himself as worthwhile, acceptable, and healthy, he has moved from victim to survivor.

A word of warning: you may find that you have anniversary grief responses on the date of some aspect of the abuse or when significant events take place in your life, such as the birth of a child, the death of a parent or abuser, getting married, or buying a house. When this happens, many people misinterpret this resurfacing of the grief as a sign that they "didn't do their recovery right or well enough." This is a time to be gentle with yourself.

A question to help you identify your thoughts and emotions:

> Draw yourself and the person(s) who abused you. How are these drawings different from the ones you drew earlier? What does this tell you about yourself?

Telling Others about Your Abuse

Sexual abuse involves the violation of personal boundaries. Therefore, people who have been sexually abused tend to have boundary problems as adults: they either don't want to tell anybody about the abuse or they want to tell everybody. As a person begins to recognize his history of abuse and the impact it has had on his life and on the lives of those around him, he may be tempted to tell everyone about the abuse. It has been a carefully guarded secret for so long that it seems as if it would be such a relief to yell it from the rooftop. However, those who have told the wrong people or spoken too soon have had regrets. We live in a victim-blaming society that tends to protect offenders. As I have described earlier, the abuse of males, particularly by women, has been a taboo subject. Therefore, many men find that they meet with hostility or ridicule when they tell others about their history of abuse. By telling the wrong people you risk setting yourself up to be mistreated again. Fortunately, as an adult you now have choices that were not available to you when you were a child.

One guideline to use in determining whom to tell and when is the need-to-know basis. Prior to telling anyone about your abuse, ask yourself (and perhaps talk it over with someone safe who is already aware of your history), "How will it help my recovery to tell this person about my abuse? What are the risks?" When in doubt, you may want to wait. Even when you do decide it is in your best interest to disclose your history to someone, tell that person in small bits. This will make it less likely that you will become ashamed or terrified, and you are less likely then to overwhelm or frighten that person so that he or she is unable to respond appropriately to your disclosure.

If you are in therapy, you may want to bring your partner in for a session when you tell her/him about your abuse. Your therapist can help your partner hear what you are saying and can provide information on sexual abuse and recovery as well as validation. Many men are afraid to tell their partner about the abuse because they think their partner won't believe them, will blame them, or will think of them as spoiled, dirty, or damaged.

CONFRONTING YOUR OFFENDER(S)

Preparing to confront an offender is more important than whether you actually confront her or him face to face. The healing takes place in the work you do to get ready for the meeting; the meeting itself is icing on the cake. Even if you do not know the whereabouts of your offender or he or she is dead, it is still important for you to follow the same steps as someone who actually meets with his or her offender.

First, determine your goal in confronting your offender. What do you hope to gain? Do you want an apology? Do you want to inform her or him that you remember what happened and how it affected you? Do you want to mend the relationship so you can be closer in the future? Do you want to put an end to the relationship?

There are two things that I would discourage you from seeking. The first is trying to obtain validation that the abuse happened. The best validation is that which comes from within. Asking if the abuse really happened gives away your power and invites denial in both you and the offender. You know if you were abused. The second goal to avoid is revenge. Striving to harm someone because of your pain is wrong, regardless of what that person did to you. The most therapeutic and spiritual thing you can do is to let the chain of abuse stop with you. Seeking revenge keeps you bonded to and focused on your offender and keeps your life from being your own. You may seek justice and compensation through the court system, but do so in the spirit of healing, not of creating further harm.

Prior to meeting with an offender, practice (and practice again) with someone safe what you are going to say. Have several plans so you will be prepared regardless of how the offender responds. Do not meet with more than one offender at a time. Bring someone safe along with you, and meet on your territory or on neutral ground, not where the offender is used to being in charge.

Some offenders will agree to attend a therapy session, but they may attempt to avoid the discomfort of being confronted by confessing to the abuse and apologizing for it before you ever get a chance to open your mouth. This can often seem to take the wind out of your sails, but it is important that you remain true to your agenda. The session is for you and your recovery, not for the offender to lessen her or his shame. If those who abused you ask you to forgive them, you may want to tell them that it is their responsibility to forgive themselves by changing their behavior. If they feel guilty, this will motivate them to take action to get help, just as your pain led you to begin recovery.

Once you have told your family and/or your offender(s) about the abuse and its impact, you may experience another ("Oh, no, not another!") grief response. Many survivors expect that once they have told the secret and confronted those who hurt them, all the effects of the abuse and neglect will suddenly disappear. They are saddened and angry to learn that many of the effects still remain and require further efforts to heal. Some survivors are surprised, sad, and angry to learn that in some cases their relationship with their families does not improve after the secret is out—in some cases it becomes even less pleasant. Be prepared to be punished if you tell the secret. It is not fair, but it often happens. This is one reason why having a strong support group is so important: so that if you are rejected by your family, you will have supportive people to turn to. Families in which sexual abuse took place rarely are one-issue systems, and numerous dysfunctions remain even after the topic of sexual abuse has been addressed. As Swink and Leveille wrote, "Incest occurs in troubled families. It is not the original cause of the problems, but it certainly intensifies them."[27] Adams-Tucker stated that "psychiatric difficulties abounded" in 79 percent of the families she worked with which had a sexually abused child.[28] These problems included alcohol and other drug abuse, suicides, "nervous breakdowns," and depression. The problems that existed prior to the disclosure of the abuse will remain. For example, a mother who refused to take any action to stop the sexual abuse of her boy is likely to refuse to take any action to assist him in his adulthood recovery, such as coming to a therapy session or providing information about his childhood.

Many survivors are saddened and angered when they attempt to tell their siblings and other family members about their sexual abuse and recovery because they are often met with denial or told to keep quiet. These siblings may also have been abused or still want to believe that the family was perfect.[29] They still adhere to the no-talk rule about what happened. If you plan to tell your siblings or other family members about what happened and what you are doing about it, remember how difficult it was for you to accept the sexual abuse and its impact—your family will have at least as much denial.[30]

If you have children, you are faced with deciding whether and how much to tell them about your sexual abuse history and when. Whatever you tell your children, it needs to be age-appropriate and done in a manner that does not overwhelm them or set them up to parent you. Before you tell them anything, I encourage you to wait until you can do it clearly. One of my clients would not allow his children to visit their grandmother because she had a long history of sexually abusing children, including him. He thought his children were too young to understand the reason why he prevented them from having contact with their grandmother, and yet it was important to him that they know someday. So he wrote his children letters informing them of the abuse and of his desire to protect them. His wife agreed to give the children the letters when they were older, in the event that he died before it was appropriate for him to discuss his abuse with them. This provided my client with a sense of peace that the secretiveness that had been in his family for so many years would not continue.

GOING PUBLIC OR CARRYING THE MESSAGE

With the growing awareness of the frequency and impact of sexual abuse, many publications and radio and television programs are doing features on the topic and are seeking men who will describe their experiences. People in Twelve-Step groups have a long tradition of encouragement to "carry the message to others."[31] Telling your story can be a very powerful tool in your recovery. Sexual abuse requires secrecy to continue, and breaking the taboo of silence can be very healing for both the speaker (or writer) and the listener (or reader). It was in this spirit that people contributed their stories to this book.

Since telling your story publicly is such a powerful experience, it also carries the possibility of harming you. As a sexual abuse victim you already know about loss of control. Therefore, you don't need another lesson in it. Remember that recovery involves changing all-or-nothing thinking into having more than two options for action. If you go totally public, showing your face and using your name, you can never take it back. Unfortunately, we live in a society that often blames and verbally attacks victims. Once you print or broadcast your story, you lose control over it. People can tape the program on which you appear and replay it at later dates in other cities. Never assume that the television program on which you plan to tell your story is only a local show or that since your family and/or offender live in another part of the country they will never hear what you say. Because you don't have any power over how people will respond to your story, you may want to tell it without using your name and without showing your face—not because you have anything to be ashamed of or have done anything wrong, but because you are entitled to your privacy and want to be able to choose who knows what about you. Privacy is different from secrecy.

Although there are still risks, I think the safest time to tell your story is when you have reached the acceptance/forgiveness stage. At this point, regardless of how others respond to your disclosure, you will be sure that the abuse happened and that it was not your fault. The risks of publicly disclosing your history at the other stages of recovery are greater. Obviously you cannot discuss the effects of childhood sexual abuse on your life when you are in the denial stage since you are denying that you were abused. At the bargaining stage you run the risk of "being talked out of" your history if someone challenges you or asks a question you aren't sure how to answer. People are resistant to hearing how widespread sexual abuse is in our society and how harmful it is. People who self-disclose while in the bargaining stage run the risk of appearing foolish, thereby reinforcing the myth that people make up or exaggerate sexual abuse, and most important of all, they may set back their recovery progress by doubting themselves and the impact of the abuse. People who disclose at the anger stage run the risk of saying things about the abuser(s) that they later regret. In addition, as I mentioned earlier, the anger stage brings with it a sense of power; being interviewed or speaking to a large number of people can add to this sense of power and make it difficult to move into the more vulnerable sadness stage. Those who wait until the sadness stage are less likely to say things that hurt themselves and others, but they are very vulnerable to being hurt by others' responses to hearing about the abuse. For example, I had a friend who decided to tell his story in a public setting. When he talked about how his uncle had sexually abused him, the studio audience was respectful and acted concerned. However, when he discussed how his mother had also sexually abused him, the audience giggled and began making accusations against him. This was very painful for him. Had he been further along in his recovery process, although the situation would still have been difficult, I think his response to the audiences's reaction would have been less painful.

Questions to help identify your thoughts and emotions:

How safe is it to be around your family when you are recovering from sexual abuse?

If it is not very safe, what measures will you take to protect yourself (your loved one)?

6

Healing the Affected Areas of Your Life

SINCE sexual abuse affects a person physically, mentally, emotionally, and spiritually, recovery needs to address all these areas. One of the most difficult aspects of recovery for both the survivor and the therapist is the sensitive issue of confronting the ways in which the survivor continues to set himself up for further abuse. Although as a child you were faultless for what happened to you, as an adult you are responsible for seeing that you do not allow your victim mentality to continue to place you in situations that lead to additional abuse. For example, if you were abused in your parents' house as a child, you are not responsible for that event. However, as an adult you are responsible for seeing that you do not place yourself at risk. If this means staying out of your parents' house, then that is what you need to do. Part of developing a survivor mentality is to take responsibility for your thoughts, emotions, and actions.

The Physical Aspects

Most American men, more so than women, associate touch with being sexual. Therefore, since the primary violation was related to the client's body, it is important that he be in charge of his body at all times during the therapy. He must be the one to decide if, when, how, and from whom he will accept touch. If the client is in a group, he can watch others and see that all touch is not sexual or invasive. The client has a corrective experience in the therapeutic relationship. He is able to interact with a male authority figure, become vulnerable and intimate, and not be sexual. At some point he may ask to be held. Many abuse victims were only touched when they were being abused physically or sexually. This lack of experience with nurturing touch may lead them to cringe, flinch, tighten, or pull away whenever it appears that someone is about to touch them.[1] I have often seen a survivor of sexual abuse being given safe, nonsexual touch or a hug, and he cries out because it is too frightening. Even in later stages of recovery, getting touched may be very painful as it reminds the survivor of all the years he was not touched in a nonexploitative manner.

One common result of sexual abuse is for the victim to view his body in extreme terms. Some men become preoccupied with their body in a negative way, believing that it is ugly, misshapen, too thin, too heavy, and so forth. Anytime they inadvertently catch a glimpse of themselves in a mirror, they see only ugliness. Others go to the opposite extreme and become preoccupied with their body in a vain manner. These men assume that their bodies are all they have of worth and that the only reason people want to be around them is to admire their bodies or to have sex. They are constantly comparing their bodies to those of others to see if they are the most physically attractive men in the room. They become obsessed with body building or with clothes. Still another type of man merely ignores his body, as if it were not a part of him. Regardless of which way you view your physical appearance, you need to put it in perspective. One method for gaining perspective on your body is to ask friends and group members to describe their first impression of your appearance or to look at you closely and tell you what they see.

People who have been sexually abused have had their bodies mistreated. As a part of your recovery you must learn not to contribute to the effects of the abuse by further mistreating your body. Take care of it. Treat it well. Eat properly, keep clean, and exercise. Exercise can be very painful in the early stages of recovery. As you move your body, you will become more aware of it, and as you become more aware of your body you will notice sensations and emotions that you ignored before. Memories often are triggered by exercise and other physical movements.

Questions to help identify your thoughts and emotions:

How can you begin to treat your body with more respect?

What one thing will you do today to show respect and affection for your body?

Who do you have in your life around whom you have a sense of safety? What could you do to learn about safe touch with him or her? Safe touch would include, for example, asking for a hug or being held when you are afraid, lonely, or sad.

Which aspects or parts of your body do you like?

Draw a picture of yourself. What does this drawing tell you about your view of your body?

Take as many of your clothes off as you are comfortable with and look at yourself in a mirror, or several mirrors so you can see your body from several angles at once. Study your body. What thoughts and emotions are you aware of?

What aspects of your body do you dislike? Find a safe person and ask what he or she thinks about those aspects of your body.

How are your perceptions of your body different from how others perceive your body? What does this tell you?

The Mental Aspects

It is very important for sexual abuse victims to be believed. My confidence in the truth of their story, even when they have doubts about it, is one of the most powerful things I have to offer my clients. Having one's reality denied is one reason that sexual abuse is so traumatic. Many people who have been convicted of sexual offenses with substantial evidence and have even been imprisoned will continue to deny that any abuse took place, so victimized people cannot depend on the person(s) who abused them to validate that the abuse took place. [2]

Unfortunately for many of the men I work with, I am the first person to believe them when they told me the secret of their abuse.

Martin Symonds has written about the "second injury" to crime victims, when "excessively detached, impersonal" personnel interact with the victimized person.[3] Therefore, I think it is not only important to believe that the abuse took place but also to have an emotional response to the information. My outrage at hearing of the abuse of someone I care about is a clear sign to him that what was done to him was wrong and that he is undeserving of such treatment. I continue to be outraged until he can be outraged for himself.

As I stated before, some worry that people lie about being sexually abused. The only distortion I have run across with my clients is a tendency to minimize the abuse. As Meiselman has written, "There is no evidence that reports of incest are more likely to be false or grossly distorted than are reports of other kinds of emotionally charged events in a person's case history, especially when the incest report is given so long after the event that there seems to be no immediate motive for fabricating it."[4]

Frequently, because of the effects of dissociation, survivors will forget what happened in a therapy session. Therefore, I suggest that my clients make notes either during the session or immediately afterward. Another method for minimizing the effects of dissociation and creeping denial is to audiotape the session and then listen to it prior to the next session. Some clients who have difficulty trusting their memories will request that hypnosis be used, to "prove one way or the other" whether the abuse happened. Hypnosis can complicate matters since the client may say, "It's not a memory, it is just something I made up while in a trance. It's just the power of suggestion." Therefore, formal hypnosis must be used carefully. It seems most useful in helping a client gain some details of the event, rather than as a means of convincing him that he was abused. It is in the best interest of the client and myself to trust the rate at which the client is able to recall painful experiences. Experience has taught me that patience is crucial when working with abuse victims. I suspect that formal hypnosis is often used for the comfort of the therapist rather than for the benefit of the client.

In order to trigger memories and to encourage further information to come into your awareness, write yourself a list of questions about what happened, how it affected you, and what you can do to heal from the effects. Don't try to force any answers; trust that they will become clear when you are ready.

If you haven't already, write and/or draw a detailed description of your abuse. Use all of your senses in describing it. Once you have done this, write and/or draw another version in which you tell the offender(s) to leave you alone or someone protects you. You may need help in constructing this version since you may not have much of an idea of how a protective, nurturing authority figure would act.

If one of the effects of your abuse is a multiple personality disorder, you need to incorporate your personalities and make them allies in recovery rather than competitors. This is such a complex disorder that I encourage you to work with a professional who understands the condition. When the time is right, sit down and write letters to each of your personalities, inviting them to be available and cooperative.[5] If you have a personality that is too young to read or write, draw a picture of yourself coming together and healing.

The mental violations associated with sexual abuse are healed by "debriefing" the abuse experience. In debriefing, the survivor recalls (this is a process rather than an event) the details of what was done to him. As he describes the abuse and as someone believes him, he grows more confident and begins to trust his perceptions of reality more. He gains insight into how his history of abuse has affected his outlook on the world. He begins to question long-held beliefs such as these: "People can't be trusted," "I deserved what I got," "I am a bad person," or "The world is a dangerous place." He then can replace these self-defeating beliefs with more positive ones. I reframe the abuse by relabeling various components—for example, "You didn't 'score,' you were molested."

The Emotional Aspects

The emotions associated with sexual abuse recovery are often very powerful, so a survivor may be afraid to be aware of them or to express them for fear of hurting himself or others. This fear of his emotions requires him to maintain a flat affect in order to "hold

his emotions in check." This flat affect keeps him from experiencing life fully and from getting intimate. My role is to affirm the
validity of his emotions and to support the *appropriate* expression
of them. Men in particular need to be taught that the expression
of anger need not be associated with violence nor the expression
of sadness with weakness.

Many survivors are afraid to experience their emotions fully.
They fear that once they begin feeling they will never be able to
stop. The emotions seem huge, "bigger than life." This is because
the abuse took place in childhood, and so a portion of what is felt
is similar to how children experience their emotions. These "child-
size" emotions are more frightening than adult-size emotions, so it
is important to remind yourself that you lived through the actual
abuse experience and that you can survive the healing experience
of recalling the emotions.

If the survivor was abused by a parent, other family member, or
loved one, I have found that it is important to make clear to him
that it is *not* a requirement of therapy that he hate the offender or
never see him or her. Most clients who were abused by family
members maintain a strong loyalty to and even love for the indi-
vidual(s) in spite of the abuse. On the other hand, some clients
need permission to talk about hatred they feel. In either case the
client's response is to be accepted as valid, and my stand is that
there is no therapeutically "correct" response that the client
"should" have if he is "healthy." It is common for some of my
clients to experience love and hatred simultaneously, and this can
lead to some confusion about which emotion is the "real" one. At
these times it is helpful to remember, "You love the person (who
was abusive), and you hate what he or she did to you."

Since victims incorporate shame as part of their identity, if the
issue is not addressed, the man is likely to continue to self-abuse
or to be vulnerable to others abusing and taking advantage of him.[6]
Therefore, the core emotion that needs to be addressed if the survivor is to recover fully is shame. No amount of insight, reframing,
or logic can heal a shameful person. Shame comes from neglectful
or otherwise abusive relationships and involves a belief that the
individual cannot be loved or accepted by anyone who truly knows
him, so an intimate and accepting relationship is required to treat

it. It is not what the client *learns* but what he *experiences* that is important.[7] The Twelve-Step program used by anonymous groups is helpful in healing with excessive shame, particularly steps four and five. You may want to do some reading about this process and make use of it in your own recovery plan.[8]

Since the relationship is so central in the healing of shame, the question of gender comes up. If the client was abused by a male, obviously he will have a strong reaction to a male therapist. On the other hand, if he was abused by a female, he still has male authority figure issues to deal with since his father did not protect him from the abuse. It either case my gender is useful in the relationship. In one sense I am reparenting the client, teaching him about manhood. This is often a topic of discussion in sessions. Rituals concerning manhood are very useful in helping my client to claim his manhood, which he may view as having been stolen, destroyed, or denied him through his victimization. At times I have met with my male survivors in a wooded setting, around a fire, and used stories to teach about manhood. Survivors report that experiences of this type are very powerful for encouraging a sense of pride in being male.

In order to become more aware of all your emotions, do a nightly feelings inventory. Using the list in figure 6–1, write or say, "Today I feel [one of the feeling words] because [the situation in which you had the emotion]." Start out by yourself, but after a week or two,

Mad

Sad

Glad

Afraid

Guilty

Lonely

Shameful

Proud

Hurt

Grateful

Figure 6–1. DAILY INVENTORY OF EMOTIONS

call or meet with another person and go over the list with him or her. You will notice that it gets easier and easier to identify and express your emotions.

Here is another thought to bear in mind. If someone is having panic attacks, or is too depressed or anxious to take part effectively in therapy, it becomes necessary to make use of medications in order to stabilize that person's mood enough to make recovery possible. Some people are strongly opposed to the use of medications. Common objections that clients have are these: fear that the use of medications implies that they "aren't doing it right" or that the therapist secretly thinks they are insane; fear that using medications would be taking "the easy way out" or would be "avoiding the real issues"; fear that use of medications will lead to drug addiction; or, for recovering alcoholics and other drug addicts, fear that use of medications means they have relapsed. When needed, appropriately prescribed, and properly taken, medication is a very useful part of the recovery process. It is not a "fix" or a magic wand. By itself it will not heal the effects of sexual abuse, but it can reduce the symptoms of the abuse so that the healing can take place. Most use of medication is short term. Use of these medications is no more a relapse or "slip" than taking an antibiotic for an infection.

Questions to help identify your thoughts and emotions:

Have you always remembered that you were abused? If so, what did you do so that you could live with these painful memories? (Drug use, compulsive behaviors, dissociation, and so forth.)

If you only recently began to have recall, how did the memories come back to you? (Through dreams, blips, emotions, and so on.)

If you were to draw a picture of your emotions about your (loved one's) sexual abuse, what would it look like?

If you were to draw a picture of your shame, what would it look like? Who do you have in your life whom you could share this drawing with?

List the people, things, or situations that you are afraid of. How are they related to having been sexually abused? What steps can you take to reduce or eliminate the fear you have?

The Behavioral Aspects

No one can merely think or feel his way into recovery. There must also be a behavioral aspect to your recovery. Many of the new behaviors that recovery requires will seem uncomfortable and unnatural at first but with practice and time will become second nature.

Sexual abuse robs a person of a carefree childhood. Somewhere inside you is a wounded child who needs your acceptance and nurturance. As long as you hate, ignore, deny, or fear that vulnerable childlike part of you, recovery will only be superficial. One action you can take to comfort that part of you that is a little boy is to get yourself a toy animal, the kind that is soft and big enough to hold and hug. Go to a store and spend a lot of time (you're worth it) looking and touching the various animals. Pay attention to how you feel as you hold each one. Don't buy one until it seems right. You may be surprised at how wrong some seem and how right others are. One of my clients had little or no reaction to the teddy bears he tried out but began sobbing in the store when he held a toy rhino. He told me, "It was the perfect symbol for me. Rhinos are big and look tough but are really very gentle, just like me."

Here are my two favorite stories about the use of toy animals in recovery. The first one involves a client I had who was a high-powered, well-paid president of a company. He never let his emotions affect his business decisions—at least that is what he told me. He was good at his job and poor at the rest of his life. I asked him to buy himself a toy animal in order to get in touch with that part of him that wasn't confident and powerful but was afraid and vulnerable. He denied that he had those parts but reluctantly agreed to purchase a teddy bear. He returned the next week with a tiny toy bear, small enough to fit in his vest pocket. He told me, "I figured the next thing you would ask me to do was to carry the damn bear around with me, so I got one that I could keep hidden so nobody would think I went bonkers." He carried the bear in his pocket for some time, until one day in a tense business meeting he absentmindedly put his hand in his pocket and touched the bear. As he did so, he became aware of how frightened he was in the meeting, how lonely and isolated he was from everyone, and how much this was like what he felt during his childhood. That noon he went out and purchased a larger bear and placed it on his desk to remind himself that he had a soft side. He found so much comfort in that symbol that he bought bears for all of the managers of his company and delivered them himself. He then found it easier to be gentle with himself and to open up in his therapy group and to be more expressive emotionally. Eventually he had a huge bear in his office that he would lean against for comfort when he was having a particularly stressful day. His ability to comfort himself with the toy helped him to seek out and accept comfort from other people.

The second story involves another man whom I asked to get a toy animal, and he also reluctantly agreed. He dragged it around with him for weeks, not seeing any use in the experiment. Finally, one day, when he was driving in his car, he had to slam on his brakes to avoid an accident, and his toy animal went flying across the car and crashed into the dashboard. Without thinking, he cried out, "Are you alright?" As he picked up the toy animal off the car floor, he became aware of how he had once been very little and vulnerable and that he had been taken advantage of and misused. He began to cry, holding the animal and rocking himself. He had finally given himself permission to know all of himself.

SUBSTANCE ABUSE

If you have any doubts (and perhaps even if you don't) about your use of alcohol and other drugs, then find a competent alcoholism/chemical dependency counselor and get an evaluation. Some county or state mental health centers have a substance abuse specialist on staff. Many states have a certification requirement, and the agency that issues the certificate will be able to help you find a qualified person. Just because someone has a graduate degree does not mean that he or she has had any training at all in identifying chemical use problems.

Regardless of where you live there is probably an Alcoholics Anonymous meeting within a reasonable distance. As the name implies these meetings are anonymous, and they are free. A collection is taken in order to pay for the meeting space, but it is completely voluntary. If you choose to contribute, one dollar is the customary amount. You need not think or say you are an alcoholic to attend AA meetings. The only requirement is "a desire to stop drinking."[9] You need not say anything when you go; you can just listen. AA also publishes literature on recovery and a list of twenty questions to help people determine whether they have a drinking problem. Most AA meetings have a supply of pamphlets that are free or low cost. You may want to read the stories in *Alcoholics Anonymous* to see if your chemical use is similar.[10] There are also other groups based on the Twelve Steps of AA. For example, Narcotics Anonymous holds similar meetings and has a book that includes stories of recovering addicts.[11] What do you work on first if you have both a drug problem and were sexually abused? Well, if you cannot stay sober while you are trying to look at your past, you have to address the drug problem first. Regardless of whether you have a chemical use problem, it is advisable to stop all use of mood-altering recreational drugs while you are in the early stages of recovery.

RELATIONSHIPS

One advantage of having a group of trusted people available to you is that you can get a "reality check" on your relationships. If you think something "just doesn't seem right," you can talk it over and get someone else's perspective. Victims often have an overly high tolerance for the intolerable and do not realize that the relationships they are in may be neglectful or abusive.

Recovery requires a sense of safety. If you are being abused or are being abusive in your primary relationship, it will not be safe enough for you to assess the memories and emotions necessary for recovery. Do whatever is required to see that name calling, threats, slapping, hitting, pushing, shaking, throwing things, and other intimidating and violent behavior are no longer a part of the relationship, even if that means a separation or ending of the relationship. If your partner is willing to agree to be a part of a safe and mutually respectful relationship, this can be an important asset in your recovery. You may also want to take part in some couples counseling.[12] If your partner does not exhibit a sense of goodwill toward you or a willingness to see the relationship change and grow, it will make your recovery more difficult.

On the other hand, you may be in a very respectful, supportive, and kind relationship and still be frightened, or, as some people say, have a fear of intimacy. I doubt that you have a fear of intimacy; I think it is more likely you have a fear of betrayal. Having been sexually abused as a child, you know about betrayal: at least one adult betrayed the trust you had in her or him by sexually abusing you or by not protecting you from sexual abuse.

SEX

Many survivors have a difficult time being playful or spontaneous when having sex or other physical contact, because it reminds them of the very serious times they were taken advantage of as a child. Others report that during sex they have a sense of becoming very small or young, often the age at which they were first abused. Since sexual abuse is someone being sexual with you in a situation in which you could not give meaningful consent, it is very important in the recovery process for you to decide if and when you want to be sexual with someone. When your spouse or partner requests or initiates sexual contact, take time to determine whether you are really interested in being sexual and how you want to be sexual. Actively and consciously decide, don't just go along with it. And remember, even if you say yes, you can always say stop or no *at any time*. You have a choice about sex now. In the past it was *taken* from you; now you are free to choose if you want to *give* it. The best sex partners are those who are clear and honest about wanting to be sexual or not wanting to be.

You may want to be sexual in a setting different from that in which you were abused so that the physical surroundings will be less likely to trigger intrusive memories of the abuse. If you were abused in a bedroom at night, perhaps at first it would be easier for you to be sexual in the living room during the day. Also, there may be certain actions or words that lead to painful recollections.

Become aware of these, let your partner know what things are frightening to you, and discuss alternatives.

Questions to help identify your thoughts and emotions:

What self-harming behaviors did you use to deal with the pain and shame of being abused? (Compulsive/addictive behaviors, and so forth.)

What resources have you got in your life to help change these hurtful behavior patterns into more self-nurturing behaviors? (Twelve-Step groups, therapy, friends, spirituality, and so on.)

What survivor skills do you have that you can make use of in your recovery?

What are some ways in which you can get in touch with the childlike part of you?

Find yourself a toy animal and hold it. What images, thoughts, sensations, and emotions do you become aware of?

If you have been engaged in self-mutilation or self-injury, write out your history. What patterns do you notice? What motivates you to harm yourself? (Look at the reasons listed earlier in the chapter on behavioral effects of abuse.) How do you feel prior to, during, and after harming yourself? How could you attain the same goal without resorting to self-abusive behaviors? For example, if you hurt yourself to prove your existence, you could call someone from your support system and ask him to confirm that you are real and that you matter to him.

What sexual issues need addressing in your life?

What actions can you take to improve the quality of the sexual aspects of your life?

The Spiritual Aspects

I have found that the spiritual aspect of the abuse cannot be effectively addressed until some significant progress has been made concerning the man's shame. Since shame is about being unworthy, it interferes with the survivor's ability to imagine a loving, accepting god figure. As with shame, spirituality cannot be productively argued—it must be experienced. I can describe my version of spirituality, but my client must discover and define his own. It is, however, helpful to point out parallels between the client's parents, particularly his father, and his view of his god(s). Once again the therapeutic relationship is a potent tool, because the client has entered into an intimate relationship with a powerful male figure and has been accepted just as he is. This experience opens the door to the possibility that a similar relationship can be formed with a supreme being or higher power of some type.

Sexual abuse robs you of things that are rightly your's; therefore you may want to find rituals that help you reclaim that which was stolen from you.[13] For example, devise a ritual that restores your innocence or your virginity. One client who had been sexually abused as a child had a virginity-reclaiming ritual in his therapy group. This gave him a sense of choice and purity when he decided again to be sexual with his partner, and this made it easier for him to see that his partner was different from the person who abused him and that what they were doing in bed was different from what had been done to him.

One useful tool in healing the spiritual aspects of sexual abuse is to find rituals that help you have a sense of being connected to the world around you and to others. You may find some of the rituals in organized worship services appealing. For example, the ritual of communion found in many churches can be used as a sign that the "badness," "dirtiness," or "unworthiness" that so many survivors experience is being washed away. If you are unable to find any rituals that you are comfortable with or that meet your needs, give yourself permission to be creative and create your own. For example, one client I had drew a picture of the shameful part of him and buried it in the company of several supportive and understanding friends. This "funeral" for his shame was very freeing for him. Another man had an "exorcism" of his bed to remove the "ghost" of his uncle who had abused him in his childhood bed and came to "haunt" him whenever he was sexual.

I went to the local legal forms store and purchased the form used in filing for divorce. Several of my clients have used copies of this to "divorce" themselves from their mothers, who had made them surrogate spouses. They told me they found it a very powerful experience to fill out the paper and to describe the reasons for the divorce.

As I wrote earlier, many victimized persons reject the concepts of spirituality and religion because they view God or other Higher Power in the same manner in which they view their parent(s) or other abusive authority figures. Meeting with a clergyperson who understands the impact of sexual abuse on spirituality can help to break this connection between abuse and spirituality. This idea can be very frightening, particularly if the childhood abuser(s) used the name of God or religion to justify the abuse or if the abuser was a member of a religious order. Some groups have a list of names of clergypersons who are willing to meet with sexual abuse survivors, are sensitive to the issues involved, and understand that forgiveness is a process, not an event, and is the result of a lot of work. Many survivors want help in understanding how there can be a God or other Higher Power that would allow child abuse to take place. They are angry at God and need permission to express it without being shamed. As one client said after describing his history of sexual abuse, "God has a lot to answer for." A patient clergyperson may be useful in helping you come to grips with this anger. Since sexual abuse involved mental as well as physical violations, it is very important that you come to your own conclusions and not be pressured into accepting someone else's answers (this applies to therapists as well as to clergy).

Questions to help identify your thoughts and emotions:

What is your concept of God/Higher Power? How has your view been affected by being sexually abused?

What are the advantages of having a God/High Power?

What are the characteristics of the God/Higher Power you would like to believe in? (Gentle, kind, wise, caring, nurturing, safe, and so on.)

If you are angry at God, write a letter saying so. Read it aloud. What feelings and thoughts do you have?

Write a letter of introduction to your God/Higher Power describing yourself and the type of relationship you would like to have. What emotions and thoughts do you have? What do you learn about yourself from writing this?

What rituals can you make use of in your life as signs of your worth and healing?

What actions can you take in order to improve your spiritual life?

What led you to seek help and to begin the recovery process? (In the language of Twelve-Step groups, what happened that you "hit bottom"?)

What do you want people to know about sexual abuse and its impact on people's lives?

Choosing a Therapist

The person(s) who abused you may have told you directly or indirectly that you are crazy. Then you may have told yourself that you are not sane. These messages and some of your family rules —like, "You shouldn't need any help; do it alone" or "Keep bad things a secret"—may make it difficult for you to seek assistance from a therapist. You may be afraid that getting psychotherapy confirms that you are insane or weak. Messages like these are good only for reinforcing denial and protecting offenders. You were mistreated, and you are worthy of getting assistance in healing from the effects of it. You didn't have a choice about whether you were sexually abused or not, but you do have a choice about whom you hire to help you heal.

The personality of the therapist and an understanding of the issues related to sexual abuse are more important than the type of formal schooling he or she has had. Many people do not believe that therapists and clients of different genders can work effectively together. I disagree with this view. I believe that the gender of the therapist is an important issue and one that ought to be decided on a case-by-case basis. A client who was sexually abused as a boy by a man will naturally have trust and fear issues if he decides to work with a male therapist. However, he will most likely also have similar issues with a female therapist since she will remind him on some level that his mother or another female guardian did not protect him from the sexual abuse. The issues are reversed when the offender was a female. I think men learn about being men best from other men. Ideally, I like to see sexual abuse survivors work with therapists of both genders at some time in their recovery— that way they learn to get both fathering and mothering. I particularly like doing therapy groups for sexual abuse survivors with a female cotherapist.

Whatever the gender of the therapist you choose to work with, he or she needs to be comfortable with the expression of intense emotion. Becoming aware of these feelings will be difficult enough without burdening yourself with a therapist who is afraid of emotions. Therapists who have little experience with sexual abuse survivors sometimes think, when their client is getting in touch with powerful emotions, that something is going wrong in the therapeutic process or that the client is decompensating (getting worse) or becoming psychotic and losing touch with reality.[14] You need a therapist who understands that safe expression of emotions can have a very healing effect. On the other hand, the therapist needs to understand that there is more to recovery than cathartic expression. Merely expressing the emotion is no more curative than just thinking about the abuse. All aspects, emotional, cognitive, physical, behavioral, and spiritual, must be addressed in some degree if the healing is to be complete.

If a therapist has never worked with a client on sexual abuse issues before or lacks confidence, two problems can arise.[15] First, the therapist will view the client as "different" from other clients. This is a concern because the therapist will not make use of the skills he or she has, thinking that somehow they don't apply, and because abuse victims already think of themselves as "different," meaning not as good as other people. If a client becomes aware that he is being treated differently, it may remind him of his "special" place in the family as the victim, and this may frighten him, or he may fear that it means he is so badly damaged that his therapist doesn't think he can recover. The second area of concern comes into play when the therapist thinks that everything in the client's life is related to the abuse and continues to focus on the abuse long after the client has successfully moved into the later stages of grief.

Questions to ask a prospective counselor or therapist: (When asking these questions, pay attention not only to the content of the answer but also to the way the person responds.)

Is he or she confident, clear, respectful, and cooperative? What do you feel as you talk with her or him?

What is your formal training? What degrees have you earned?

What certificates or licenses do you hold?

What type of services do you offer? (individual, couples, group, family therapy)

What are your fees?

When is payment expected?

Do you accept insurance or other third-party payments?

Where are sessions held?

How long have you been working as a professional helper?

What type of people and issues do you work best with?

What type of people and issues would you rather not work with?

Do you have any specialized training in the treatment of sexual abuse?

What is your definition of sexual abuse?

With how many sexual abuse victims have you worked?

With how many male sexual abuse victims have you worked?

What diagnostic category do you usually use with sexual abuse victims?

What are your goals for working with sexual abuse victims?

Recovery Issues for Partners

When it comes to the topic of sexual abuse, the only people who have been overlooked more than male victims are their partners.

As you have seen in the earlier chapters, childhood sexual abuse has broad and long-lasting effects on men's lives. These effects influence the lives of their adult partners as well. Therefore, it is likely that partners too will experience a healing/grief process. It involves many of the same steps.

You may have known that there was something "wrong" in your relationship with your loved one before you learned that he had a history of sexual abuse.[16] You no doubt tried to figure out what was wrong, what was keeping you from being as intimate as you wanted to be. You may have blamed yourself. Once you learned that your loved one had been sexually abused, you probably experienced many powerful emotions.

EMOTIONAL RESPONSES

Denial. For many people their first response to hearing that their partner was sexually abused as a child is relief. Suddenly so many things make sense. However, they may not realize what is involved in recovering from sexual abuse, and so they assume that since their loved one has acknowledged his sexual abuse, all his problems will disappear. They are quite disappointed to learn that awareness is only the beginning of recovery.

In many cases, the partners of men who were sexually abused were themselves abused as children. If this was true for you, beginning to discuss the topic of sexual abuse can be very threatening. It can trigger memories and emotions that you would have preferred to suppress. In order to deny your own abuse, you may deny your partner's abuse, and this dynamic can be very hurtful to the relationship.

Even if you do not have a history of being sexually abused, you may still find yourself denying your partner's abuse. Often this is because of a belief in the stereotypes concerning male sexual abuse victims that I discussed earlier. You may find yourself thinking things such as these:

"He can't have been victimized—that would mean he is weak and I can't count on him."

"I can't believe this; he must be a homosexual. Now he's going to leave me."

Fear. Many people respond to the news with fear. They are afraid that children are no longer safe in their home. They assume that because someone was abused as a child he is fated to become a child molester as an adult. It is important for these partners to have accurate information about pedophilia and compulsive sexual behavior so they can determine whether children are in any danger.[17]

In many cases, the person who abused your loved one may be an in-law or other family member, so you may still have a relationship and interaction with him or her. Realizing that this person you have known for some time abused someone you love can be a very frightening awareness. Do *not* assume that just because the sexual abuse you know about happened years ago this person is safe for you, your loved one, and your children to be around. People who have abused children and do not receive treatment are very likely to continue to abuse.

Partners in homosexual couples often fear that their loved one will be pressured by the therapist or will somehow decide that he is not really gay but is merely reenacting his childhood sexual abuse and will leave the relationship. In my experience, I have found that dealing with sexual abuse merely helps people become more comfortable with their sexual orientation and that there is overall improvement in the relationship.

Disgust. Upon first hearing that your loved one was sexually abused you may have experienced disgust. It may have been difficult not to view your loved one as tainted, damaged, or dirty. If you have had this reaction, it is important that you talk about your reaction with someone safe. Sexual abuse victims already think of themselves as disgusting, and unless you have someone outside of the relationship to talk with about your reaction, your loved one will probably be aware of your disgust, and it will reinforce his negative view of himself.

It is equally important that you do not "beat yourself up" for having this common reaction. Most people experience disgust when they hear about children being grossly mistreated. Your task is to separate what was done to the person you care about from who that person is. In other words, what was done to your loved one was disgusting, but your loved one himself is not.

Guilt. Some partners experience guilt for not knowing that their loved one had been sexually abused. They assume they should have known somehow. I hear statements like this: "I should have guessed. All the signs were there. I missed all the clues." In most cases this guilt is not appropriate or useful to you or to your loved one. It is more important to focus on the here and now than on your regrets about the past. If you feel guilt about something you did or didn't do, say so, make amends, and forgive yourself.

Many people do not understand how hurtful sexual abuse is. Some partners feel guilty because they think their loved one is "making a big deal out of something that happened a long time ago." This is one of the reasons why a group made up of others who have been victimized and can better understand the pain is important in your loved one's recovery.

Powerlessness. The most frustrating thing about caring about someone who has been so mistreated is your inability to eliminate his pain. You know he hurts, you know the reason why he hurts, yet you can only stand by, offering your support, while he experiences it. You are equally powerless when it comes to ridding your loved one of shame. You cannot talk someone out of the shame he is feeling. You can only treat him in a nonshaming, nurturing manner. Your actions, the respect that you show in the way you interact with your loved one, will show him that he is a worthwhile person, even when he doesn't believe it.

Anger. There is plenty to be angry about when it comes to the topic of sexual abuse. Perhaps the first anger you felt was toward the person(s) who abused your loved one. You may have been angry at your loved one for " letting it happen" or for not telling you sooner. A common target of anger is the therapist who may have brought up the topic of sexual abuse in the first place. You may get angry when the therapist questions you about your past, seeking clues concerning the possibility that you were also sexually abused. And you may get even more angry if that probing triggers memories showing that you were abused. The only thing more upsetting than one person in a relationship dealing with sexual abuse is both people in a relationship dealing with sexual abuse.

Awareness of sexual abuse never seems to come at a convenient time; it is always disruptive somehow. Your loved one's awareness of the abuse may seem like a burden instead of a breakthrough. You may find yourself longing for the days when sexual abuse was something that was only an issue for other people or something you merely read about in newspapers. You may resent the money your loved one is spending on therapy or the time he is spending with his support group members. You may be jealous of how important they have become to him. He may have become very self-focused and preoccupied. You might find yourself being angry over his mood swings, unpredictable behavior, and inconsistent responses. As one partner told me, "Well, at least one thing is predictable—that he isn't predictable!" He will have a change in priorities. What was vital before will now seem meaningless to him, and vice versa. It is not unusual for someone who was very tidy to become sloppy, or for someone who was very lax about housekeeping to become a "neatnik" and vacuum the floor three times a day. One day you will want to scream, "Get responsible!" and the next day you will want to yell, "Lighten up!" Living with a newly recovering person can be like an emotional roller coaster ride.

Don't be surprised to find yourself angry at your loved one's family for not protecting him from the abuse. You may be so angry that you need to take a break from socializing with them for a while. In these cases I suggest that you let family members know that you won't be coming around, but don't tell them the reason— it only adds to the problems. I have suggested to my clients that they write or phone, that they say for personal rasons they prefer to keep private at this time and will not be having contact for an unspecified lengthof time, and that they ask that their desire for privacy be respected. You may find that the more dysfunctional the family, the larger the protest over this limit-setting will be.

Many sexual abuse survivors need to stop being sexual for a time because they have a difficult time knowing the difference between sexual abuse and sex. You may find that the person you have been sexual with doesn't want to be sexual, is angry, afraid, or cries if you are sexual. All in all, it is a pretty safe statement to make when I say that dealing with sexual abuse really messes up a couple's sex life. Try to find comfort in the idea that as a person heals from sexual abuse, his sex life tends to become much more rewarding.

You will know that you have reached a point of acceptance when you are able to touch and be sexual with your loved one without being hyperaware of your every move and his every reaction. Part of the recovery from sexual abuse is to claim responsibility for one's life. Therefore, it is imperative that your loved one learn to be in charge of his own body and sexuality. This means that he must be aware of what he wants and doesn't want, and he must communicate that to you. It is not your duty to try to anticipate his reactions or read his mind. Offer him your honesty, your respect, and treat him like an adult.

One appropriate target of your anger is the person(s) who abused your loved one. Whether you know that person or not, you are likely to have fantasies of telling her or him off, or of being violent. These thoughts are very understandable. They are useful in coping with the sense of powerlessness you have about the situation. You may find some relief by telling someone or writing an unsent letter to the persons who abused your loved one, describing what you would like to do to them or what misfortune you would like to see them suffer. Denying the anger only prolongs it. Remind yourself that you are in the anger stage of grief and that when the time is right, you will move on to the next stage. Give yourself permission to indulge in putting a curse or two on them. I know a couple who got a great deal of relief sitting around one night and describing their revenge fantasies to each other. They ended up laughing together, something they hadn't done for months.

Periodically you may find yourself wanting to throw a tantrum because you are just fed up with therapy, support groups, a crying, vulnerable, unavailable partner, and books about sexual abuse lying around the house. Go ahead, have a tantrum. It will relieve some of the tension. However, may I suggest that you are less likely to feel guilty and will enjoy it more if you don't direct your tantrum at your loved one. Have it with a third party who won't take it personally, like a therapist or a friend who knows about the situation.

Acceptance/Forgiveness. Just as the actual victim must forgive his offender(s) to heal from the effects of the abuse, so too must you forgive if you are to have peace. Holding a resentment against the person(s) who harmed your loved one may give you a sense of power, but the emotional energy you spend keeping that resentment alive is energy you won't have to put into other more rewarding relationships. If you are in therapy, you may want to enlist your therapist's help in facilitating your working through the stages of forgiveness. Writing letters, which you never send, can be a very potent and safe method of expressing your emotions. Remember that hatred is as powerful a bond as love.

As I discussed earlier, partners tolerate a lot of stress while their loved ones are in therapy and in early recovery. Keep your eyes open for resentments about the inconveniences you experienced because of being in a relationship with a sexual abuse victim. These will prevent you from being very intimate. If you are having trouble forgiving him for his past behaviors, you may be holding on to the resentments to avoid noticing some guilt that you feel about something that you did or didn't do. If this is the case, you may want to forgive yourself first, which will make forgiving him easier.

Joy and Pride. Although it may be difficult to imagine right now, there is a great deal of joy that comes from working through a painful issue such as sexual abuse. Even when it seems that your relationship is being torn apart, there is still a part of you that can see how strong your bond is becoming as the two of you struggle to become intimate and whole. Once the two of you have overcome the effects of sexual abuse, your relationship will never be the same. You will know a new strength and pride.

GUIDELINES FOR RESPONDING TO SOMEONE WHO HAS BEEN ABUSED

Hearing that someone you care about has been mistreated is difficult. Here are some suggestions on how to respond. Since you are reading this book, you probably have already heard your loved one disclose something about his abuse. Regardless of how you responded then, the topic is bound to come up again, and again, and still again. Victimized people need to talk about what happened many times and in various ways. Your task is merely to listen as best you can. You can't fix him or make the pain go away.

Respect the person's privacy. Keep the details to yourself or within a confidential relationship, like that with a therapist, clergyperson, or support group.

Don't confront the abuser(s) yourself. It is your loved one's responsibility to do that when he is ready. Don't rob him of that experience.

Don't touch him without asking permission *each time*. His comfort with touch can change from moment to moment. What was okay an hour ago might be terrifying now.

Be open about your emotions. It is a sign that you care and that he matters. If you are sad when he tells you about what happened to him and want to cry, go ahead. But watch out that he doesn't then focus on your emotions and ignore his.

Pay attention to the emotions he has, rather than getting wrapped up in the details of what happened.

Comply with reasonable requests for special attention or safeguards. For example, if he is afraid to answer the phone for fear that it will be the person who abused him, then do more than your fair share of answering the phone or buy a phone answering machine and screen the calls.

Avoid telling him what to do.

Talk less, listen more.

Learn the healing power of silence shared.

Find a safe place to express *your* emotions.

Let him move at his own pace. Don't try to talk him into getting angry or talk him out of his sadness. Let him know you will be sticking around.

Remind him of how much you care about him.

Be patient.

Treat him as a worthwhile person.

Treat *yourself* as a worthwhile person.

GETTING SUPPORT FOR YOURSELF

Being in a relationship with a newly recovering person is very draining. He will be constantly reevaluating his beliefs and values.

He won't be sure what he is sure of. He will be questioning his relationships and studying every interaction. Often he will ask, "What did you mean by that?" thinking that there is some covert message hidden in what you are saying. He will be experiencing very powerful emotions. Many of these emotions will have nothing to do with you, but that doesn't mean that you won't be affected by them or that you won't be the target of them when he expresses them. When victimized people become aware of their pain and anger, they sometimes unfairly lash out at others. Being understanding is one thing, but don't allow yourself to be mistreated. Part of the recovery process is learning to express emotions *appropriately,* so *don't* tolerate verbal or emotional abuse from your partner.

Just as your loved one benefits from being in a group with others who have been sexually abused, you too will find comfort in becoming a member of a support group for partners. This will provide you with a safe place to complain, cry, get information about the recovery process, get a hug, and hear that things do get better.

PART
II

Survival Stories

Secrecy is the cement that holds incest firmly in place.
— Mike Lew, *Victims No Longer*.

Shut in
Locked in
Incoherent
Inarticulate
In a shell
Shell-shocked
Thunder-struck
Dumb-struck
Deaf and Dumb
Stupefied
Shut-down
Stunned
Oh, Wicked Mother of the Kingdom of Silence
I have obeyed you long enough.
— Roseann Lloyd, "Exorcism of Nice,"
Tap Dancing for Big Mom. p. 54

Jesus said, "If you bring forth what is within you, what you bring forth will save you. If you do not bring forth what is within you, what you do not bring forth will destroy you."
— Gospel of Thomas, in Elaine Pagels, *The Gnostic Gospels*

Having had a spiritual awakening as a result of these steps, we tried to carry this message to others and to practice these principles in all our affairs.
— The Twelfth Step in the recovery program, Al-Anon,
Living with an Alcoholic.

7

Greg's Story: The Son They Never Had

M Y name is Greg, and I am a recovering incest victim. I am writing my story to say that what happened to me was real, my feelings are valid, and that my family can't wish or pray away the tragedy—no matter how hard they try. I am an incest victim of my maternal grandparents. In putting my past on paper I am fighting the family rules that echo in my mind.

The following messages from my family have made writing this the hardest task in my life:

1. If I signed my name to the bottom of my story nobody would believe me because I am insane. Everyone knows I am insane because . . . .

2. My grandparents loved me so much there is no way they could have abused me. Anything that did happen was not abuse.

3. Everyone knows how religious and morally upstanding Grandma and Grandpa are, and since Greg is an admitted sex addict he must have been responsible for initiating any sexual contact *if* any did take place.

4. I am scarred and defective. I have an invisible "leprosy" inside me. If I open up and let anyone see the true me, they'll see how bad I really am and leave me.

5. Since most of what I recall about what my grandparents did is in the form of feelings, not visual memories, all of it must

be my imagination. I am confused and insane. None of the incest actually happened.

In spite of all the family messages to be silent, I am revealing what happened to help my healing and acceptance of the past.

Childhood Experiences

I am the oldest of four children, with two sisters and a brother. My father was the fourth child of seven. His father was an immigrant from Ireland, the twelfth of fourteen children. He ran away to America at the age of thirteen. He was a steamfitter and weekend alcoholic. My mother was the youngest of two girls. Her mother was very driven to be financially successful. Both my maternal grandparents worked while my mom and aunt were growing up and they had to raise themselves. Mom was her "daddy's little girl."

When my mom and dad were married, they moved in with her parents and continued to live with them for four years, until after I was born. They finally bought a house half a block from my maternal grandparents. I believe my mother had me because my grandma wanted a grandchild, not because my mother wanted or was ready to have children. I became the son my grandparents never had. If I was sick or crying, my mom totally relied on her mother to remedy the problem. Until the age of three, I don't believe I emotionally knew who my actual parents were. Looking back as an adult on my childhood I feel both anger and sadness that my parents relinquished all power in their relationship with my grandparents. I was just "leased" out to my grandparents, giving my parents one less child to have to deal with and, more importantly, fulfilling my grandparents' wish for a son. Early on, Mom and Dad were frightened by me, while my grandparents couldn't do without me. Although I do feel they all really loved me very much and considering how much attention I was being showered with, I never understood why I always felt so alone and frightened.

Growing up I was totally ignorant about sex. "Good Catholic families" don't talk about things like that. I had no idea that such a thing as sexual abuse existed. As an adult, the stories about incest I saw in the newspaper were hard for me to believe. *Could that actually happen* in a family?

Six years ago one of my sisters, Ann, asked me to a family counseling session at the local rape crisis center. As I sat there, both of my sisters described a family that I didn't know at all. I was shocked, but I could also see they were telling the truth. Both of my sisters revealed that they had been sexually abused for six years by Grandpa. My ultimate male role model turned out to be mentally ill. I thought to myself how glad I was that my grandparents hadn't done anything to *me*.

Two years ago I found our differently. I went to see a therapist for depression after being demoted at my job. I had been using compulsive overeating and compulsive sexual behavior as my primary tools for coping with life since my high school days. These behaviors eventually left me unable to deal with adulthood, severely depressed, and were seriously affecting my job performance and marriage. I went to a therapist for help, totally lost and not knowing why. I was very confused about my past. At first I couldn't remember any of my childhood. I couldn't remember what my mind had spent years blocking out. My memories of the incest only started to surface after I had been in therapy for a while. It is important for me to say that even now my memories are few and sketchy.

After completing a clinical program for my compulsive overeating and sexual addiction, I decided to share my insights with my younger sister, Stevie. After hearing about my stories of what happened with Grandma, she started telling me in more detail what our grandpa had done to her and Ann. Her memories were the key that opened the door to my past. Stevie would start a sentence and I would finish it: to my own amazement. The words spilled out of me without any conscious effort. It was almost spooky the way we jogged each other's memories. What was even spookier was what kind of feelings I was starting to feel about *my* being with *Grandpa*. Two years later, those feelings continue to haunt me.

The first memories to come back involved my grandmother. I am not sure how old I was, probably twelve, just entering puberty. My grandma had called me from the kitchen to tell me something. She came out of her bedroom and her blouse was wide open and her bra was undone. I stood there looking at her breasts for a second and then turned away, ashamed and excited. She asked why I turned away, saying, "What are you so embarrassed about? I bore your mother, you know." I became confused, wondering how I had stumbled into her, not remembering until later that she had called for me.

After this first time, a sort of ritual developed, where she would announce that she was going to need to change her blouse shortly. Then she stayed busy for five or ten minutes, giving me enough time to hide in her closet. The high (fear and excitement) of being "caught" looking at my grandma undressing and the mixed message I was receiving left me feeling dirty and shameful.

As I became more and more aroused, I became bolder. I started asking Grandma to show herself to me, and for a while she consented. I was allowed to sit at the foot of her bed and look up her nightgown. I was also allowed to sleep with her on weekends. My grandma seemed dismayed by my requests to explore being more sexual with her. She was never very direct, but she acted disgusted and seemed reluctant to consent. I touched her breasts and her pubic hair, but this must have intimidated her because the next time I came to visit I was told I could no longer sleep with her but had to start sleeping on a mattress she had put on the floor next to her bed. I felt as though I must have been very sick to have pushed her this far. Twelve years old and corrupting my grandmother.

Another clear memory I have is that of my grandma trying to get into the bathroom while I was bathing. I was about thirteen. Although I don't know why, I had taken the hidden key for the bathroom with me when I went to bathe. There was Grandma banging on the door begging to be let in so she could "visit" me. I told her she could visit me when I came out. I wanted my privacy. Her words are still clear as a bell: "Darling, honey, let Grandma in to see her little boy. Don't you love me anymore?" That memory still makes my skin crawl. As I grew into a teenager I found myself repulsed by my grandmother. I was pretty hostile towards her, and it intensified when I became sexually involved with girls my own age.

At first I had only two clear memories about being sexually abused by my grandpa. I recall sitting on his bed with the bedroom door closed and the curtains drawn, listening to his tape recorder with him. The tape he had made was a story about a pretty young girl named Sally and what happened to her during her long walks in the woods. The story revolves around her and three "healthy" young guys in their car. Tom, Dick, and Harry find Sally while going for a ride. She gladly agrees to have sex with all three of them. Sally was even happier to have sex than the boys were. Grandpa supplies all the voices, and there was much dialogue during the gang bang.

Grandpa actively questioned me as to which one of the boys I wanted to be. I remember at first not knowing how to answer, but Grandpa was patient and willing to coach me. I finally told him that I wanted to be the second guy, not wanting to deny him the opportunity of having Sally first. Other times I asked to be Tom, since he got to go first. Grandpa had told me I "wouldn't want sloppy seconds." (Getting in touch with this memory drains all the emotions out of me. The pain of how sick this was seems to be too big to feel.)

Sharing these fantasies with Grandpa seemed important to him, and he seemed to enjoy my taking part in it. I don't know exactly how often or how long I was subjected to this, but I do know it was frequent and probably lasted from age six through eleven. I have a lot of shame writing about this because I remember asking to hear the tape. Listening to the tape was our "special time together." His funny voices and the way he would get so excited would make me laugh. The time in his room became "our secret club." My parents never knew about the fantasy tapes; that was Grandpa's and my secret. He made other tapes of us telling ghost stories or singing songs that everyone else got to hear. My grandmother was happy that Grandpa and I had so much fun in his room. She would let me bring my favorite pop and cookies into Grandpa's bedroom when he and I were listening to tapes. But she used to scold him about his tape recorder, not understanding why she was left out. He went to great lengths to keep those tapes hidden from her.

The other clear memory I have is of him showing me his penis and testicles. We were getting undressed for bed. I asked him why his penis was different than mine. He explained what circumcision is in a matter-of-fact manner. He said that being circumcised made it easier for a man to keep clean, but since he was uncircumcised his penis was more sensitive to touch since it wasn't numbed from rubbing against his shorts. He was quite proud of the fact that he was uncircumcised. I don't think he encouraged me to touch him— but some gut feeling says if he didn't that time he probably did other times. Trying to remember, I get confused and nervous that I have to be *absolutely certain* before I have the right to write about it.

One of the most powerful experiences I had recalling my past began in a Reiki session (which is a form of physical therapy). I was trying to learn to relax and get in touch with the pent-up feelings inside my body. During one session, I was in a deep state of relaxation, when I suddenly felt a dull pain in my shoulders. It felt as though someone was bearing down on them. While the therapist continued to ask about the pain in my shoulders, my face started stiffening. The pain in my face was intense and growing. Gradually I became aware that my face was somehow changing shape without any conscious effort of my own. Trying to visualize what kind of facial expression I was making, I realized my mouth was shaping the letter O. The therapist later confirmed this happened. I became short of breath, completely terrorized, and started crying. I begged the therapist to let me leave. She assured me nobody was preventing me from leaving.

I was unable to move. I felt pinned down. As the fear increased, my mind raced faster. Thoughts and images seemed to shatter inside my brain, and a silent scream from within kept telling me that Grandpa could *not* have done *that* to me. At the next session at my regular therapist's office I told him that I was beginning to believe that my grandpa had forced me to perform oral sex on him. Even now I feel as though either I'm crazy for writing this, or somehow responsible that such a thing happened. My therapist believed me and that the abuse could have taken place. He did much to help me deal with the family messages and to see who was really responsible for the abuse occurring.

Three weeks later I did some memory regression work with my therapist, trying to improve the link with my childhood memories. Through hypnosis I went back to my grandparents' house. Most of the scenes I recalled were through the eyes of a child.

I remember going into my grandpa's bedroom and seeing him sitting on the edge of the bed, with only his T-shirt on.[1] I look up into his face and all of the sudden I'm watching a little boy of three or four years in front of my grandpa. The little boy looks just like me, but I'm up in the corner of the room, hovering by the ceiling. I can't see what is going on. Grandpa has his back to me, and his body is blocking my view from the corner.[2]

I become scared. With my therapist and wife I sat shaking, crying and paralyzed. I couldn't move or open my eyes. As I started to cry, I began to talk in a higher and more frightened voice. A few moments later I was frightened enough to ask my therapist to help me out of my memories and end the session.

The most compelling reason for writing my story is to be able to confirm my feelings about being an incest victim. I have had very strong emotional and physical response to certain situations, both in and out of therapy. These feelings lead me to believe that what I have remembered so far is only a small part of what actually happened. I now know that I need not minimize the impact or seriousness of what was done to me. Some of the consequences of the sexual abuse have been severe. In adolescence, I became a compulsive overeater to physically keep people away. I also believed that my size would give me the appearance of power or strength.

I am intimidated in one-to-one relationships with men. On a recent trip with a friend, I found myself terrified to sleep in the same room with him.

Other experiences I have had that support my belief that there was incest are:

Becoming dizzy and nauseated while watching any movies that contain any sex where force is used

Waking up in the middle of the night, convinced there is a man in the room

Being afraid to meet women, fearing that if they are sexually attracted to me I won't have the right or ability to say "no" to them

Believing that my body is repulsive and unattractive, even to my wife, and that I'm genitally underdeveloped

The most devastating effect of the incest is how much shame I have. Shame is a reaction that becomes self-perpetuating and self-triggering. It creates binds that are difficult to see through or past. It flooded all areas of my life and who I am. My self-perception was clouded and my self-esteem was nearly nonexistent. My most frequent response to others' anger was to assume that it was about *who* I am and not about what was done. I've always taken on everyone else's ill-feelings. The other half of the bind is I feel just as badly when praise or compliments are directed my way. I've felt so deceitful and unworthy. If they only knew who I really was. Since shame is about who I am and not about feelings or behaviors, there seems no chance for change or forgiveness.

My shame severely clouded my view of reality. I always thought my wife was entirely in control of our relationship. I felt I had very little say in anything that happened or how we interacted. The truth was that my behavior had a very large effect on the course of our relationship. My unconscious or underlying belief was that I needed to get affirmation from her to prove my worth as a human being. The patterns I was taught as an incest victim were that someone important really showed her love and approval through being sexual with me. Any signs of affection or attention were simply methods to manipulate me. I refused to kiss or hold her unless it led to sex. Being sexual was the only selfless gift another person gave that did not require repayment.

Since I needed daily affirmation and assurance that I was an acceptable person, I asked my wife to be sexual at least every day. If she declined, I knew that it meant something was wrong with *me*. This was very painful to accept, so whenever she said no, I would continue to ask, plead, beg, and badger her for sex. She felt attacked, yet I assumed she was the one that was in control of the situation.

When we were sexual I often asked my wife to be aggressive and take control of the lovemaking. There seemed to be something comforting in having her take responsibility for the outcome of the sexual encounter. I now realize that I was trying to recreate the same feelings I felt when I was being abused by my grandfather and grandmother. Due to my fear of intimacy, I would often fantasize out loud about sexual things, hoping my wife would fulfill these fantasies. This also distracted me from what was actually happening and helped me to cope with my shame about receiving love from my wife.

Sexuality is a big part of a person's core being, and the people who were supposed to care and protect me were the ones who shamed and violated my sexuality. The double messages about sex, what was right and wrong, left me feeling the incest was somehow my fault. My parents were always treating sex as taboo, while my grandparents concurred in word only, not in action. I was always being told sex was dirty and bad, yet physically it felt good. The real message seemed to be: "There's something wrong with Greg." This shame, combined with the belief that the only way to feel affirmed was to be sexual, led me to become a sex addict.

There is much confusion in my mind about what parts of my behavior are due to being an incest victim and what parts are due to my sexual addiction. I see evidence that the beliefs and values about sex I was taught in an incestuous family led me to become compulsive about sex.

With the help of my Twelve-Step groups, sponsors, therapist, and support from my wife, I have made many strides in my recovery. Still, the shame about my abusive behaviors in my marriage makes it difficult to be close to my wife. Many times this shame prevents me from viewing myself as equal to my wife. I am afraid that my wanting to be sexual will be judged as addictive by her and that she will leave me. It is very hard to share my fear of abandonment with her or anyone. I feel like people will think I am crazy for having feelings like that. Any healthy urge to be sexual with her is accompanied by the thought that there must be something wrong with me for wanting to be sexual. I also think of the old shame-bound messages: sex is something only I want and she only consents to please me. Of course I don't deserve anything, therefore I shouldn't even ask in the first place. If I do ask and she says no, it proves I was wrong to ask. If I ask and she says yes, she's only doing it for my pleasure. I end up feeling so unworthy of any nurturing that I can't even enjoy the lovemaking. It becomes physically painful.

My defense of dissociation had become so ingrained that it was almost a reflex reaction to any changing stressful situation. Although dissociation was useful when I was being abused, it became a handicap in my ability to respond as a spouse, parent, and employee. Many times when faced with the possibility of a highly emotional conversation or argument I imagined what was going to happen. I planned what I would say and what the other person would say. When I was actually with the other person, I was so frightened by my feelings and those of the other person that I retreated into a fantasy. Since I hadn't been totally present during the actual event, afterwards I had an extremely difficult time separating what had really gone on and what was fantasy. Dissociating while my wife was looking to me for support was very painful. I was unable to listen to her feelings, figuring that anything negative that was happening to her must be my fault and I would just space out. Consequently, I never really knew what was on her mind and I felt very distant from her.

These are the consequences and effects of being sexually abused I am most in touch with today. Being a sexual abuse victim left me with an impaired ability to see the world and my place in it. With the exception of the sex fantasy tape, my family of origin explain away and excuse everything that happened as not sexual abuse, but as merely a coincidence, or Greg exaggerating things or making things up. The reactions and feelings I've had are the only real proof I can hold on to that the abuse was real and damaging.

The help I received from my therapist was twofold. He helped clear away the "fog" covering my past and he introduced me to the Twelve Steps. The therapy I've done is important; learning about the abuse has helped me accept why I behaved and felt like I did all those years. I also need to say that insight alone is not enough to change one's life. That is where the Twelve Steps come in. By joining Overeaters Anonymous I was able to start treating my body in a healthier manner and begin to love myself. Shortly after joining OA I joined Sex Addicts Anonymous. In SAA I learned that I was in the throes of a terrible and progressive illness and that willpower alone was not enough. With the help of my sponsor and friends in the program I was able to start finding out that there is such a thing as healthy sexuality. I have stopped my destructive behaviors towards myself and the ones I love.

The struggle to use, or not use, sex and food to deal with my fears, hurts, and anger is still there. The difference is that I have a choice in what I can do. I no longer have to fight this battle alone. As a matter of fact, I don't have to fight at all. I have learned about a higher power, one that I can trust. I just have to work the Twelve Steps to the best of my ability and turn the rest over to my higher power. It's a daily reprieve from the insanity of the past. I only need to be willing to work the steps and face my feelings.

Twenty-three months after joining OA and SAA I have eighteen months of "sobriety" in both programs. I weigh two-thirds of my former weight. For the first time in my life I am eating to nourish my body, not stuff my feelings. I have some struggles in learning to accept my body as it is; a lot of the old feelings still pop up now and then. I have been blessed with a loving and patient wife. Together we are finding out about love and a healthy sexual relationship. I've also found out that women are people, people with a lot to offer, not just walking objects of my lust. For the first time in my life, I have men friends. Men that care about me as a person, not as someone to use or abuse.

Knowing that I was a sexual abuse victim is still painful and difficult to accept. I still carry a lot of hurt and anger towards my parents and grandparents. Understanding doesn't produce immediate acceptance or relief from pain. The ability to forgive them is something that I have prayed for and need to continue to pray for. It is a process that takes time. The most important thing I want to share about my story is that there is hope and healing. I can't change the past, but I have been gifted with some tools that are helping me accept that past and move on to a better and happier life.

Additional Thoughts Six Months Later

I have continued to have new awarenesses about the family I came from and how they've influenced me. I failed to mention earlier that I work in the same office my dad does. This has become very difficult for me. His daily physical presence reminds me how little he was, and still is, available for me emotionally.

I've started to look at and accept that a lot of the attitudes I had in my sexual addiction came from my parents as well as my grandparents. My dad always shamed me about my sexuality and any interest in sex. I now see the same man ogle women in the office, and I've heard him make repeated inappropriate sexual comments to female co-workers. I now wonder why he always locked himself in the bathroom every morning for one hour. If we needed to use the toilet, we just had to wait. I question whether he too used compulsive masturbation as a tool to face the pressures and stresses he met every day.

Memories of having to share my closet with my mom while growing up are becoming clearer and more unsettling. She was always parading around in her bra and panties while my dad was hollering at her from their bedroom to "cover herself up." He'd tell her to cover up before coming in my room so I "wouldn't get sick in bed."

My mother has exhibited some current behavior I would call at the very least unusual. During one visit to my home she sat across the living room from me and continued to hike her dress up while talking to me. She seemed to be doing it unconsciously, and my dad told her three times to "pull her damn skirt down" before she finally acknowledged him with a cold, raging stare.

I also saw my mom sit on the edge of my sofa, pull my son and then daughter between her legs "to give them a hug," while she rocked back and forth against them with her legs round them. I'm still shocked at that one-time incident. My wife and I put a stop to that behavior.

I don't know if I was ever abused sexually by my parents, but I do know what kind of families they came from.

I am writing about this because I am a parent in recovery and I have responsibility to my children. My children deserve a chance to grow up in a healthy system. Therefore, I called my mom and dad into therapy a month ago to share some facts and feelings with them. I told them that I had been sexually abused and that I deserved better. They acknowledged that the abuse from my grandpa had occurred, but their prime concern was that I wasn't accusing them of anything. I also told them I would not allow them to baby-sit my son and daughter. The most frightening part of this decision was that I didn't offer them any reason other than I was uncomfortable with them sitting. I did this as respectfully as I could without allowing them to challenge my feeling and reality. Standing up to my mom and dad as an adult confronts all my fears of being abandoned by two people who were never there while I was being abused.

I am not happy that I was sexually abused, but I am very grateful that I've been introduced to the Twelve Steps and the opportunity to live life in a new way.

Questions to help you identify your thoughts and emotions:

How is your (your loved one's) story similar to Greg's?

How is your (your loved ones) story different from Greg's?

What emotions did you have reading Greg's story?

What was the most powerful section of the story for you?

What did you learn about yourself from reading this story?

8

Katherine's Story

Early in 1986 my husband, Greg, went to see a therapist for his anger and depression. After his first visit he notified me that he was going into treatment for five days. Upon returning home he shared with me that he was a compulsive overeater, an incest victim, and a sex addict. I remember how sad and frightened I was. He was deserving of much more and had been betrayed by both his parents and grandparents. My trust in Greg's parents and grandparents was shattered. The very people who were supposed to love and nurture him had left a long path of destruction. I now understood my husband's reaction when our first child was born. He had been left a legacy of fear: Would he have to struggle now to avoid abusing his own child, or in trying to maintain a "safe" distance? Could he give our daughter the love and nurturing she deserved? I was scared. However, I finally had words to affirm the craziness I had been feeling all those years. My many prayers for help had been answered. I started to feel there was hope after all.[1]

I had felt such emptiness. It was always like I was walking ten paces behind Greg. I would start to get close, only to get a door slammed in my face. I always felt responsible and knew that I could never make Greg happy. I was aware that he never felt content. I had felt the unhappiness in my marriage had been my fault. My family message was strong: "If you would only try harder, everything will be all right."[2]

It was a year after my husband was in recovery before we began couples therapy. I was scared. More old family messages came up: "Don't ask for help. You can handle this yourself." It was in reaching a point where I feared that I had *lost myself* that I agreed to go for help with our relationship. Accepting that my husband was an addict and victim seemed easy compared to accepting that I had any problems. Saying that I was codependent or a co–sex addict seemed devastating. Seeking out support from other women at a Twelve-Step group (Co-SA) was very difficult but crucial to my acceptance and recovery.[3] This process continues for me even today. Greg and I started working hard on our communication, anger, and intimacy issues. The roadblocks seemed endless. For years I was unaware that Greg even masturbated. It was hard to hear that he compulsively masturbated during our entire marriage, even immediately after being sexual with me. Even worse was how he was always comparing me to other women. I never had big enough breasts, I never made enough noise while we were sexual, I never wanted to be sexual often enough.[4] The list of complaints seemed to go on and on and on. Now all that seemed important was that all my anger and hurt *had* to be expressed and validated. Our old patterns of interacting were *so* engrained.

I remember a few sessions when my husband did memory regression work to recall additional details of his sexual abuse. My biggest feeling was wanting to hide. I was confused and unsure of what my fear was about. Greg and our therapist worked with hypnosis and started to unlock many more of the secrets from his past. It felt good that Greg would allow me to be present during these sessions. I felt that he *trusted me.* It seemed to be a very big statement about our relationship that he shared his realities about his past with me, no matter how sordid the details. At the same time the sexual struggles in our relationship heightened. Many times while making love, Greg became frightened and said that he felt like he was being sexually abused again. These waves of feelings seemed to come and go without notice. I was confused and frightened. Seeing Greg's courage helped me believe that I could unlock the door to my past and accept my life too. My denial, *anger*, and *fear* couldn't stay locked up any longer.[5]

When our therapist suggested that I go into group therepy, I started sobbing. Thinking of going to group therapy by myself was terrifying. I was painfully aware that during my couples work with Greg, whenever my family was mentioned, all I could do was cry. Once starting group, for months all I could do was cry. Talking seemed like an impossibility. I found my memories of childhood are very few up until about the age of six. My father had died when I was four years old, very unexpectedly. I was not allowed to grieve or express any anger about losing him. Conversations about my father or his death were nonexistent. My mother set me up for a lifetime of never expressing or even having any feelings. My family rules were *strong:* "Don't have any feelings, or at the least never show them to *anyone.*" Locked inside, however, these feelings festered.

I remember as a child coming home from kindergarten to an empty house; Mom was working, trying to make ends meet. I always felt so alone, even when my mom was home. My greatest fear was that no one would ever miss me, or even notice if I were gone. I learned well at an early age to take care of myself and be responsible. The memory of just playing seems nonexistent.

Six or seven years after my father's death my mother remarried. My stepfather turned out to be an alcoholic. It was readily accepted that I could drink alcohol with my mom and stepfather, even in my early teens. Drinking was something we all did together as a family. The years to follow were filled with drinking and fighting. When there were fights between my mom and stepfather, my role in the family was to be the mediator. I was coaxed into this role by both of them. I was beginning to act more like a parent than a child. A memory that stands out is my mother asking me if I thought she should divorce my stepfather. She also confided in me her frustration about their sexual relationship: he was impotent and they had never consummated the marriage.

My stepfather's comments to me were always so negative: "You're fat and lazy!" Fat maybe, but not lazy.[6] How could this be? I was the one to clean the house, cook, do the laundry, and mow the lawn. My mother's reaction to his harassment? *None.* Her unspoken message was clear: *"Try harder."* In addition to taunting me about being fat, my stepfather began grabbing at my breasts, always stopping just inches short of touching me. Again, my mother's reaction? *Nothing.* Years later, she did ask more than once if he had sexually abused me. How strange it seems to me now that my mother watched this happening and never saw it as sexual abuse. Considering my mother's attitude, it's no wonder that I had such a hard time accepting that, although he never touched me, this really was sexual abuse. It took me many months of therapy to accept that I too had been sexually abused. It was painful that after hearing about the abuse my husband had been through, I never made any connection to my own.[7]

All these people around me and I felt so alone. I am now starting to feel the tremendous anger and hurt that she never stood up for me, never reaffirmed that I was a good person, deserving to be treated with respect. By adulthood my self-esteem was nonexistent. It was no mistake that my husband and I were a match.

The struggles and the pain I have felt in my marriage have been strong. I also realize that in accepting my past, I can now look forward to the future. I can now plainly see that my childhood set me up for the adult life I chose. The covert nature of being sexually/ emotionally abused and abandoned has made it harder to accept and deal with. My stepfather never *physically* touched me while sexually abusing me. My husband was never *physically* unfaithful to me, so where is the *real abuse*, I thought. Now I know *it was there*, and I feel stronger than ever.

Today I still sometimes struggle in my attempts to assert myself and ask for what I need. Sometimes it seems easier to ignore my feelings, my anger, than to confront people with it. I also know that my family messages lead me through a lot of pain and that I have the tools to cope and grow in relationships. I feel that the spiritual growth in my life is responsible for the happiness I feel inside. I feel hope and joy in the future, and I don't have to be the only one "trying harder" to achieve it.[8]

Questions to help you identify your thoughts and emotions:

How is your (your partner's) story similar to Katherine's?

How is your (your partner's) story different from Katherine's?

What emotions did you have reading Katherine's story?

What was the most powerful section of the story for you?

What did you learn about yourself from reading this story?

9

The Story of Sonny Hall

My name is Sonny Hall. I am fourteen years into the recovery process, but it has only been in the last year that I have known that I am recovering from incest. About a year ago I was able to face that I am recovering from incest and other types of abuse. Until I faced and came to terms with the abuse in my past, it affected every part of me, every day of my life, and I continued to be victimized in many ways.

My recovery began when I entered a Buddhist monastery in California. What I learned there formed the cornerstone of my recovery. The meditation practices I started there provided me with a way of stilling my mind, looking inside myself, and becoming aware of what was there. Even though overt memories of sexual abuse did not begin to surface until years later, meditation helped me to become aware of some of the other scars which I bore from my childhood.

This religious training helped me through some of the destructive ways I had lived in the past. If I had not had the good fortune to have this experience I probably would have committed suicide.

After studying at the monastery, I married. My wife gave birth to a son. I began working at a social service agency. About five years later a change in jobs required me to work under a weak and dependent female supervisor. In some ways she reminded me of my mother. Unaware of the deep and unresolved issues in myself, I became severely depressed and entered counseling. Unfortunately, the counselor was ineffective at dealing with the depression.[1] I was desperate. I turned to alcohol. My eventual alcohol dependency led to serious problems with my marriage. My wife and I began working with a family counselor. We got my drinking under control. Unfortunately, the shit kept hitting the fan. At work, my weak and dependent supervisor was replaced by a radical feminist. She attempted to dominate me; that made the situation much worse. The next two years brought academic and behavioral problems for my son. My wife had an affair; I began having anonymous sexual contacts with men.

Near the breaking point, I found another job. Slowly we began to pull our lives back together. My self-esteem improved. I left therapy for a year, although my wife continued. She frequently requested me to accompany her to these sessions; one day I gave in. We rehashed many old issues with the therapist that day, but for some reason he seemed to dwell on dynamics present in incestuous families. Some of them fit the struggles for autonomy and closeness which had troubled my life. Curious, I scheduled to see him privately five days later.

For five days my anxiety raged. I knew that Mom and I had slept together frequently, but we didn't have intercourse. That couldn't be incest—or could it? Could I have been abused? How could I even talk about it?.

The next meeting with the therapist confirmed my worst fears. I explained to him the situation between me and Mom. "Yes, that's incest," he replied. His words struck me like a left hook to the head. Tears began to flow. In my mind an image appeared of an infected wound. It is lanced; the wound drains.

Slowly, the relationship with my mom comes into focus. For a number of years, until the time I was about fourteen years old, my mother and I slept together every night. Even though we never had intercourse, the relationship was highly sexualized—we often hugged and kissed. Overall, it seemed like the husband/wife relationship in our family was between Mom and me. There were problems with that, of course. First, she was already married, to my dad, and second, the person she was choosing to have the relationship with was thirty years her junior. I suspect that Mom was terrified at the thought of having sex with Dad, so she manipulated me so that I came between the two of them. I can remember actually sleeping between the two of them—I must have been ten or eleven at the time. What seems striking about the memory is the emotional tone: best described as frigid. (Until recently I couldn't recall any other mistreatment.)

Over the next few weeks in therapy I tell the news to my wife. She is shocked. Slowly she understands my pain. Our therapist leaves for sabbatical, we begin with a new counselor. In the new counseling relationship I explore the environment in which I was raised. I recall images of my past: a house with a wood heating/cookstove, no firewood in the woodshed, the toilet stopped up for months, using a hastily built outhouse, the roof catching fire on the house—Dad putting out the fire, with the family still inside. I begin to realize that my home was chaotic and dangerous.

There were six people in my family. I am the youngest. My father was a distant and troubled man with an explosive temper. He slept just a few hours each night. Generally he would stay up until early morning reading before coming to bed. Mom was a dependent and infantile woman. A strict Christian, she went to church every Sunday. Yet she also molested me. We lived on a small farm. We were exceedingly poor. The six of us lived in a two-bedroom house. Due to the lack of space, my brother and I had to bunk in our parents' room.

My brother, who was ten years older than me, was fascinated with guns. Once, while cleaning his shotgun, there was an accident. He almost blew off my foot. I recall my parents scolding him for being careless with the gun; after they finished with him he took out his frustration on me.

At school he was frequently in trouble for fighting. At home, he and I fought continually. I think my brother was jealous of the "special" relationship I had with Mom. Maybe that was why he was so tough on me. He was a strong merciless bully and frequently beat the crap out of me. I fared poorly against his strength. When I was about eight, I came up with a way to end his bullying. I saved up my money and bought a large bowie knife. I planned to kill him someday.

I can't recall trying to let anyone know about the abuse. My family was very isolated. There seemed no one to tell. I used fantasy to cope. The *Perry Mason Show* was popular in those days. He seemed so capable, and I admired his smooth way with words. I borrowed his voice to run a narrative in my mind as if I were explaining my action to a jury. It really came in handy if I needed to explain my actions to my brother too.

When I was in the sixth grade one sister dropped out of high school and eloped with a Marine. That same year my other sister and my brother married and left home. I continued to live at home with my parents. The stress must have been unbearable, because that year my eyesight deteriorated from 20-20 to 20-400. To deal with the pain of the situation I ate compulsively and gained twenty pounds.

My mother continued not to respect my boundaries. She would enter my room without knocking—pretty embarrassing for an adolescent boy. She would also manage to find the "dirty" magazines I had hidden in my room. They would just disappear, without a trace, no discussion, no confrontation, nothing. I imagine she spent hours looking at them.

After my dad died of a stroke, Mom and I lived together for another three years. Living with her, dating and socializing were impossible. I felt I had to lie just to get of the house and visit friends. I think she might have been jealous. One time when she refused to let me go out I asked her why. "You're just growing up too fast" was her reply.

I continued to gain weight. At high school graduation I weighed 220 pounds. Despite miserable SAT scores, I was accepted to college. When I was ready to leave home for college, my mother attempted to find a job in that city and move with me. During the the first year away from home she pressured me to come home every weekend. The first year brought acceptable grades. But then I discovered drugs. The next three years brought LSD, grass, speed, mescaline, opium, trips on morning glory seeds, and peyote. Some of my pain began to surface, but more drugs kept it down. When I graduated I quickly moved to another part of the country to flee my mother.

As the weeks passed in therapy, other information emerged which points to other abuse in my childhood. I began to have nightmares of being raped in the mouth. I felt fragile and anxious. I felt as though I was digging through granite. My counselor and I decided that I should meet with yet another therapist for hypnosis.

With the hypnotherapist I learned self-hypnosis. My anxiety decreased. Slowly, other memories of abuse began to surface. I recalled an image of my mother assisting me on the toilet when I was about three years old. She stroked my penis to erection, saying she is cleaning it. I struggled and tried to move away from her. Her facial expression was ghoulish and frightening.

Another memory emerged of myself as a very young child—possibly around one year old. Someone lifting me and spreading my legs. I struggled against the lifter and moved my legs to cover my genitals. Confusing feelings were associated with this memory: sexual excitement and terror.

I became aware of an intense feeling of spiritual darkness in myself: I was raised by parents who were insane, and I lived as I was raised. As an adult I had continued with illicit sex, alcohol, and other drugs. I had caused incredible difficulty for myself, my wife, and my son.

The "darkness" thickened. One night it became unbearable. There was intense pain. I meditated, struggling with the darkness. But in the darkness there was a kind voice saying, "Now that you fully understand the problem, you can set about changing yourself." I would remember a contrition verse from seminary and recite it. The darkness would clear and I would be at peace. However, I was still unable to sleep. I would get up and read, overtaken by anxiety. I tried to relax with self-hypnosis. The anxiety intensified. Slowly, the pieces of my past began to fit together. In an attempt to regain my father I had sought the sexual contact of older men. My mother seemed to live in fear of my father. He probably abused her. For her own protection she manipulated me so that I came between her and Dad. Eventually she began to use me to meet other needs as well. The special relationship between me and Mom enraged my brother. Suddenly, my body began to tremble uncontrollably. I went into spasms, as if I am trying to struggle against someone who pins me down. There are intense anal spasms and gagging. Tears came, with old and deep emotions: fear, anger, rage, and shame. I recalled my brother and a friend holding me down and raping me anally and orally. This memory had been too painful to remember.[2] For years I had kept it down any way I could— with food, then alcohol and other drugs. Hours later, drained, I return to bed. Waking in the morning, my wife tells me that I clung to her as I slept.

The next day brought relief. The anxiety cleared. In my mind an image appeared of an empty circle, perfect and clean. Another image appeared of a circle blackened except for a small sliver. It is clear that I have avoided living in the immaculate, empty circle in favor of living in the sliver of the other circle. A small voice inside says, "Because of the abuse in your family, you have cut yourself off from the fullness of life. You have cut yourself off from the tender, nourishing side of yourself. If you wish, you may choose to change. You may live in the whole circle." I went into town for lunch. I met a friend whom I hadn't seen for months. He commented that in some way I looked different.

That evening I can finally sleep. The next morning I wake from a dream feeling refreshed and relaxed. In the dream I am in a pickup truck delivering fertilizer to my garden. The brakes fail, the truck careens wildly, destroying the rows of plants. The truck comes to rest and I survey the damage. It seems the whole garden is destroyed. An old man appears; his face is familar. I expect him to blame me for the damage, but he laughs, "Don't worry about the plants, they will regrow. You haven't destroyed the fertilizer and the irrigation, that's the important thing." The dream had the intensity of an explosion. I began to realize that the way I lived most of my life was in reaction to the abuse. I began to grieve the pain it had caused me, the pain I had caused others. I could finally forgive myself for what I had done. Finally there appeared to be an end to the incredible suffering.

My therapist diagnosed me as having posttraumatic stress disorder. As is common with this syndrome, I have frequent sleep disturbances. I often wake from a nightmare in the middle of the night and am unable to return to sleep. Tender and loving emotions are difficult for me. If I feel threatened I have trouble with my memory. For a number of years I had a major depression every winter. A number of times I felt near suicide. I felt as though I had to struggle to stay "normal." Many times I felt as though I was losing the struggle. I think in some ways the abuse caused a major split between my public self and my true self. I seemed unable to integrate these two parts of myself. To heal this split I had to come to terms with the abuse. For years that had seemed too painful.

Frequently elements in my environment will trigger intrusive thoughts or emotions which relate back to the abuse. When this happens I feel spaced out. Often these triggers cause me to feel as though I am again being abused. Some of my triggers have an obvious reference to the abuse: feeling trapped, people who violate my personal space, the scent of Avon cosmetics, weather which reminds me of childhood winters, and people with characteristics of my abuses. I have a hard time trusting people who in some way resemble my mother or my brother, especially if they are authority figures. In my personal life I can generally avoid people whom I can't trust, but my professional life has been difficult. Working under a female supervisor is almost guaranteed to cause problems. Among feminists at my office I've gotten a reputation for being a male chauvinist. If they only knew.

Other triggers seem more symbolic: working in the wind brings on a feeling of resistance, of something demanding my attention. Still other triggers are symbolic to the point of being humorous; my dog can often trigger intrusive thoughts of my mother when he begs for attention or gives me adoring looks with his big brown eyes.

One of my perpetrators, my mother, was a fundamentalist Christian. While she was sexually abusing me she was also dragging me to church several times a week. That mixing of goodness and badness in one person really did a number on my head. It strikes me as ironic that my mother looked so positive but committed the ultimate sin with one of her children. To this day I have trouble trusting people who seem too good or too positive—I can't help but wonder what they are trying to hide. In many ways I feel that I have survived multiple kinds of abuse: sexual, physical, emotional, and spiritual. Although as an adult I have managed to find a spiritual peace in myself, as a young man, in an attempt to shield myself from the effects of my mother's abuse, I turned against Christianity, turned against God, and turned away from the positive, nourishing, and sensitive side of myself.

The problem of my mom's intrusiveness continues to this day. Recently I brought an answering machine for my phone. Now I don't have to worry about picking up the phone to Mom's saccharine voice on the other end saying, "How's my boy?" Last Christmas Mom sent me a gift she had made: a coffee cup on which she had painted SONS ARE FOREVER & SONNY IS MINE. One day I saw the cup on my counter and got really angry about the sentiment in the inscription. I picked it up and threw it in the sink, smashing it. Several days later my wife was running the disposal and heard a clattering sound. She reached in an pulled out a broken piece of the cup—the piece with SONNY painted on it. We both looked at one another laughing. What a perfect symbol for my recovery: I've been through the disposal and ended up intact!

My body is very important to me. I have finally learned to treat it well. Adequate exercise and healthy recreation have been vital to my recovery. Initially, I began jogging to counter depression— but I got more than I bargained for. I also made a group of healthy friends. I learned to relate to men in more positive ways. The relaxed and friendly atmosphere of the looker room and sauna helped undo some of the damage that was done to me. Skiing and rafting have also served a major role in my recovery. Through these activities I have been able to change my relationship with fear. Now I am much less likely to freeze up when I'm afraid. Recreation and exercise have really helped improve my self-esteem.

I still haven't talked to Mom about any of my memories or therapy. I'm not sure why; maybe I'm afraid of hurting her. Perhaps I'm afraid of her denying that she did anything wrong and dismissing it as my fantasy. Or maybe I'm afraid of her saying something insincere, like "I'm sorry for that. Will you be my Sonny-Boy again now?" Or worse yet, she might want to have a relationship with me and my own family again. I don't think I could allow that.

The question comes up of how to end a story such as this. That's a hard one to answer, because the story is still being "written." The pain and conflicts which I have borne for years yielded to gentle understanding. The future seems very bright, much brighter than the past. So to answer the question, the ending to my story is still being written and *I'm* writing it.

Questions to help you identify your thoughts and emotions:

How is your (your loved one's) story similar to Sonny's?

How is your (your loved one's) story different from Sonny's?

What emotions did you have reading Sonny's story?

What was the most powerful section of the story for you?

What did you learn about yourself from reading this story?

10

Ruth's Story: Falling Together

Dear Mic,

Here's my story. Don't know if I've really conveyed how hard this year has been, how we really hung in there through lots of totally crazy days . . . no sleep, he would forget things, couldn't go to work many days, somedays didn't feel together enough to drive. We gave up all of our socializing pretty much. I managed a cross between honest concern, total availability, and good humor most of the time. We are truly fortunate to be so open with each other. I guess what I really would want to tell another spouse or mate is that there will be a time when your man is really not available for any interaction, and needs a total commitment and tending to by you. It felt that the entire resources of the universe centered around Sonny, and sometimes I did feel resentful.

But I *knew* that things were mending, that he was falling together rather than falling apart. The second really vital thing was for me to have an understanding of what he was going through in therapy and not feel left out or weirded out by his meditations and all of the time he spent writing in his journal. Knowing the therapists and having access to therapy both for myself and with Sonny was essential.

It has been a whirlwind year and we kissed it goodbye gladly! The new year has got to be an easier one! Thanks for giving us both the opportunity to write. It helps to bring things into focus, and we have shared our writings with each other as summations of where we are.

Hope you can use some of what I wrote.

Sincerely,
Ruth Hall

JANUARY 1 . . . Thank God this year is over. Today marks at least the start of a new calender year and new changes for Sonny. We have been through a lot, to say the least. In February, while I was in the hospital having surgery necessitated by an injury, Sonny opened up the wound he'd been hiding from all these years and discovered with our therapist that he had been in an incestuous relationship with his mother as a child. I knew nothing about this, nor did he as he had total amnesia about it. So just when I needed him to be there for my physical recovery, he was reeling from the emotional blow of recalling and reliving the pain of his past. This was when he needed me, but since I was hospitalized I wasn't home to see how upset he was or to comfort him during his painful period of discovery. Sonny and the therapist decided not to tell me what was happening but alluded to something really important that they'd fill me in on when Sonny was ready.

Due to these circumstances, I did not find out about his incest issues and his pain until a week or two after he had his first memory. The way in which I found out was none too pleasant. I was home recuperating, and he was ignoring me and spending lots of time alone and being very distant. I really felt angry and abandoned. So one day while he was reading downstairs I asked him what he was reading and he said some books the therapist had suggested. I pressed him as to what they were about. He resisted till finally I blurted out something like, "Well, what the heck is going on around here, incest in your past or something?" Saying what I now realize is nearly the worst thing I could have said. When he answered yes, I was stunned. Then he refused to talk about it, leaving me to imagine every possible variation of hurts that could have been heaped on him by various family members.

Finally, a day or two later he started to talk to me about the few parts he remembered and what he was feeling. I was feeling quite raw also, yet he had no emotional leeway to see to my needs. I was not even physically able to get to our therapist to talk at this point, and he was going a few times a week. Had I been mobile, we would have had a joint appointment and could have discussed it in a more supportive atmosphere. Actually, the worst part of hearing it for the first time was not knowing what had gone on, and my mind raced around opening frightening door after frightening door in a long corridor of possibilities. Later I learned that the same was true for him. Since he had suffered such total amnesia, he never knew what he would recall next.

So, what did I think when I first learned of his incestuous relationship with his mother? I was very, very sad about it. Total sadness. I have never liked his mother anyway, so I had no need to rearrange my emotions towards her. I had never communicated much with her, leaving that up to Sonny and knowing he disliked the task. Her visits made me anxious, and Sonny always seemed distant and distressed for days, even before she arrived. Our son had always disliked her intensely. He even took a pin and scratched out her face in a photo we had on the wall. So I wasn't that surprised to learn what she had done. I had always known she was somehow poisonous.

As to my feelings towards Sonny, I felt a new wave of the old fear that he would abandon me, especially now that he had recalled how badly he had been hurt by a woman. Luckily, the therapist reassured me that he didn't feel that would be the outcome at all, since Sonny was going to face the consequences of the abuse, rather than run away. He foresaw for us a brighter future than ever before and helped quell my fears a great deal. It was vitally important for me to have access to a therapist and be able to check my feelings out. I would talk about my feelings in my own therapy before I would tell them to Sonny.

I didn't turn away from Sonny physically when I heard of his incest experience, but I knew that he would be unavailable sometimes. Though this has been painful, it seems to be improving. Sexually, we have been estranged from each other sometimes, and very close other times. My feelings for him didn't change when I learned of his past behaviors. Well, that's not exactly true. When he told me about his sexual contacts with older men when he went on trips I was hurt and shocked, but the pieces started to fit together. I had always been paranoid about his "really" being gay and leaving me someday for a man, and when he got out of bed to pout or read immediately after we made love, it reinforced this fear. When we were in therapy I learned how, when we made love, memories of his mother, a woman, threatened to come up, and to block them out he fantasized about men. So my "paranoid" thoughts weren't all in *my* head after all. He was thinking about men, although he isn't homosexual. It was just a method he'd devised to deal with his incestuous past.

After the initial shock of learning about the incest we were both quite open with each other, often coming back from our individual therapy sessions and talking about what we had each learned. I was really glad to have someone who was understanding to talk to until the wee hours of the morning, exploring the possible effects of our behavior on one another in the light of the new information about incest. I started to understand why Sonny never kissed me on the lips, and why he always rebuffed me when I made the first sexual advance. Not that these things cleared up right away, but I understood them better and had the notion that they might one day change. So we were either in a deep meaningful dialogue with each other about new revelations or he was totally self-involved and moody. I felt that all of the energy in the entire household was being used to hold Sonny together and keep the family on an even keel. I felt that I was carrying an extra burden for many months, and in fact I was. But at least I now know why. My understanding of the therapists and meditations he was doing really helped alleviate the feelings of estrangement that were inevitable as he focused all of his energies on recovery. Since I was in therapy too, nothing he was doing to me was foreign to me. I didn't feel as left out of his healing process and could talk to him about the things that were happening. So understanding what goes on in Sonny's head, even the painful parts, helps. Before therapy his bad moods always seemed like the tip of an enormous iceberg, and I walked on eggshells when he was in a bad mood, afraid his moods were my fault or that I would make things worse.

One of the saddest things about the past months has been the inability to share my pain with friends because of the nature of the problem. I often felt that I was carrying the weight of the world on my shoulders, walking on eggshells, and not getting my fair share of anything. Once, for example, I told Sonny I was depressed, and he snapped, "Well, do something about it!" I was furious and told him so. It was taking three therapies, two types of meditation, all of our energies for *him* to get better, and he had the nerve to tell me just to "do something about" *my* feelings.

There have been times when I've wanted to tell him to take his "soap opera" somewhere else for a while, but I have not said those kinds of things to him, as they seemed only spiteful. However, I didn't let them fester; I acknowledge these feelings to myself, in my journal, and to my therapist.

So, here we are, almost a year into the process I call Sonny's falling together. What has changed . . . our understanding of a lot of the problem dynamics in our relationship, for one. Anytime I remind him of his mother or of the situations he was abused in as a child he balks completely. I used to think that he just put my demands at the end of his list because he was angry and sullen by nature, so now his reactions make more sense. I feel free to call him on things, like saying to him, "Hey, I'm not your mother and I made a reasonable request." Or, "Let's try that conversation again and see if we can get somewhere without pissing each other off."

If I had *not* known what he was going through in the last year, if he had kept it secret from me, I doubt if I would have stuck it out. I might have taken him to the psychiatric ward the nights he was having flashbacks and really feeling awful. But I had faith in him, in us, and in the therapists we were working with. I have faith in the future, and I have always really loved him. There is still lots of unfinished business, let's not kid ourselves. I now have to face the fact that I have endured close to twenty years in an emotionally neglectful and abusive relationship with Sonny. He was unable to be there emotionally for me. At times, because of his past, he was unable to meet my real needs, or even hear them, and I believed that my needs were excessive and that I was the only one who needed to change. I always felt guilty. The unmet needs festered and grew till there were angry outbursts and I searched for relationships in the willing arms of other men. These things are in the past, but there are wounds yet to heal, new patterns to practice, and miles to go. I feel we'll go them together, Sonny and I, with our eyes open this time.

Questions to help you identify your thoughts and emotions:

How is your (your partner's) story similar to Ruth's?

How is your (your partner's) story different from Ruth's?

What emotions did you have reading Ruth's story?

What was the most powerful section of the story for you?

What did you learn about yourself from reading this story?

11

Al's Story

What Happened

I was standing in front of the toilet. It was probably a Sunday morning, because I had a white dress shirt on. I had to have been over two years old because the house I was in was bought by my parents in 1962 and I was born in 1960. I couldn't have been very old because as I stood in front of the toilet my penis barely made it over the rim. (Whenever I recall this memory I get that ominous feeling I had whenever my dad was angry, and it always seemed the less I moved or spoke or was visible the better.)

To say that the first time I noticed him was when he came into the bathroom would be false—I could feel him and his rage throughout the whole house. When he came into the bathroom I don't think I looked up, but I knew he was very mad. I must have gone on the rim or something because as he grabbed me by the arm he mumbled something about showing me how to do it right. When he grabbed my arm it hurt. I think he had been drinking. I knew I had better cooperate. He pushed me to the floor of the bathroom. I laid very still as he urinated on my back. It was very warm at first, but the shirt held it so it soon got cold. I had my hands near my face and turned my head straight to the floor so as not to get it in my face. (To this day the thought of that smell makes me sick.)

I think the next thing he did was take off my clothes, but I don't really have a concrete memory until I was in the bathtub watching him wipe the urine off the floor. He had a very "man with a mission" type energy about him, like what he was doing was right and he was going to show me!

Then he took me into the bedroom of my older brother. The bed was right behind the door and the dresser across from the bed. The carpet was white. He sat on the bed and had me stand in front of him. He put his hand on the back of my neck and pulled me down so his penis was in my mouth. This didn't last long though. I think he was frustrated and angry because I didn't do a good job of it. He stood me up, spun me around, and lifted me onto his penis to penetrate my buttocks, but I squirmed and stiffened up, so he quit. He said something to calm me down, but I don't know what it was. Then he put his penis between my legs and masturbated between them. He had me all bent over. His chin was above my right shoulder. I could feel the hair of his chest on my back. The only time I was physically hurt, besides when he was squeezing my arm, was when he began to ejaculate. He squeezed my whole body and that hurt. His semen ended up on my chest. At that point it seemed he finally realized he had done something wrong. As he was cleaning me up he was acting like everything would be all right. It was like the release of come was a release of rage. He had to clean me up because my mom was coming home. (The night I began writing this I had one of my worst nightmares. For the week after I had trouble with canker sores, losing my vision, anxiety, trouble keeping my balance, and giddiness.)[1]

I've also got a memory of my dad putting a broom inside of me—that is the most active memory right now. (By active I mean while I write, my lower stomach begins to cramp, my throat begins to tighten up, my anus won't relax unless I concentrate. I'm a little bit afraid of sleeping tonight after writing this part. I want you to know that I can't touch this stuff without a reaction. But my choices are to touch it, or have it reach up and grab me.) I'm walking into the porch of the same house I've just described. I step over the threshold of the door. It's blond wood. The floor is red and black tile. The walls are knotty pine.[2] I walked into the porch off the garage while my dad was cleaning it. My dad always got mad when the garage would get dirty. He sat on a beer case, put me over his knees, and put a broom handle up my anus. I felt numb before he did it. It was like that feeling you get when your hand falls asleep and feels swollen—but my whole body felt that way. (This is hard to write.) I can feel the pressure inside of me and the wood inside of me. He used to have three-foot brooms around for his business. (There is no rationalizing this act. There is no excuse. At this time I believe my dad made an agreement with his dark side.)

The house we lived in before 1962 was also the scene of other episodes. My uncle raped me when I was quite young. (This is the uncle that used to pick my cousins up by the hair and throw them across the room.) My memory starts on the top of the stairs.[3] They are painted gray with no risers and lead to a cement floor. My uncle is holding my hand. I had to reach up to grab his hand. I feel no fear at first because he's being really nice and he's paying special attention to me. As we start down the stairs I can remember hearing laughter and sounds of kids playing. He's talking to me, but I don't remember what he's saying. But I know the tone of his voice. He's being kind of icky sweet. I have to step sideways and use my hips because the stairs are so big; he's very patient with me and he smiles. He let me walk all the way to the bottom of the stairs and then picks me up. The next thing I know he has me over a wooden box in the corner. He has my pants down in the back, not in the front—I think just in case someone comes down the stairs. He's trying to put his penis inside of me. It hurts. I can feel it up my tailbone and down my legs. I feel like I'm going to break in two, and it's not even really in. I can feel my face, it is numb. It looks confused and scared. The box he's got me over is unfinished, rough, and hurts. He's mad, I assume 'cause he can't get it in. Then the memory gets a little choppy. I think he did some things with himself against my back. I think he might of come against my back. I don't remember walking up the stairs. I think he carried me. But I remember standing by some tables in the living room, and the other kids were running and playing. I don't envy them, though, I'm sure they got it much worse than I did. The parents were busy. I stood there, dizzy, weak, and numb. I was disoriented, much like I get sometimes now. Everything looked as if I were looking through a convex lens. I think I was in someone's way.[4] I think I was torn but have never gone to a doctor to see if they can find scars.

This same uncle would come up to my room in the night and molest me. (I doubt this memory because I have always wondered how I could remember so well something that happened when I was so young.) I remember being in my bedroom, the door cracks open, and the light blinds me. He comes in and reaches over the crib side. I hold very still, but he picks me up and has me lean against the bars. He sticks his penis through the bars and pokes me in the face, eyes, and mouth. Then he masturbates on my face.

The next episode I remember is with my mother and is one of the ones I trust the least (and also the most). In this memory she gave me oral sex. I was very young, an infant. I can remember being confused because it felt good, but I was afraid. I also remember her breath being bad, which sounds trite, but it's a detail that makes the memory more concrete.[5]

The last memory I have to tell you is of my cousin. I trust it the most because all the other memories were from five years of age and younger. In this case I was six or seven. My older female cousin was baby-sitting. I was going to the bathroom, and she came in and lowered herself down to my level. She was very scary. She talked to me with a very mocking, patronizing tone in her voice. (Just like her dad, my abusive uncle, used.) She used a pencil to play with my penis. She asked me questions like "Can you make it hard?" (It makes me sick to think about how she talked to me.) As with many of my abuse memories, when I remember this I'm above, looking down at both of us.[6]

The next thing I remember she punished me by standing me in the corner by the front door. I was barefoot and shirtless, and it was a freezing cold winter night. I remember the cold blast of air from the door as my parents came home while I was being punished and asking why. I don't remember her response, except that she said I had been bad. When people ask me why I didn't tell my parents what she'd done I just freeze up and giggle. I just wanted to get through it and not make waves.

My mother has told me that when I was an infant this cousin was ten years old, and she had beaten me and bit me on the face to the point of drawing blood. This cousin was the daughter of my uncle who raped me. My parents were obviously not able to, or didn't care enough to, choose a sitter with proper boundaries.

I have to take inventory of validations before I can believe any of this abuse happened.[7] The facts that I have that help me to believe that I came from an abusive family are:

I've been told my cousins have the record for the youngest children to be severely beaten (broken legs, etc.) in the 1970s in the state where they live

I've also been told that my other cousin's kitchen utensils were confiscated by child protection to examine for signs that they were used to sexually abuse their children, and the children's butts were examined for signs of abuse

My mom sent my brother dogshit in a box through the mail

All of my cousins in that family are obese

My brother and aunt are "bibleholics" or religious fanatics

Many of my family members are alcoholic

I don't remember being bathed or dressed or being helped to do these things by my parents. My father once cornered me in the kitchen and was screaming at me to clean up vomit I had thrown up when I was sick with the flu. I barely reached his belt loops, and yet he threatened me with a closed fist. He is a very violent man. I have very few memories of my mother and father together. They are now divorced.

This is as detailed as I will get about my abuse. The only memory that I've always had was of my cousin. I even talked to a friend about it over dinner a long time ago. At that time I didn't think of it as abuse. The rest of the memories started to come round about age twenty-five.

How It Affected Me

With all the new information I've got now, I'm able to look back when I was a child and see how I dealt with my situation. Lots of things I don't remember, but I do remember some things: like spending a lot of time in closets and under my bed. My dog used to come and visit me, which I think helped me to cope. I was very shy, quiet, and afraid.

As an adult I believed that I had to keep the abuse secret and that I would die if I faced it. I thought that men were evil. I believed that I was to take care of others, not myself, and that emotions were to be unexpressed. I was always too afraid of other kids to get involved in sports or social activities. Being schooled in a Catholic grade school didn't help. I think it just drove the shame deeper.

As a child I had several ways of coping with the abuse. I don't remember a lot of my childhood. I was always impressed by other people's ability to recall last year's weather or a birthday. It wasn't until I was fourteen or sixteen that I knew January was in the winter. I think I was walking unconsciousness. Although I had perfectly healthy eyes, I started having trouble with loss of sight. My mother would disappear when I would talk to her in our living room. I used to think the paint in that room had some kind of special effect on my eyes. Even though I have gone totally blind for seconds at a time, I never told anyone about it until I was in therapy. I have had eye examinations, and nothing abnormal was ever discovered. I've since been told this blindness is the same as going into shock.[8]

I also remember one obsession that I had when I was young. When I would sit and watch TV, I would have to make a fist, otherwise my fingernails would grow through the wall and kill someone. I've since been told this has to do with anger.

By far the worst childhood symptom I had was fear of the night. I was always petrified when the lights would go out. I once went to the bathroom in bed because I was too afraid to get up. I also consistently wet the bed in my sleep until I was seven years old. Lots would go on in the night in my house. I remember getting up in the morning and there was a hole in the wall. My mother explained that my alcoholic father had gotten into a fight over a drink. Being a child I pictured a glass of milk and wondered why anyone would fight over a drink of milk.

As a young adult the symptoms I've suffered were less obvious; a strong, resilient body and an undeveloped mind can keep the darkest of the dark at bay. In addition to being workaholic and being very shameful, I think my repeated violent relationships reflected my past the most. I was always the victim of any overt violence. I was attacked three times by two different women, and my life was threatened by a third. When I was attracted to a woman, I would talk myself out of noticing warning signs that she was violent. I thought I could change her, be her knight in shining armor. When things didn't go the way I had expected, I would use sex to smooth things over.

When I started to take a look at myself (thanks to my third violent relationship) the worst symptoms surfaced. The night I first remembered part of the picture of my dad urinating on me I made a picture of it and tried to figure out what it represented—not considering for a moment that it was a real memory. The next day it started: I woke up feeling anxious, my legs felt fatigued and weak, my mouth was dry, and I had a sore throat (which has continued for over two years). I also had my first panic attack. I continued to work in absolute terror for one full year. For the next year I experienced anxiety and following symptoms:

Nightmares—usually of being chased by a bear, a demon, or a severed arm. Then I would wake up too afraid to get out of bed.

Fear of AIDS. Even though I don't belong to any of the high-risk groups, I was convinced I had AIDS. Although I'm not gay and I don't see being gay as bad, I now see this fear as a self-guilt trip where I thought I deserved to die for sexual crimes.

Obsessions. I call them blurps because they were short and varied (a credit to my creativity). I would see things like being knifed, sodomized, and beaten by people I was with. I would picture myself being shot in the head. I also had perpetrator blurps in which I was on the delivering side of the violence, which added to my shame. These were constant and took hard work to accept.

Gagging. Many days I would constantly be on the verge of a full gag.

Loss of vision. I would lose sight for seconds at a time. I was fully conscious and aware but could not see.

Hallucinations. Things would appear to shoot across the room or buildings would move. People would melt into walls and their faces would distort.

Weakness. I just felt weak and run down, which is probably just a result of having to deal with all the other symptoms.

Bleeding from the anus. I believe this was due to the muscles around my anus being in a constant tense state.

Intense emotions. At times I would sob for up to an hour. I would be grumpy or in a rage. For days I would get up, vomit, cry for a while, get ready for work, and then off I went. I'm very proud of making it through these times.[9]

I had my first symptoms approximately three years ago. I recently watched a TV show about torture victims and was validated when they reported that torture victims have the same symptoms I have had, and they even missed a few. The body reactions I've experienced are extreme, but I'm now learning to see them as just misguided energy. I've learned from one of my advisers how to make better use of my body. I also think of the body reactions as helping me because they wouldn't let me forget "the monster in the closet." The symptoms are much less intense now than before, and I plan on another year or so of work before they disappear completely.

The Work

Now for my favorite part. The first part that helped me was realizing that there was no way I could get better by myself. I needed the help of trained professionals, support people, and friends. Finding properly trained professionals is not an easy thing. I had to go through three different therapists before I found one that would help me bring this stuff up instead of suppress it. When I described the abuse, I had one therapist ask, "How are you going to *prove* that? Let's just work on helping you cope." This was terribly abusive. But I went on and finally found people trained for what I needed.

I found I needed to change some friendships. I found I had chosen several friends that were much like my family. Even though five of my friends suffered from many of the same symptoms I did, they couldn't or wouldn't talk about my symptoms or the causes of them. When the shit hit the fan they headed for the hills. Other friends were supportive. I was also lucky enough to find a support group of other men who had been sexually abused. I needed this so I didn't feel so alone and didn't feel "dirty." I know that someone who understands is only a phone call away.

One huge obstacle for me was that in everything that I read and saw men were portrayed only as perpetrators or as only victimized by men. I couldn't find a publication or program that represented women as perpetrators. If they were mentioned at all it was only as being blind to the abuse done by men. My experience shows that women do abuse. There are many sympathetic ears when I talk of my anger towards men who abuse, but I've still got tons of anger for women and few places to go with it.

Two things I needed to avoid were silence and isolation. Coping techniques that I found useful were meditating, focusing on simple body movements, concentrating on my work, writing down affirmations. For example, I wrote these notes to myself:

Mental goals:

Come to the realization that my thoughts belong to me; I don't belong to my thoughts.

Ingrain into myself that thoughts are not necessarily reality and not to take my thoughts too seriously (lighten up).

Accentuate good thoughts.

Have patience with my thinking now. My thinking is a foundation, and it takes lots of work to change foundations. I will be patient with my thinking during change.

This stuff is a part of me, therefore it can't be bigger than I am!

Physical goals:

To run at least twice a week, three miles.

To skate, swim, or bike weekly.

Remember, it is very important to move a depressed body gently, but move!

I will be sure *not* to use exercise as a way to escape my emotions or problems or to punish myself for guilt feelings or shame.

My reasons for working out are to feel good and to bolster my self-image.

Massage is a great way to experience healthy touch.

Nutrition—feed a hurting body.

I will nurture my body. I will love, take care of, and caress my body. I will affirm that my body is loved and that it is *my* body. Feeling good is my birthright.

Spiritual goals:

Not to form a picture of what god is like so I can believe in god, but rather to trust god.

I can't do god's job.

God will take care of me.

God is my true parent.

There is nowhere I can go where god is not.

God and I will work together in this life.

Sexual goals:

Have sex only after I get to know a person well.

Sex was used to control and punish me. I will stop that cycle now.

Sex is a way to express love, to get close to someone, to feel good.

If to have sex puts me in a dangerous situation I will not have sex. It is my body.

Sex is another way to love my body. I love my body.

Emotional goals:

Let my emotions flow. I must jump at every chance to cleanse my emotions.

I will be patient. I was told not to let my emotions show. I now reject this notion. I am an emotional person.

I will share more emotions with men that I can trust. I was told men were evil. This isn't true. There are tons of good men out there. I will meet them and make friends of them.

These techniques helped me get by. I depended on them for months, but I began to wear out under the tremendous stress, so I reluctantly agreed to go on medication. This turned out to be a smart move. I used the medication inconsistently for approximately four months, which intermittently took the edge off my panic so I could begin to examine where the fear and pain were coming from. The meds. helped me to face the pain, not run from it, which is an important distinction. I began to touch the immense amount of emotion I had tucked away for twenty-five years. As a child I went numb. My family wound me up like a toy that when set off would spin out of control.

At first I only felt comfortable crying or raging alone. I would watch TV shows or ads that would show some kind of compassion for children, and I would begin uncontrolled sobbing. I'm just now getting to be able to express emotions in my support group, which is a safe place to do it. I have found that the facilitator is a safe, paternal person to practice my anger with. He lets me express my anger but doesn't take any abuse. My final goal will be to bring my parents in and respectfully express to them how they have hurt me.

Finally, I'd like to mention humor, which helps me greatly, and will help you too, so there.

Questions to help you identify your thoughts and emotions:

How is your (your loved one's) story similar to Al's?

How is your (your loved one's) story different from Al's?

What emotions did you have reading Al's story?

What was the most powerful section of the story for you?

What did you learn about yourself from reading this story?

12

Allen's Story

GREETINGS, dear reader. You may ask yourself why someone would ever want to write about their experience as a victim of incest. I too have asked myself that question many times since agreeing to this undertaking. Well, there are a couple of reasons. First of all I would hope that through works like this others may benefit, either in working through their own issues, or professionals who will be helping others to come to grips with incest and related sexual abuse issues. Secondly, my motives are self-serving/self-helping. The more I work through all the pain, shame, and fear that I experience of my past, the healthier I get. You see, it's by bringing my issues out of the shadows of the past and exposing them to the light of truth that I take away their power to control my life. So, I will bless myself and say a prayer for myself that I may honestly and accurately share my experiences and for you, dear reader, that rather than a story of horrors it may be a message of hope.

My story begins, oddly enough, at the age of thirty-three. I was married, four children, a success by many standards. My one weakness was always my weight. I was six feet tall, but weighed 384 pounds. That's right, 384 pounds, and most of it was all between my chest and my knees. My hands and arms were more or less "normal." I didn't have a pudgy face or anything. I was just big and thick through the middle. I was feeling very frustrated with life, wanting to know what God wanted me to do. You know—feeling "unfulfilled." Well, in my search for meaning I took on a spiritual director who confronted me on my weight problem. He insisted I seek out an Overeaters Anonymous (OA) group and begin to deal not only with the pounds but, as I know now, the issues that brought me there.

I began going to a local group with two of my sisters. As my sisters and I all had weight problems we all were looking for a solution. Having my sisters go with me helped a lot since this happened to be a predominantly female group. Things were going well, I began working the Twelve-Step program of OA, and for the first time in my life began to deal with the fact that my eating had less to do with appetite and more to do with feelings and emotions than I had ever imagined. So, my sisters and I were on the road of recovery, all losing weight and gaining awareness, when we heard a guest speaker one night talking about dysfunctional families. We all reacted the same way: "That's *our* family he's got up on the chalkboard!" After the meeting we shared with him some of our thoughts, and he gently suggested that there might be something in our past family life that should be explored.

Well, we went home and began talking about this with an aunt of mine. She said, "You know, your father sexually abused me when I was five years old." We were, of course, horrified. As it turned out, my aunt and grandmother had kept this a secret for thirty years to avoid hurting my mother or causing any family trouble. My father was dead and the children grown, so now she felt it was safe to share this with us. Well, that opened up all kinds of speculations on our part. My sisters began to put pieces together in their own lives. Past things that seemed to suggest that they may have been victims of my father as well. No conscious memories at this point, but lots of other things: dreams, sexual problems, the way they reacted to certain situations or individuals. For example, one sister had recurring dreams, or rather experiences, where she would wake up in the middle of the night gagging. Two of my sisters had very similar "tiger" dreams, as they called them. These nightmares consisted of some great gnashing teeth, biting and hurting them, tearing them apart. They all had some kind of sexual dysfunction. One sister had been married for ten years and her husband had never seen her naked. She expressed the desire to be celibate the rest of her life and feels resentment towards her spouse's "recreational" sexual advances, because in her mind sex *can't* be fun.

All of my siblings shared my reactions towards reminders of the past: problems with men who physically resembled our father, reacting to stress with binging on food. Even little things, like the click of a cigarette lighter or a cough like his, gave us a sick feeling inside and sent our stomachs churning.

It was decided that my sisters would go to a treatment program for five days. It consisted of marathon, small-group therapy sessions all centered around compulsive behavior of one kind or another. I decided to go "to support my sisters," and since I was definitely a compulsive overeater I would attend this clinic with them.

In one of the first sessions with my small group after sharing "my life story" I was asked if I thought that since my father had abused my sisters perhaps he had sexually abused me as well. My reaction was strong and violent: *"No!"* The tension in the room was very thick, and later many group members told me they thought I was going to hit the counselor who had made the suggestion.

Well, I was confronted with many of the indications that I may have been abused. Things like how I carried my weight, how it served as an "insulator" for my genitals, my exaggerated response to the suggestion that I may have been abused, my insecurity with my sexuality and identity—there was enough to make me try and open myself to the possibility that I too may have been abused. The therapist remarked that sexual abuse is no more about sex than alcoholism is about thirst, meaning that my father could still be a heterosexual and sexually abuse male children. I was counseled to just relax and let myself feel what was going on, don't force anything, don't block anything, just let go.

I began what was one of the scariest processes of my life. I had never had a memory of any of my childhood before I was six years old. Now I was all of a sudden getting flashes in my mind, like a disjointed slide show. Things like black pubic hair, the head of a penis, my father's glare. There were feelings too: fingers around my throat, some sticky fluid all around my mouth, my rectum would start to pucker, a hand on my head. I thought I was going crazy. This couldn't be. "Please, God—no!"

I kept to myself and stayed with the feelings. I was promised by the staff that if I worked the program I would find that which I sought: truth. It came to me one night as I laid in my bed naked (which to me is the ultimate in being vulnerable). I laid there trying to listen to my body, my spirit. Many things came to me. My mother's words: "Your father was always so good about getting up with you in the evenings, but once you got older he never wanted much to do with you." I remembered things, those "slides" in my head again. My mouth felt like it was leperous, all rottening filthy flesh. As I lay there I started some rhythmic contractions of my tongue. This went on for a few minutes until I started gagging. It was then I knew the awful truth: I was getting in touch with, recalling the abuse I had suffered at my father's hands.[1]

As I allowed the memories to return I recalled more: the way he would squeeze my testicles until they hurt, making me cry and promise not to say anything, how he would put his finger in my rectum, how he had his hand on my throat and choked me and how awful it all was. So many questions answered: why I hated turtleneck sweaters, neckties; anything on my throat brought me back at some level to my father choking me. I never wore hats even though I live in a cold climate; the feeling of it was too much like his hand on top of my head, forcing me to present my mouth to his penis. I realized how as a manager in business, whenever I had to deal with a man who physically resembled my father, no matter what I showed on the outside, inside there was a frightened little boy running away. The memories explained why I was so insecure in my masculinity/sexuality. All of my life I was so afraid that I was a homosexual because I was so insecure, so lonely. I had no close male friends—I might be gay. No girlfriends because I was scared to death and couldn't risk the chance of rejection; my self-image couldn't handle it.

In my sexual life I had always been very uncomfortable, not only with my body but with being sexual at all. Sex for me was like a bowel movement, necessary and maybe even a welcome release, but never intimate. My wife had my body only, my mind was elsewhere. Whenever oral sex was suggested I became terrified, although I had never known why. All these scary thoughts would well up inside me, like wanting to ejaculate angrily on my wife's face. What was most fearful was not that it was "kinky" but that the drive behind the compulsion to do it was some perverse degradation I wanted to enact on her. These "monsters" inside me were not me—they were all the undealt-with rage, anger, and other emotions from my childhood. Though I never acted them out with my wife or anyone else, I now understand how abuse is passed from generation to generation.

That night at the treatment program I had a dream in which I was a superman shackled hands and feet to a brick wall and breaking the chains, bursting through the shell that had confined me all my life—free at last! I now knew that I could be or do anything I wanted. I was no longer going to be controlled by the events of the past. I had been held in bondage all my life, and now the truth, no matter how awful it was, had set me free.

I learned/recalled my father's abuse; from the time I was an infant (four to six months) until age six my father repeatedly sexually abused me: forcing me to suck on his penis until he had an orgasm in my mouth (that is still difficult to write) and inflicting a great deal of pain on me by squeezing my testicles and by sticking his finger in my rectum, squeezing my throat, choking me, and threatening to kill me if I resisted or spoke a word. I came to realize that to resist his pleasure meant pain.

I also realized that my father never wanted children. I can see today the rage and vengefulness with which he committed these acts of abuse on my sisters and me.

I remembered him setting all kinds of bad examples: lying, stealing, and physical abuse. He would be very violent and call it discipline. Once I remember him kicking me all the way home when I was late for school. His abuse was passive as well as aggressive. You see, not only was it what he *did*, it was also what he *didn't* do. I never remember my father saying he loved me. Which makes sense, given everything else. He never fathered me. All those things a boy needs from his father were denied to me. You see how I couldn't exactly use him as a role model, yet I did. So much of what I became was a result of my experience with my father.

My father was well liked by people outside of the family, and that set up terrible conflicts within me. As a child I couldn't stand up to my father's peers who were saying how swell he was and say he was really a jerk. Also, I wanted a "good" father. Every boy wants "Dad" to be a superstar, so you allowed this "fantasy father," so different from the truth, to grow in your mind until you almost believe it yourself. Additionally, if all those adults thought your father was so good, you as a child must be wrong. This just serves further to put all the shame, blame, and guilt back on yourself.[2]

What did all this abuse do to me? Well, first of all, I grew afraid to fail, afraid of being anything but perfect (for we never knew what would set my father off). I attempted to eliminate anything imperfect out of fear of being judged, of trying to live up to my father's expectations. To this day I have to fight the urge to tear up letters nearly completed because of a misspelled word.

I was a very, very lonely boy, frozen to the world. I never allowed myself to feel anything. When the pain was too great, or in reaction to any stress, I began to eat, stuffing my feelings. So from the earliest pictures of me onward I was always fat.

I was almost impervious to anything that might hurt me, at least I thought I was. I could "run" to this faraway corner in my mind where I could huddle up with myself and no one could hurt me.

Growing up I always dreamed of being a hero, so people would know I was "good." Yet at the same time I rebelled, trying to prove how "bad" I was: shoplifting, drinking, destroying things, always a "hardass" on the outside, while a scared little boy on the inside. I resented authority and continued to rebel, yet I hated myself for it.

I would cry at Walt Disney movies, for they were a safe outlet for my emotions. I also loved music, the sadder and more tragic the better, especially if the singer projected the tragedy in their voice. As a teenager I remember listening to Janis Joplin's painful melodies which she virtually screamed out. I cried, consoled that I was not alone in these feelings.

I never dated, never went to a high school dance. I was so afraid of rejection that I could never being myself to ask anyone out. My male friends never really gave me what I needed, an intimate relationship, someone that I could trust in. I guess that's the biggest part of my loneliness; I could never trust anyone. My mother was there, but she was my mother and "had" to love me; besides, why hadn't she protected me from my father?

There isn't an area of my life which hasn't been affected by the abuse. In my married life I was so fearful of intimacy, so afraid of being vunerable. Before I was set free I would have all this rage inside me that I kept locked up tight—gutting it out until something would happen and I'd go over the edge and then all the rage and pain would come gushing out and God help whoever was in the way. I always thought this was some genetically inherited trait. I never realized the true source, yet even in my rage I always saw my father's eyes.

It is now some four years later and I continue in the healing/recovery process. It takes lots of patience, time, and prayer—for the scars run deep. For me recovery has been like a big dark room. I found the light switch, but it's like a rheostat. The light is coming on slowly, dimly at first, so I can go about the cleaning up, dealing with that which I can see. Just as I finish, the light gets a little brighter, and I see more that needs to be done which I had never seen before. Believe me, there are times when you will feel like just turning the light off and forgetting the whole thing. Those are the times when the alcoholic drinks, or the compulsive overeater stuffs himself. Whatever way it translates in your life, "If you don't deal with it, it deals with you."

The next step in my story is to share with you how the recovery process has worked in my life, or, what is recovery all about? Well, first of all for me it is working my eating program. If I'm not dealing with my compulsive eating then I'm medicating some hurt, anger, or other emotion. The first clue that I'm not dealing with something going on in my life is a desire to binge. I swear that I could binge on rocks and it wouldn't matter. The binge is not about food but about the need to stuff my feelings. Working my program doesn't mean being perfect in my eating—that will probably never happen. What it does mean is going to OA (Overeaters Anonymous) meetings and not giving up. I try always to stay sensitive to what's going on—what's driving and motivating my eating and emotions. You know, I heard it said once that the difference between saints and sinners is that saints keep trying.

One of the wonderful things about belonging to a group was that I found out that I wasn't alone. I discovered others who shared all the same feelings, fear, and shame that I had. I could talk about stealing others' lunches, hiding somewhere, and binging—and they all understood, and loved me, unconditionally. The greatest gift they gave me was the fact that I felt loved at my very worst, and that I was not alone. I kept coming back to OA, whether I had a "successful" week or not, because I could trust, truly trust, for the first time in my life, that they would not judge me but love me for who I am. That was a unique experience for me. This was also the first step in my beginning to love myself; if they could love me, maybe I could too. I believe this is the key to my recovery. Only as I begin to love myself will I be able to receive love from others.[3]

I find that I also need to be patient, understanding, and forgiving of others. When I am patient I don't get down on myself for my "failure" or frustrated with my lack of progress. Recovery takes time, and by realizing that, and living that, I'm more likely to succeed than fail. If I look for too dramatic results I get frustrated with the lack of instant success and start that downward cycle of guilt, shame, and panic which led to binging and sabotaged all of my previous efforts at weight control.

So, that's the eating side of recovery for me. But recovery is not one dimensional. We are all body and soul, and all levels need to be healed. For me, healing my soul, which I define as personality, intellect, and feelings, has been through work and study to help me understand the mechanics of what happened to me and why. It is also critical to be free to feel my pain, anger, and rage. I need to get out all those pent-up feelings towards my father. They were coming out all along, but sideways, through eating, or in other relationships, such as my unreasonable responses to small irritations. All this crap was inside me waiting to come raging out. This is where professional therapy came into play in my life. I first attended the five-day clinic and then in an aftercare group I was able to safely get in touch with what was going on inside and get it all out. The other group members provided the essential elements of safety, confidentiality, and support, while the counselor offered his experience and expertise. This all combined to help me honestly uncover what has been stifled and suppressed for so long. The difference between fact and fantasy in my life was great indeed. However, that ability to cope with stress was what kept me from committing suicide a long time ago.

As I gained an understanding of abuse and its effects I have learned how there is not an area of my life that wasn't affected. It's like a big hanging mobile; if you disturb one part of the mobile it sets the whole thing in motion.

So, as with the body, so with the mind, it is truth that has set me free. It's not that I have all the answers or ever will, but I'm no longer held in bondage. I know I'm good and lovable; it's okay not to be correct all the time. It's okay to fail; I'm still good. I don't have to do it all right now. I can be patient with myself and the process and not worry about my self-worth. As I write this I realize that most of all I'm not afraid of myself anymore. I'm not a lunatic. I'm not an evil monster. I'm not a twisted pervert. I'm a victim.

Working through the mental and emotional rubble has allowed me to reorder and rebuild my life, ideas, and attitudes. I am able to "give back" to my father all the crap his abuse thrust upon me, the shame and guilt that was controlling me thus far. The biggest freedom is the ability to be vulnerable. Unless I risk, I will never grow. I will never be able to extend myself to others.

The last dimension I'll write on is the spiritual. This too was affected in a very deep way by the abuse. I am Christian, Roman Catholic, and we profess a belief in a triad God: Father/Son/Holy Spirit. Prior to dealing with the incest I struggled with the fact that I could never seem to develop a relationship with the "Father." My God was not the father figure I wanted: kind, loving, forgiving. No, God the Father for me was an extension of the earthly father I experienced. He was someone I lived in fear of, whom I had to be perfect for, I dared not approach, who could never really love me.

After recalling the abuse I was angry at a God who allowed it to happen to me. How could He (God) do this to me if he really loved me? Well, I'm working through this too. I know that God didn't cause the abuse to happen. We all have free will, and God allows us the freedom to abuse, steal, wage war—all sorts or awful things, but we do them to ourselves. If I am consumed by my anger and cannot forgive God, my earthly father, mother, and all those who contributed to the abuse and all the other pain in my life, I will still be controlled and the evil of the incest will continue to run my life. Now there is a fine line between hating the sin and forgiving and loving the sinner, but that is what I feel I am called to do. I forgive what my father did but still hate that he did it. Without this forgiveness the healing process will be incomplete (patience is again the key). These things come in degrees, small steps, slow progress that moves, even if imperceptably at times, ever forward.

The other spiritual dimension is my ability to love others. As I have learned to love and forgive myself and my God, I have been able to extend to my fellow man these same virtues. As I was unable to love myself I could not accept love from my God.

To sum this dimension up, I am now gaining in my ability to love and forgive. I am at peace with my God, myself, my father, and my fellow human beings. This is a wonderful place to be. I try never to judge others. We all have our own stories, and I know how fragile we are.

So, dear reader, that's about all I have to say. I'm not a professional writer; I simply wanted to give you a window into my life and how it has evolved regarding the issue of sexual abuse. Let me close by saying that while there is a wonderful world out there just waiting for all who are being held in the chains of abuse, there is no magic. Recovery takes time and lots of work. The work I speak of is not an oppressive work, however—it's life giving. It's like the difference between slavery and freedom—you are working for yourself now and will reap great rewards. One thing to remember is just because it doesn't feel good doesn't mean it isn't. Change is hard, very hard, and today's reality may seem preferable to change, but reach out. I love you. I'm praying for you and waiting to take your hand and help you from a life of human-imposed hell to the joy and peace that God intended. I'm as close as the nearest Overeaters Anonymous meeting or any of the other groups where men and women like me anxiously await your reaching out. God bless you.

Questions to help you identify your thoughts and emotions:

How is your (your loved one's) story similar to Allen's?

How is your (your loved one's) story different from Allen's?

What emotions did you have reading this story?

What was the most powerful section of the story for you?

What did you learn about yourself from reading this story?

13

Daniel's Story

MY sister tells me that when I was born it was like Jesus Christ had arrived. The second child and the first boy. I could do no wrong. She seems to think I had it good. I suppose good or bad is a pretty subjective experience, although in our family I don't think there was a whole lot of good. Anyway, my sister thought I was the fair-haired boy my mother was waiting for, which knocked my sister out of a rather tenuous first place. She had been around five years before me and so got what little nurturance was available until I came along.

I don't remember having it good. But I don't remember having it so bad either. I don't recall getting much from my mother, but then "Jesus" gave a whole lot more than he received. I think my mother was looking for someone to build her self-esteem. I didn't have a lot to give.

My father was gone a lot. He was a salesman and on the road. I know he would bring me presents when he came home, and I was always excited to see him. Then he and my mom would argue. I don't know what about. They also had separate bedrooms. My brother and I would sleep in the same room as my dad when he was home. I didn't really think much of it at the time. My sisters would sleep in the room with my mother, and my grandmother had her own room. It was her house.

I did all the things that most kids do. I had a paper route and was in Cub Scouts, then Boy Scouts. I played the bugle in the drum and bugle corps and the cornet in my grade school band. My father would take me with him sometimes when he played in the city band. I would take out my cornet and pretend I could play music with the grown-ups. I was a dedicated altar boy. I remember getting up at 5:30 A.M. so I could serve mass for the priest at the convent. I got good marks in school, at least in the early years. I had a few unsatisfactory marks in conduct and citizenship, but most of the nuns liked me, even though I didn't quite measure up to the image of Jesus to them.

Sometimes my dad would give me part of a pill when I had trouble sleeping at night. I know the pill worked really well because shortly after he would give it to me I would fall asleep like someone had knocked me out. He had a big bottle of those pills, and he always seemed to have them. He died from them.

My first experience with anything sexual was one summer at Boy Scout camp when my tent mate showed me how to masturbate. At that time I couldn't ejaculate, and he couldn't either, but doing something secretive together seemed exciting. He also told me where babies come from. I didn't believe him, so I asked my mother. She confirmed what my friend had said. That was the first and the last conversation we had about anything sexual.

Sexual curiosity and experimentation escalated after Boy Scout camp rather quickly. I continued to masturbate and finally was able to have an ejaculation. For a long time before this was possible, I would fake having one when my friends and I would masturbate together. I felt ashamed of my inability to orgasm and put a handkerchief over my penis and pretended I was coming. My father sold calenders, among other things, and had some samples in our garage. There were pictures of nude women on them, so our garage was a gathering place for many circle jerks. One friend and I began experimenting sexually. We would perform oral sex and masturbate each other. One time my father caught us in the act of oral sex. He gave me a lecture on where babies come from but never mentioned the incident between me and my friend. He had a lot of rather trite sayings, like "The hardest word in the English language to say and the easiest to spell is 'no'" and "You can't tell the depth of the well by the length of the handle on the pump." I know they had some meaning, but I think it was lost on me. They didn't seem to relate to the particular incident to which he was attempting to apply them.

My father was the emotional warmth in the family. He wasn't there very much, and one day he wasn't there at all. He left when I was eleven or twelve. I still don't know why he left. My mother had lots of answers, but none of them satisfied me. He was a different person to me than to her, but I don't think she knew that. She thought I should see him the same way she did. After he left, my mother looked to me to fill in for him, and I tried to. We used to go to the bars together, like we were on a date. She would buy me a beer (you could do this in our state at the time), and we would talk and dance together. I thought I was really special. She needed me.[1] I even thought I should have sex with her. One time while she was sleeping, I went into her bedroom and started to touch her genitals. She woke up and was quite startled. I don't know if she realized what I was doing or not, but I didn't try it again.[2] She eventually found a boyfriend, and I was rejected. I felt like I lost a girlfriend, and I hurt a lot. She didn't seem to care; she had a big replacement for my dad, one she should really have sex with.

My dad finally showed up after a while, and I began to visit him, even though my mother wished I wouldn't. Sometimes I would hitchhike several hundred miles to visit him. A dad is pretty important to an adolescent male, but my mother didn't know this. I still feel angry at her for her insensitivity and preoccupation with her own needs.

My dad had a girlfriend, Mary, who was twenty-five years old. My dad was twice her age. She used to come into the bedroom I was in at night. She would kiss me and stick her tongue in my ear. It seemed pretty strange, and I was frightened. It was also exciting and felt good. I didn't tell anyone, even though she never told me not to.[3]

By the time I turned sixteen I had been in lots of trouble with the law and had spent one year in reform school. I know now all of my acting out was because I was so angry. It was my way of getting even for the hurt I felt was inflicted on me. I remember some adults who tried to help me. I would only trust them so much, and then I would close up and do something to push them away. I kept myself isolated from most people and managed to stay safe. Girls were terrifying to me. I wanted to have a girlfriend, but I was totally ignorant about how to talk to a girl or even how to approach one. I had a few friends get me dates, but they were disasters. I felt so vulnerable and scared that I was mute. I longed inside for a girlfriend, or was it for a mom?

Eventually my dad married Mary and moved. I told my mother I wanted to live with him and that there wasn't much she could do about it. When I moved in with my dad and Mary, she continued to come into my room and stick her tongue in my ear, and now she would rub herself against me. I was confused. What did she want? It seemed like sex, but she was my dad's wife and my stepmother. We would make out a lot and she would pull me towards the bedroom, but still I wasn't sure what she wanted.[4] I was getting the message, however, and eventually we ended up in the bedroom and had intercourse. I was sixteen. It was my first sexual experience with a female.[5] I was ecstatic, guilty, frightened, and ashamed. I fell in love with her. After a while all I wanted was sex. I would come home after school and want to have sex with her.[6] I wanted to marry her. Isn't that what a boy does with his mom?

I think my dad knew what was happening.[7] Mary told me that he had asked her if we were being sexual. She used to compare me to him sexually, and I usually came out the winner.[8] I should write a book: "How to Compete with Your Dad and Win." She didn't care about me other than how she could use me sexually. She probably didn't care about my father either. I hate her now.[9] She committed suicide by drinking herself to death.

Two women in my life that only gave a shit about what they needed. No wonder relationships were so difficult for me as I became a young man. The first woman I dated as an adult was just like my stepmother. She was much older than I, and all she wanted was sex. I obliged until she got tired of me and found someone else.

Then I met Diana. We were going to be married. I don't know why I asked her to marry me. I guess I thought it was the right thing to do. Much of our relationship revolved around sex. She would do just about anything sexually that I asked her. Now that I look back on it, I know some of what we were doing must have hurt her, but she never said anything and I didn't ask. Eventually I got tired of her but was too afraid to tell her I wanted to end our relationship. I had bought her an engagement ring and even told her mother that we were going to get married. I eventually stopped seeing her but never even asked for the ring back. I also sold my first new car. I picked it out in her favorite color. I hate orange.

Then I met Lisa, the goddess. I thought she was the most beautiful woman. I was going to a junior college. One of my fraternity brothers was dating her. Once, when we were at a party, she began to flirt with me. I found out later that she flirted with everybody, but it didn't matter, I was hooked. I would have done anything to be in her favor. I gave her my fraternity pin and thought we were a pair. Then I found pictures of other guys who she was also going out with. I took the pin back, but then I gave it to her again. She continued to flirt or go out with just about everyone, and yet I couldn't let her go. This relationship was based on sex too. As long as I could get her to be sexual, I felt some security that she was mine.

I asked her many times to marry me, and she finally agreed. I think she did because I sold myself to her mother. I paid a dowry of giving her mother my car and continued to make the payments because without Lisa she wouldn't have the same income. Lisa was working and helping to pay the rent.

So we were married, and off we went to the big university so I could be a doctor. I always thought that sounded good when someone asked me what I wanted to be when I grew up. It lasted about six weeks. We were broke; Lisa was depressed and lying around the apartment all day, not even bothering to get dressed. I dropped out of school, Lisa had a baby, and I was drafted. While I was in Vietnam Lisa had become involved with an old boyfriend and divorced me. I gave up my rights to my child. I know now I wasn't able to give Lisa very much; I was looking for a mother who would take care of me emotionally. However, I don't think I could have tolerated anyone who would have really given me what I needed. It just wouldn't have seemed right to me. All my experience was with women who were out for themselves and who really expected me to take care of them.[10]

Vietnam is where I discovered drugs. Up until then I had only used alcohol. Several times I could have killed myself by driving when I was totally smashed. I was either extremely lucky or there was some divine intervention working. In Vietnam I became acquainted with opium, marijuana, hashish, LSD, speed, THC, and heroin. I would have used anything anyone offered me. I had no ability to say no or to respect my own vulnerability. I was lucky to have come out of it alive. I really didn't give a shit about myself. I was on a suicide mission, trying to obliterate the memories and pain of the past. I was angry at my mother for placing me in the role of husband and then rejecting me for this asshole that treated her like shit (and still does). I was angry at my father for not intervening and breaking up the incestuous relationship between me and my stepmother. I was angry at my stepmother for using me for her sexual enjoyment and excitement and not really seeing my needs.

When I was discharged from the service I quickly found another woman whom I could attach to and avoid my loneliness and pain. She was a lot like the other women in my life. We quickly moved in together and began a very chaotic relationship. I continued to try to blot out my feelings with drugs. I overdosed one time on alcohol and barbiturates and woke up to the paramedics and police trying to take me to the hospital in the ambulance.

I finally realized that I needed some help and sought out a therapist. He was a good therapist, and both my wife and I saw him together. I remember telling him about the incest between my stepmother and me. He took it seriously, but we never talked much bout it. My wife blamed me for it, and I think I quickly put it away again. I didn't talk about it again until eight years later when we were divorced.[11] Our marriage was built on denial, both mine and her's. She was also a victim, and that was never dealt with either. I think we supported each other's denial through conflict. We knew how to fight with each other, but nothing was ever resolved. I think the continual fighting kept us from our internal pain. It was easier to do that than face the really hard stuff inside.

When she left, I felt scared and uncertain of my ability to care for myself. However, I did finally get some help with the incest. I attended a workshop on incest where a film was shown of women talking about their incest experience. During the film I got a big knot in my stomach and felt physically ill. I asked one of the workshop leaders if I could make an appointment to see her. She had never seen a man who had been sexually abused before, but she used what she knew about women incest victims, and it was helpful.

I did much grieving about the many losses in my childhood. I felt my rage but not at my stepmother. I hadn't accepted the fact that I was a victim. Perhaps this therapist assumed that because I came to her for help I knew I was a victim. I knew something ugly had happened and that I felt shameful, but I believed that it was my fault. After all, I enjoyed it and sought it out. I still thought I was the only man that anything like this had ever happened to. It wasn't until I met other men who had been sexually abused that I began to realize that there wasn't anything I had done to encourage or invite it.[12] Only then could I recognize the way I was used for her release and pleasure. She didn't really see my needs even though she pretended to. Even as I write this I am confused about her feelings towards me. She acted like I was important. We even talked about marriage. I was in love with her, I thought. She said she didn't think she could leave my dad. She told me I was a better lover and had a bigger penis. I was special, or at least I thought so. The craziness of this became more and more evident. I can still feel the rage at her for what she did. Not so much for the sex, but for the disregard of what it meant to me.[13] It wasn't the sex as much as it was the attention, feeling that I was important because she wanted to have sex with me. But there was also a phoniness to it that I didn't realize until later. I'm angry because she didn't respect my feelings and recognize the impact on me of what she was doing.

Maybe I had a difficult time with this because men aren't supposed to have such intense needs for nurturance and affection. I have had a difficult time believing that my feelings are normal. What wasn't normal was the depriving and ignoring of my needs as a child. What wasn't normal was the meeting of these needs by a mother who used me as a surrogate husband to meet her emotional needs and a stepmother who used me as a sexual object. I have to keep telling myself that my feelings and needs for love and affection are normal and I can have them met in healthy ways.[14]

I am getting my needs met in healthier ways more often these days. I have good friends who care about me and support me. I care about my emotional and physical self. I have a spiritual self that is concerned about my fellow human beings and the world around me. I have a wife that loves me and is available emotionally. I will soon have a son to whom I believe I can provide healthy, nurturing parenting.

There are still problems too. I have to continue to work on them, which will probably always be true. I have a compulsive side that is less voracious than it once was, but I still go out of control. I have to set limits and be able to follow through on them. I still have difficulty with intimacy. I don't let people know me as often as I would like. I am afraid of feeling vulnerable and being used in some way. I still get hooked in my family and think I can get what I need from them, even though I know that it will never happen.

Overall, as I look back on the sexual abuse and what it meant in my life, it is still painful. I think it always will be. However, I don't think I am a bad person because of it. I can put the responsibility where it belongs, and I can take responsibility for my own life now. I didn't cause the abuse but I was stuck with its effects, but they don't have to ruin my life.

Questions to help you identify your thoughts and emotions:

How is your (your loved one's) story similar to Daniel's?

How is your (your loved one's) story different from Daniel's?

What emotions did you have reading Daniel's story?

What was the most powerful section of the story for you?

What did you learn about yourself from reading this story?

14

Henry's Story

M Y story starts on a small farm.[1] Although it was nearly fifty years ago I still remember crawling into my parents' bed, getting face to face with my father, and reaching down with my feet to feel his penis. How excited I was being able to touch it and feel it grow. How I longed to see it. How pleased I was that he didn't know what I was doing and make me stop.[2] At age three I was moved into my brother's room. He was big, fourteen years old, and best of all he used to hold me every night. I enjoyed it when he held me and didn't even mind when he rubbed up against me, even though I didn't understand what he was doing or why I got wet when he did it. I just wish he wouldn't make me move over when he quit rubbing up against me.

Before long he showed me a "game" called "playing farm." I didn't like this game. I was always the "cow" and he the "bull." Whenever he got behind me and crawled on top of me it hurt very much. At first he just rubbed his penis between my legs, and he entered my butt for a few seconds. But in a few weeks' time he started to enter me as soon as he crawled on me. He stayed on me for a long time. The pain made me cry till a long time after he stopped and left me alone. I was sore all the time, even my stomach hurt. If he played the part of the "cow" I had to be the "calf." This didn't hurt, but I had to suck till the "milk" came. When he held my head tight I choked on him and got a stomachache on his "milk."

As much as I liked when he held me, I was glad when he went off to the war. I missed him, but most of all I envied his penis. It was not like mine; it was like Dad's. I didn't know what it was, but I knew there was something "wrong" with my penis. I had known that for as long as I could remember. I can see me standing to the left of my brother while we were urinating, his penis at my eye level, watching, fascinated, wondering why I was not able to move the skin on my penis like he did on his.

When I was age nine, a sexual relationship with my cousin, who was four years older than I, started. We played in the hay barn at Grandmother's farm where there were many tunnels and small hiding spots. He picked up on my fear of the dark and confined spaces, and at first he just told me to stay by his side. This soon led to us lying side by side, then holding each other, and later to him pressing against me with his erection very apparent. Then he took my hand and put it on his pants over his erection. After a few Sundays he had his penis out and erect within a few seconds of us getting into a hiding place in the hay. He showed me how to masturbate him. Afterwards I asked him what all the sticky white fluid all over my hand was. He explained what it was and how it came out. I started to understand what my brother had been doing to me all those years before.

As our sexual activity continued, he soon tried oral sex on me and the fear of being held tight and forced to swallow semen returned from the times with my brother. With the first taste of semen I started to choke and spit up. He let me go. I think we were both afraid to try it again.

After many times of masturbating him I asked him to do it to me. He said he could not because I had no skin to do it with and that mine would not work like his or the other guys'. The shame of being different came back stronger than ever. It was too late to hide my nakedness from him, but none of the other guys saw me. Our sexual activity lasted until he turned sixteen and got a car. After that I didn't see him for years, and this hurt.[3]

About this time I met the cousin of the boy on the farm next to us. His cousin called him "skin-dink." I asked him why, and he became embarrassed. I got him alone and asked him all the questions I could think of. He would not show me his penis unless I showed him mine. The embarrassment I had felt about being different from all the other males I had seen was overridden with the hope that I had found someone like me. I'll never forget that day in the shed when we both pulled out our penises and they were alike. We touched and examined each other's like we had found the most important thing in the world. When we found out we were alike, we became friends like no one I had ever known before.

After playing with each other a few times, he showed me something he had done on another farm. We went into the chicken coop and took turns putting our penis into a chicken. The heat and the new feeling was unbelievable. After a while I didn't wait for him, I did it every chance I got. This soon led to trying it with other farm animals. Before long I was having intercourse with an animal every day, and this lasted through my teenage years.

As I got old enough to leave grade school and start junior high, I was filled with fear about being different every day. For many months I had feared going to gym class. The terror of having to shower with the other boys and being found out. I tried every way I could think of to get out of going to gym. But nothing worked. Soon that dreaded day came. How hard I tried to become invisible; thirty boys in a shower with only twenty sprayheads and no place to hide. I just wanted to sit down and cry. Why were the rest of the boys laughing and joking? Was I the only one afraid? As I walked towards the showers my fears seemed to choke me. I wanted to turn and run. I held my towel in front of me to cover myself as long as I could. As I neared the shower room I saw most of the boys were already in there. Some faced the wall, like I planned to do, but most were facing out, talking and laughing. Then I saw for the first time almost every one of their penises were just like mine! Those facing the wall were the only ones who were like the males I had seen as a child. Could they now feel like I had felt? Could I be almost normal? No, I must just be lucky to be with the few who were like me.[4] It was to take many gym classes and four years of observing other boys before I saw that I was like most of the males. The few males in my childhood were the exception, not me.

Yet the summer of my thirteenth year the fear of being different and inferior returned. I started to caddy at the golf course. I saw boys being "depanted" by bigger boys. I soon dreaded having to go to work. I hoped my size and aloneness would keep others from trying to pull my pants off. But a few weeks later, when I refused to go skinny-dipping in the lake by the clubhouse, my clothes were dragged off and I was thrown in the water. I stayed in the water and hoped that they hadn't seen my penis. I noticed that two of the boys' penises were like mine. One of the boys told me that the skin over the heads of our penises had been cut off when we were babies, that's why I was different. Then he gave me the word I came to use every day of my life; a word I came to look for in every book or paper I read; a word that I used to decide who my friends would be; a word I've come to hate like no other: *circumcision*. The word that explained all my hates, fears, and anger. The word about my feeling different, inferior, less of a man, and deformed. Now I knew why my dad called me his "little Jew boy," why he always said mine "didn't work like his," and why everyone else in my childhood always said, "Yours is different." Why did they do this to me? Was I bad? Was I a freak? I still struggle with these feelings forty years later.

As my summers at the golf course went on, I would make friends with the boys that I caddied with during the day. During the evening I would then get them to go with me to look for golf balls.[5] When we would undress to look for golf balls in the lake, I would start talking about sex till they got aroused. At first mutual masturbation kept me satisfied, but by the second summer and for the next four, any boy who said anything about circumcision I would get them alone and overpower them and anally rape them. Soon it did not matter if they were uncircumcised or not. I started to set up any boy I felt attracted to. Before long I was molesting four boys a week. Some of them more than once. Often I threatened them at the start of my attack, but after having climaxed I would keep going with my movement but sound concerned, tell them I would quit if it hurt or if they didn't tell anyone. Most of them thanked me for stopping, and in a sad way we used to act like friends. I felt bad after each time I did this to a boy. But the next time the sexual urge came all was forgotten. I did what seemed important at the time. The shame and regret was pushed aside, only to return after I had satisfied some uncontrolled feeling that only sexual activity would help.

The sexual activity at the golf course soon was not enough. If I could not find a boy to set up during the day I would come home to the farm to find an outlet. I tried to use the chickens again, but I had grown so large that I killed the first two chickens I tried to have sex with. I then turned to our dog and used her. One time my father came into the barn when I was having intercourse with our dog. I acted like I was just sitting behind her. My clothes were on, but my penis was sticking out of my fly. I didn't withdraw from the dog or move for many minutes while my dad talked to me. Nothing was said about what I was doing, and I thought he didn't know what I was doing.[6] However, shortly after that he talked about how large the dog's vulva was the last few weeks. Though I didn't know the meaning of the word I knew what he was talking about. I tried to stop having sex with the dog, knowing that Dad now knew, but didn't. Then she was gone for a few days, and I was told she had died. I felt shame and regret because I believed I had caused her death. I told myself that I would never do that again. I had killed chickens and now our dog. Only a very bad person would do something like that. I often told myself how bad I was.

During my thirteenth year no amount of sex seemed enough. When I came home from the golf course I went straight to where some of the cows were near a wooden fence. I got behind a cow and carefully put my penis in her. (This was the start of twenty years of sex with cows.) I climaxed and was getting down when I realized that the cow had wet the front of my pants all the way down to the cuffs on both legs. How was I going to get into the house and my room without being seen? Everyone was in the kitchen talking. I finally got my pants wet all the way around and told everyone as I went into the house that I had fallen into the lake looking for golf balls. They laughed, and I swore to myself I would never have sex with an animal again.

When we got a new dog I began masturbating him and having him lick my genitals and anus. I put my penis in his anus, and he put his in mine one time. There was a lot of fear and pain, but that never stopped me.

I then started to have sex with a calf. At first it seemed impossible because her opening was so small. I pushed so hard I got blood blisters on the head of my penis. But before long I was doing this morning and night when it was milking time. Besides that I was masturbating five times a day. I also started molesting boys on other farms or visitors from the city.

At times I hated my penis so much I even tried to cut it off. Using a razor blade I cut straight across the scar from my circumcision. But the pain and blood made me stop. It hurt and bled for a long time, so I hid in my room so no one would find out. Over the years I hated my sex organs so much that I stuck pins and needles into them. I tied ropes around them, I pulled till the pain was too great to continue. I burnt my penis with a hot wire. I laid it over my circumcision mark.[7] This burn left a scar and more hatred for myself.

One spring day when I was fourteen when everyone had gone away for the weekend I went into the barn, took all my clothes off, and started having sex with a calf that was tied up there. All I thought of was the pleasure I was receiving, and for a few minutes the feelings of worthlessness were gone.[8] But suddenly I panicked as I felt two hands on my back holding me, a body pressed against mine, and the probing of a penis between my legs. The pain that followed is hard to describe. It seemed to be worse than any I remembered from when my brother had entered me. Only one person I knew had such a large penis, my dad. My fear of being caught having sex with an animal had come true. No amount of crying or begging could make him stop. He said I had to be taught "what the calf felt" and that I was "going to remember this lesson for a long time." It seemed like forever before my first "lesson" was over.[9] As he withdrew I fell to the barn floor. The pain in my stomach and my sides prevented me from standing. I crawled over onto some straw and just laid there for a long time. The hate for my dad was now matching my hate for my body and my life. As I lay there looking up at him with his erect penis sticking out towards me, covered with blood and semen, hair matted down, all I could do was hate and hope someday to be able to do it back to him.

Once more I swore never to have sex again. But soon I was back at it. I realized that Dad was watching me every time I was anywhere in the barns or sheds. Even standing urinating near a calf brought on an accusation and another "lesson." Then came the oral sex. That too was "a lesson."[10] If I "didn't scream out" during anal sex, I would not "have to suck it." The pain of anal sex matched the anger of being held tight by my head, forced to suck something that stretched my mouth till it hurt. I was cursed for choking when he tried to put it deeper in my mouth and made fun of when I threw up the semen he forced me to swallow. The real lesson I was learning was that I could not do anything right. I was learning that real well.[11]

As much as I hated my dad and was glad when I would not see him for days at a time, he only had to walk into the barn to urinate and I would become fixated by his penis and the way he drew his foreskin back and forth all the while acting like it was a part of urinating. And then he let me take his penis and draw his foreskin back and forth. He even let me put my penis by his and draw his foreskin over the head of mine.[12] The envy I had for his penis grew as strong as the the hatred for mine had become.

I remember that Saturday afternoon going to church with some friends and their laughter afterwards when they talked about what the priest had said when they confessed to having masturbated. Now for the first time I learned that even that was a sin. Now I also had to fear God. The guilt increased, and the feeling of having a big black hole inside of me grew strong. My religion had become a strong influence on me. I not only felt guilty about everything I had done, but I felt I could never be forgiven. Death seemed like the only way out. But someone so bad was sure to go to hell. The "policeman in the sky" was sure to judge me too bad to spend forever in heaven.

In high school and the years right after I tried to be straight and "normal" with my friends. But all the while I lived a totally different life at home and on the golf course, where my life revolved around boys and sexual acting out. My life was out of control and I didn't even know it. Every time I started a relationship with a girl and it became sexual, I broke up with her and looked for another. I just kept searching for that unknown person to make me feel good, never realizing no one else could do it for me.

At age seventeen I was arrested for sexually molesting a nine-year-old boy. I was handcuffed and taken away in a squad car while my friends stood by and watched. The night in jail was frightening, shaming, and sleepless. I just laid there with my clothes on, staring at the light overhead and wishing I had been successful during one of my suicide attempts. I had lost what little self-respect I had. My closeness with my family was now gone.[13] My secret was out. I had lost my family, friends, and job. Life seemed to hold no reason for going on.[14] I just wanted to call it quits. Lost in self-pity, with no one to turn to, I became even more of a loner than ever before. Going to school and having to face everyone was more than I could stand. The silence and the other kids ignoring me hurt more than I ever could have imagined. I just told myself that I really did not care if they talked to me; that way I wouldn't have to lie or make up stories about what I had done.

I got out of school, got a job in a factory, and hoped I would never see anyone I knew again. It was a chance to start over. No one knew me, the real me, the me I hated and tried to hide.

But then I started being sexual with older men, one after another. Soon I felt all the same shame and discomfort at work I had felt at home and in school.

At twenty-four I had a chance to get married. It was a way to gain some respectability and to prove to myself and others that I was not a homosexual. The marriage worked, for a while. But the feelings of holding and being held by a boy became so strong that soon I had every boy in the neighborhood playing in our yard. I spent the next ten years playing with, teaching, coaching, setting up, and molesting every boy I became attracted to. I would take them hunting, fishing, boating, swimming, and hiking. I befriended them, made them feel indebted to me. I tried to be the father that all these boys did not have.[15] But most of all I held them and loved them. The one thing they were all missing and looking for. I gave them that special closeness that made them feel it worth being sexually molested just so they had someone to hold and love them. They didn't know what a high price they were paying to get this attention.

My secrets increased in number as did my shame, anger, denial, fear, and the gap between my wife and me. My world came crashing down when she divorced me. I moved away and tried to hide. After two years of total isolation I started answering ads in a gay paper. I soon had one or two guys a week. But it just was not the same, so I started working with boys again.[16] I soon had one living with me and one who was always coming over to visit or go places with me. I had that good feeling again—mixed with the shame and guilt of using these boys' vulnerabilities to set them up.

There was never a shortage of boys who were hurting for love, who needed some one who cared for them and gave them time and understanding. How sad that the good acts were done for my sexual satisfaction and the boys lost out.

I wanted to be closer to my children from my first marriage. I bought a house a few blocks away from them, and my oldest son moved in with me. It wasn't long before I started setting up my son's friends. Even in this upper-middle-class neighborhood there were the same hurting and vulnerable boys.

One teenage boy I met not only had a body just like mine but he also revealed that he had suffered the same abuse and shaming I had known. He even hated being circumcised. (It seemed that every boy I set up had a part of them that they hated, something that they were led to believe was tangible "proof" that they were less than a whole person.) I molested this boy for a whole summer.

I went to my family doctor to see if he could help me. He put me on a drug for treating depression. But I became so tired and drowsy that I feared for my job and stopped taking it. I went to another doctor who wrote down my whole sex history. He asked me every question I think there is about sex but never let me ask any questions. He measured my penis when it was soft. Then he rubbed it and measured it erect. When I questioned him on how this was going to help me stop sexually abusing boys, he became angry and told me that there is nothing anyone could do for someone like me. After six months of weekly meetings with him I was no better off than when I started looking for help. I still didn't understand the reasons I acted and felt the way I did.[17]

The help came four years later when I was arrested for having molested that boy that was so much like me. He had gone to alcoholism treatment; only then did the abuse come out. He was getting the help he needed and started the process of my getting the help I needed. I was under arrest and locked up, but for the first time in my life I felt some sort of freedom.

When I was released from jail that day the anger, fear, shame, and hate were all there, but a new feeling was also there for the first time. It was a feeling of not knowing how to act. My secrets were out. I had nothing to hide. My secrets, my books, my films, my pictures, and my "other life" were all out in the open.[18] I had nothing to keep hidden. Nothing to deny. Nothing to have to control. My whole way of life was swept away. I walked around lost. I cried tears of self-pity, fear, and anger for days. But most of all I cried because I had never let anyone inside my "walls." The loneliness and isolation of my way of life kept me from reaching out to someone, anyone. I needed to talk. I had a lifetime of questions, starting with: "Doesn't everyone live like this?" and "How can I tell someone all about myself and still expect them to stay?"

I told myself:

Counseling is not for me. I never hurt anyone. The boys wanted to do what we did. They asked me, so I taught them. Hell, I was doing them a favor. No one else would answer all their questions about sex. They needed me. I was the only one who was good to them. What does this counselor know? Why don't she get a real job? Victims! I had no victims, just boys I had sexually molested. Why does that hurt so bad? I've got to get out of here. She's going to blame it all on me.

But there is only one way out of this mess. I have to go through all the junk of a lifetime, forty-five years of garbage.

I can't tell them what my dad did. What if they find out about my brother? What does that say about me and my family? Only a sick family does those sorts of things. My family was perfect. I dare anyone to prove that it isn't.

What does she mean denial, compulsive behavior, sex addiction? What does she know? Next she'll say I pumped up my ego by be-friending confused, needy, or inadequate boys, or that I focus on friends who have problems rather than deal with my own. If things went wrong in my life it must be someone else's fault; don't blame me.

Okay! Maybe some of those things happened to me when I was a kid. Really? It wasn't my fault because I was only three years old when it happened to me? What do you mean I was programmed? I was twenty-one years old and still playing with my dad's penis. I was thirty when I went to confession, and the priest told me to come to his house for sex. I was set up? You make me sound like a trained animal! All this makes me very confused. Okay, I'll take some chances. I'll share a little. But don't ask too much. Yes, that happened. Yes, he always called me "useless." So what? It didn't hurt. Well, maybe a little. No, I didn't like being hit. But everybody does it. What do you mean there are other ways to raise kids besides name-calling and put-downs? If I come back, will you tell me more? It feels good to talk with others and to know I'm not the only one who feels like this.

And so recovery very slowly started for me. The negative side of me was very strong. The shaming messages I've learned about being unlovable and about my body will take time and help to overcome. I have had to look at the ways my family influenced me. How I was taught, programmed, and conditioned by the way they treated me.

Growth is painful and time consuming. But I also have a lot of hope and faith because I have found a better, healthier way of living. I had to decide to change, to trust and risk. I also had to learn there is a Higher Power that is accessible to me. I'm learning that I don't have to be a martyr, victim, people pleaser, or emotional cripple to get what I need from people. Slowly, a little bit at a time, I'm learning to care about myself, to love myself, to know I'm important and that I have worth. Slowly I'm learning I don't have to hurt or be hurt to have a relationship with someone else. This is the real beginning.

Questions to help you identify your thoughts and emotions:

How is your (your loved one's) story similar to Henry's?

How is your (your loved one's) story different from Henry's?

What emotions did you have reading Henry's story?

What was the most powerful section of the story for you?

What did you learn about yourself from reading this story?

15

Jim's Story

WHEN I was first given the opportunity to write my story, I leaped at the chance. I said, "Of course I will! Thank you for thinking of asking me. I'm sure my story will help a lot of people. I'll get started right away." But later that day, I thought, What if my parents find out about it? What will they think? In the days to come the old defenses surfaced again: Now why did he suggest to *me* that I write my story? My story isn't as bad as most guys'. People will think I'm just being a baby about it.

After a week I was thinking, I still don't understand why he wants me to write. I don't have anything to say. I'm not even sure anything really happened to me. I could be making the whole thing up just to get pity. And even if it did happen, it really wasn't that bad. I could just have misunderstood what they intended to do. They didn't mean to hurt me.

I told my wife about my *thoughts,* as I was unaware of my *feelings,* my fear. She knowingly smiled and said, "Sit down and start. I believe it happened. I have seen what it did to you." Still, I was confused. I had trouble concentrating. My body felt "funny."

All this was familiar to me. Before I went to therapy I spent a large part of my life walking around in a fog. My therapist has since taught me to say *dissociation,* rather than *fog.* I didn't know what he meant when he said that I "wasn't in my body." I didn't understand what my girlfriend wanted when she insisted that I interact with her on a "feeling level." I just thought, Here is another woman that I can't satisfy, that wants more than I can give.

I didn't go to therapy because I wanted to deal with being sexually abused.[1] I didn't think I had been. I went because one of my college professors suggested it. My girlfriend had been suggesting it for months, but I thought she needed it much more than I did. After all, she had been sexually abused for years by her father. If anyone needed therapy, surely it was she. (At that time I wondered if there were any women who hadn't been sexually abused. All my girlfriends eventually told me about how they had been sexually abused as children.)

I don't remember what I told the therapist when he asked me the reason I was at the first session. (I don't remember a lot about my life.) But I kept coming back to see him, and I got to like him. I assumed that he didn't much like me and just tolerated me because I was paying him. We sat there while I told him stories about my family. One day he interrupted me, saying, "That sounds like sexual abuse to me." I responded flatly with one word: "Really." He explained what sexual abuse is and the reasons that what happened to me was abuse.

The hour was up, and I walked to my car thinking, "You know, I was just beginning to like that guy, and he comes up with this outrageous idea that I was sexually abused. No doubt *he* was sexually abused and just sees sexual abuse everywhere, even when it isn't there. The poor guy." But before I realized it I had driven twenty-five miles out of my way.

I had already scheduled another appointment, so I decided to keep it. We again talked about the so-called sexual abuse. I left that time feeling very guilty and shameful: "What kind of a son am I that I say things that make it look like my mother sexually abused me? I must be some kind of a pervert or something."

The next time I returned, I said, "You know I have been thinking. I wonder if I'm not wired right, that I have something missing inside me. That would explain why I feel so different from other people and why my girlfriends always complain that I don't express my emotions. Maybe I don't have any emotions." It made sense to me. However, try as I might, I could not convince him that I was crazy or some kind of mental freak. "Is it less scary to be crazy than to have been sexually abused?" he asked. "Well, if you're crazy at least you can take medications or do something about it," I replied without thinking.[2]

The more I talked, the more "trouble" I got myself into. Every few sessions my therapist was claiming to see another example of how I had been sexually abused. I just couldn't believe it. Things like sexual abuse just don't happen in a town like mine. I came from a small farming town in the West, "God's country," we used to say. Besides, my parents were successful, respected, church-going members of the community, not the kind of people who have a kid who gets sexually abused. If I had been sexually abused I must have done something to cause it or deserve it since there was nothing in my background to explain it. At least that is what I thought at the time.

I was born the first of three children. My father was a writer who traveled in order to do research for his books and to give talks. He was rarely home as I remember. When he was home he was busy writing. He sometimes told me how proud he was of how I took care of Mom and my sisters while he was gone.[3] When I was older he told me that he had a couple of affairs, one-night stands really, when he was away. Somehow I wasn't surprised. He talked and joked about sex frequently. His friends used to call him a "dirty old man" and gave him birthday cards with sexual pictures on them.

One time we were at the neighbors' house after church, and he was sitting next to a woman, talking with her. I was sitting across the room from them just listening. I don't remember what they were saying, but I do remember what she was doing. She kept spreading her legs farther and farther apart, and pulling her dress up higher and higher. She wasn't wearing anything under her dress. I was nervous about looking. I figured I would get in trouble if I got caught. Maybe my dad and she had forgotten that I was in the room. How could she not know how high her dress was? How could my dad not see what was going on? I felt very shameful for looking at her.

This same woman had a son my age. One summer she and her son came to spend the day with my family at our lake cabin. We were all sitting around after lunch when she announced that she was going to go for a swim. As soon as she left the picnic table to go into the cabin to change into her swimming suit, her son turned to me and said, "Here's our chance." I followed him as he went around the back of the cabin. His mother had opened up the bathroom curtains and was undressing in front of the window. Just as before, I was curious, frightened, and embarrassed. I kept wondering why my friend didn't get mad at me for looking at his mom naked, but then he was doing it too. It seemed impossible that she couldn't know that someone could see her if she opened the window like that, yet she was acting like she didn't know we were there. I was really confused. I couldn't figure out what was going on.

I seemed to have had a pattern of finding myself in places where women "accidently" exposed themselves to me. When my parents traveled, they would leave me at a neighbor's house. I was young enough that I was getting up and watching cartoons on Saturday morning. Although it was very early, Mrs. Wright would get up too. She came downstairs in her nightgown and would sit on the sofa next to me. Periodically she would go to the television and adjust the controls. She would do this numerous times, and I never saw that the TV needed adjusting. However, what I did see was that each time she leaned over to reach the controls, her nightgown would raise up, showing that she wasn't wearing anything underneath. It was confusing for me. I was excited but embarrassed. I hated myself for looking, for "taking advantage" of her. I was sure she didn't realize that I could see her when she was merely trying to fix the TV for me. No matter where I sat in the room the view was the same. After an hour or so of this her husband would come downstairs and tell her to "get dressed properly."

My mother also used to expose herself to me. She would go into the bathroom, undress, and get into the tub. After a while she would call to me through the closed door and ask me a question. I would come to the door and answer her. She would say, "I can't hear you. Open the door." I would talk louder. "I still can't hear you," came her reply. I could hear her fine; why couldn't she hear me? Finally, I would open the door and we would talk. She would be lying in the tub. She would look at me and talk, all the while rubbing herself. Sometimes she would cover her crotch or breasts with a washtowel, but only after I had seen her. Every time it was the same. I would try to avoid opening the door, she would insist, and I would feel horribly shameful for looking at her.[4]

Once as an adult I had parked my car and was on my way to a therapy session. I was walking down an alley, and there in a picture window in the back of a building was a woman dressing. I imme-diately felt shameful that I was violating this woman by window peeking. When I got to my therapist's office he asked me what was wrong and wanted to know the reason I was so dissociated. I con-fessed to him how I had just been voyeuring on that woman in the alley and felt very shameful about it. I told him that she wasn't intentionally dressing where someone could see her, that she didn't expect anyone to walk through the alley and catch her. He told me that he thought just the opposite, that she wanted someone to see her. Just as when I was a child I wanted to believe that I was at fault and that the woman was blameless. I kept arguing that it was my fault because I was the one that had chosen to go into the alley. I had a very difficult time not thinking that I was a pervert for walking through an alley in the middle of the day.

I had difficulty seeing any of these women as being sexually abusive. For one thing all of the television shows, radio programs, and newspaper or magazine articles I had ever seen only talked about women as victims and men as abusers. Secondly, since they never touched me I didn't see how it could be sexual abuse. Finally, when I told other people about it everyone said that I was a lucky guy to get "free strip shows."[5]

As a youngster I was also sexually abused by a male. When I was in junior high school I started staying after school to watch the high school kids rehearse their plays. After a few weeks the director, Mr. James, started asking me to do him little favors: "Go get that" or "Hold this for me." He said that when I got old enough he would let me have a part in a play. I loved his attention. Within a couple of months he and I were walking home from rehearsals together. We both lived in the same direction, and since it was getting late in the year and getting darker earlier he thought it would be a good idea for my safety. He even walked me right to my house, even though it was out of his way. I invited him in and introduced him to my mom. She thought he was a nice man.

There was another teacher, besides Mr. James, that directed plays too. She and he were rumored to have dated each other. It was also a rumor that she invited senior high boys over to her apart-ment for parties. I don't know if she ever really did or not. But I do remember how she would always pick the really cute boys to be the leads in the plays she directed. She would spend hours going over the love scenes with them. She always had to show them how they were supposed to kiss. She would kiss them and then have them kiss the female actor, tell them they were doing it wrong, and then she would kiss them again. I saw her use her tongue when she kissed them.[6] I knew I was too ugly. I would never get a part in one of her plays and she would never want to kiss me.

Eventually I got a part in one of Mr. James's school plays. In one scene I was supposed to sit on a couch with another actor with my arm around him. Mr. James kept telling me that I was doing it wrong, and he would sit down and put his arm around me. I was nervous when he did that, but I figured it was because I was acting so poorly and not because he was doing anything wrong.[7]

Then Mr. James made me student director. We would sit in the theater until late in the evening and discuss how the play was going. One night he offered me a ride home in his car. On the way to my house he said he was going out on a date that night and needed to swing by his house to pick something up. Now I knew where he lived. I thought to myself, He must really trust me to let me know where he lives. Everyone knows how important his privacy is to him.[8]

When I went to play practice the next day I was kind of smug. I thought, I'm his favorite. The rest of you are just students to Mr. James. I'm his friend. As we sat in the darkness of the theater watching the play, Mr. James patted me on the shoulder, telling me what a good job I had done and how proud he was of me. I enjoyed the attention, but I got uncomfortable when he left his arm around me. I figured nobody could see anyway, since we were sitting in the dark.

One day as we were leaving school Mr. James gave me his unlisted home phone number: "Maybe you should have this in case of an emergency and need to get ahold of me. Just don't give it to anyone else." I memorized it so that I could throw away the note. I didn't want to risk violating his trust by misplacing the note and having someone find out his number.

A few months later he asked me to do some set designing and to call him when I was done. When I did he asked me to bring them over to his apartment. He met me in the entryway; we stood and talked. He said I couldn't come in because he had company.

A former student was visiting him. I was a little jealous, but I knew that Mr. James and I would remain friends even after I graduated.

That spring Mr. James began to loan me records. Each day I would pick one up from him at school and listen to it at night. The next day I would return it and borrow another one. When summer vacation came I figured I would have to wait till school started again to borrow any more records. The last day of school he brought me a huge pile of records. "This ought to keep you busy this summer." I was thrilled. I also liked it that the other kids at school saw that a popular teacher was trusting me with his personal property.[9]

When my parents saw all the records they asked me where I got them. I told them that Mr. James had loaned them to me. They told me to be careful with his records, that he was being kind and I ought not to violate his trust.

About a month into summer vaction Mr. James called and asked if I had a certain record. It turned out that I did, and he said he needed it. He said he would come by and pick it up. I volunteered to bring it over to his apartment.[10] When I got there he stood in the doorway. I had always wondered what the inside of his house looked like. All I could see from the doorway was shelves full of records. I knew he must have a great stereo from the quality of the music I could hear.

One day I decided to return the albums that he had loaned me. I just showed up at his house. When he answered the door I told him why I was there. He responded, "I suppose that you want to borrow more records since you are bringing these back. Wait here and I'll pick out some more." I stood in the doorway as he disappeared around the corner. A few minutes later he returned with more albums.

A couple of weeks later I found myself back at his door. Mr. James opened the door with something all over his hands. "Here are those albums I borrowed," I explained. "I'm baking, my hands are covered with dough. Bring them in and set them down in the living room," he directed. I was excited to finally be able to see his house. It was just as I had imagined. The walls were filled with shelves of records. He had several tape recorders and speakers in every room I passed. I really liked the way he had decorated the

house. I wanted my room at home to look just like his house. He
came in the living room wiping off his hands. "I'll pick out some
more albums for you," he said as he started putting away the borrowed records. A minute or two later he exclaimed, "Why am I
putting out all the effort in this relationship? You pick out the
albums." I chose some records and left, apologizing for interrupt-
ing his cooking.

The pattern continued throughout the summer and into the next
school year. I would come over to his house, return some albums,
and pick out some new ones. One night I started to take a certain
album when he said, "You can't borrow that one. It's too rare." I
protested, "But I borrowed it a couple of months ago." "Well, you
wouldn't have if I had been paying attention," he retorted, somewhat gruffly. Then he added, "If you want to listen to it you can
listen to it here." So that's what I did. I began to spend afternoons
and evenings with him listening to music. He had a nicer stereo
than I did, and he always had pop and chips to munch on. One
time I asked him for a cigarette, and he gave me one. Then he
offered me wine. Soon that too became part of the ritual. One day
he really honored me and said that I could call him by his first
name, Roger, rather than Mr. James. He even let me call him Roger
at school, where it was a written policy that students never address
their instructor that way.[11]

Each year of junior high school I spent more and more time with
Mr. James. I stopped spending time with my friends. I thought they
were too immature. My parents asked me where I was spending
all my time. When I told them I was at Roger's they didn't seem
to think that it was unusual for an adult to spend all his free time
with one of his junior high school students. They did call Roger
and asked if I was being a pest. He assured them that I was be-
having myself.[12]

Some of the kids at school made fun of me for hanging around
Roger. They said that he was gay and that I must be gay too. I
told them that Roger couldn't be gay because he had been married
and I had seen him go on dates with women.[13] I knew the other
students were just jealous of Roger and me.

Roger told me that he was entering a photo contest and needed
a model.[14] I said that I would pose for him if he wanted. We did a
series of portraits of my face. It was fun getting all that attention.

He said because I had helped him he would teach me how to use a 35mm camera. The next time he wanted me to pose he said that the contest rules required that the model be nude. I was somewhat uncomfortable with that idea but went along with it. Later he told me that the photos had won a prize and had been published in a magazine (which I never saw). He gave me some money, saying it was my share of the prize money. Next, he said that instead of taking still photos he wanted to take movies and then would pick the very best frame, enlarge it, and submit that to a contest. I was really uncomfortable moving around his house naked, but I had promised to help him. Finally he said that the latest trend in photo contests was to have the male models appear with erections. I was really uncomfortable and said so, adding that I refused to take part in photo sessions anymore. Roger sat down beside me, saying, "You don't have to do anything you don't like. Have I ever done anything to hurt you? You act as if I'm a pervert or something. It's no big deal; I can find somebody else to do it. You don't owe me anything." I felt guilty that I had suspected him of something bad after all he had done for me.[15]

There was a large city about three hundred miles from where I lived. Roger used to go there to buy records and see movies that never came to our town. One day my mom came to me and said, "Roger called and asked if we thought it was okay for him to take you to the city for your birthday. Do you want to go?" I was excited because I hadn't done much traveling.[16]

When we went we stayed in the same room, but in different beds. Each morning Roger would wake me up by rubbing my back. He would ask me to roll over and offer to rub my chest, but I always declined. I would press myself into the bed when he would try to reach around me and touch the front of my body. When I would dress he would stand at the sink shaving and watch me in the mirror. When I noticed that he was watching me I would turn away.[17]

One night I woke up and he was playing with my penis. The physical sensations were pleasant, but emotionally I was very frightened. I was angry that he was touching me without my consent. My body felt all distorted and strange. I didn't know what to do, so I pretended that I was asleep and tried to roll over. He held me down so I couldn't move. I became even more afraid and angry.

My erection went away. He kept touching me, but eventually went back to his bed. The next morning he acted as if nothing had happened. I was really depressed. Throughout the day he kept asking me, "What's wrong? Aren't you having fun? What good does it do me to spend all this money on you if you're going to act like this. You're no fun to be around."[18]

When I got home from the trip I was still depressed. All the things that the kids at school had said seemed to be true. Maybe Roger was gay and maybe I was too. It had felt kind of good when he touched me, and I did like to spend time with him.[19]

By this time I was dating girls. Most of them of were older than I was. I couldn't drive yet, but I would hitch-hike to see them. Roger would let me have the keys to his house when he was gone. I figured I could really impress girls with his stereo and record collection. He started to leave condoms out for me. I started having sex with lots of girls older than I. Roger would ask me about what I did in bed with different girls.[20]

He said that one way to impress girls and get them really ready for sex was to give them a massage first. He offered to teach me how. He heated up oil on the stove as I took my shirt off. He rubbed oil on my back. It felt good and relaxing. Then he asked me if I had underwear on under my jeans. When I told him I did he asked if I wanted to take my pants off and he would rub my legs. I figured that since I had on underwear he wouldn't touch my penis. Once my pants were off he kept saying, "Why are you so tense? Relax and enjoy it." Then he told me to roll over so he could do the front of my legs. Suddenly, he just reached in my underpants and started fondling my penis. The warm oil felt good, but my head started spinning. I thought I was going to faint. The music on the stereo sounded miles away. My body seemed like it was contorting in impossible ways. Some parts of my body seemed huge, while others seemed minute.[21] I couldn't hold on to my thoughts long enough to form a sentence to tell him to stop. After what seemed like hours I felt his mouth on mine. I was disgusted. His beard hurt my face. My face burned with anger and shame, but I seemed helpless to do anything. He put his mouth by my ear and said, "I want to suck your cock." I started to shake my head and wanted to cry. I just kept shaking my head violently back and forth. He got up and went away. After what seemed like a long time he came back into the room, saying, "You fell asleep. It looked like you were having a bad dream so I left the room." I was so angry. He was treating me like I was an idiot and didn't know what was going on.

When I got home that night my mother took me aside and asked, "Has Roger ever tried anything weird with you?" "Like what?" I asked. "You know, anything *weird,*" she replied. I was afraid to tell her. I didn't know what kind of trouble I would get into. I was sure that she would call Roger or the police or the school and there would be a big scandal. It would be written up in the paper, and I would be an outcast at school. "No, he hasn't," I mumbled. She dropped the subject.[22]

About this time a family friend, a married woman about twice my age, started inviting me over to her house when her husband was away. The first time it was to "help her with a household chore." But then she started offering me drinks, and we ended up in bed. (I don't recall how it happened. I can't remember the first sexual encounter of most of the sexual relationships I have had, even as an adult.) I never found her attractive and didn't really enjoy the sex very much. I was so afraid that her husband would come home and catch us. I would make excuses to keep from going over there, even though she would offer me money. I managed to avoid her for months until she called me and said that if I didn't start coming over she would tell her husband that the baby she was pregnant with wasn't his and was really mine. She added that if he didn't kill me she would take me to court and force me to make child support payments for the rest of my life. I didn't think she could make a sixteen-year-old boy pay child support, but I didn't know whom I could talk to about it and decided that I had better not risk it. When we would have sex I was very detached. I did what she said to, but didn't show any interest. She would get angry, saying that I wasn't doing a good enough job and ordering me to try harder. The longer I was with her the more disgusted I got with her body. The more angry I got, the more things I did to try to hurt her. I would pinch her and bite her. I would slam my penis in her joylessly, hoping she would get sore and leave me alone. I called her names in my head. I hoped her husband would come home drunk some night and kill her. Eventually, she told me I was so bad in bed that she never wanted to see me again, which is exactly what I wanted and exactly what happened.

By my senior year in high school I had started to see Roger less and less. He said he disapproved of how many girls I was sleeping with. He also didn't like the amount and types of drugs I had started taking and selling. When I did go over to see him he began to *give* me albums instead of loaning them to me. He continued to offer me back rubs and asking me to pose for photos. I began to refuse. He got angry and began insisting. I became stronger in my refusals. One night I showed up at his house at the time he had asked me to be there. When I opened the door at the bottom of the stairs, I looked up and saw him standing there holding his typewriter over his head. Without saying a word he threw it down the stairs at me. It crashed into the wall, smashing into pieces. I fled. The terror of the event did not come to me until hours later. I decided, though, that I had better go back to see him because I had seen him be violent with other people and I was afraid of what he might do next. He blamed me for destroying his typewriter: "You drove me to it. You're so ungrateful. I made you what you are. You're nothing without me. You'd be just like the other hicks in this worthless town if I hadn't taken pity on you and made something of you."

I sat there while he yelled at me. The doorbell rang, and he answered it. There was a junior high school boy standing in the entryway. Roger said, "You can't come in. I have company." He stood there and talked to that kid the way he had talked to me only a few years ago. I suddenly saw his patient, intricate plan. How he set kids up to come to him to use them. I wasn't special, I was just one of a series. He was always setting one up as he was using another. I was just one of many. I left overwhelmed with a sense of betrayal, telling myself what a fool I had been to believe that I mattered to him. I thought of how I would kill him. I went home and stared at my father's guns. I imagined killing Roger: quickly, slowly, in private, in public.

At this same time I was going out with a girl younger than I. She came from a lower-class family. Her dad was known as a drunk, and her mom slept around. She had spent a lot of her life being moved from one relative's house to another. I didn't have a lot of respect for her. I thought of her as below me. Whenever she would complain that I was seeing other girls I would just say, "If you don't like it, you know where the door is." One night she said she was tired of me treating her so poorly. I told her I could do anything I wanted to do. I forced myself sexually on her. At first she resisted, but I was twice her size, and I held her down. Towards the end all she did was cry and beg me to stop. After that she ran away. She left the state, and I never heard from her again.

Roger knew something was different in our relationship. He called me up, being very nice. He said that he knew I had always liked his car. He offered to trade my old car for his new car. I knew he was afraid that I would tell someone what he had done to me and that he would lose his job or be arrested. I was smug. I traded cars with him. My parents asked how I got the new car. I told them that Roger was only loaning it to me. I decided to punish him even more. I went over to his house with my key when I knew he wouldn't be home and took a bunch of albums. The next time I went over to see him it was my turn to act like nothing had happened. I even rubbed it in. I asked to borrow one of the records I knew was gone because I had taken it. He acted like nothing had happened. He said that he must have loaned that album out to someone, but he would let me know as soon as it came back.

After that I all but stopped having any contact with Roger. He would call and invite me over, offering me "gifts." But I kept telling him I was busy. Although I was acting smug I was afraid that he would somehow get me in trouble. He knew that I had used and sold drugs. I was afraid he would tell the police. I was afraid he would be able to change my school records so I couldn't get into college. Maybe he would tell my parents something to get me in trouble. They would believe a schoolteacher before they would believe me. I didn't know what extremes he would go to in order to hurt me.

Finally, one night he called me and said, "I'm going on a trip this weekend, and you're going with me." I told him I was busy, that I had plans with a girlfriend. He shouted, "You'll be with me this weekend or you'll never see me again!" I was both afraid and excited that I would be free at last. "Can't make it," I said softly as I hung up. The next few days I was terrified each time the phone rang. I was afraid it was Roger calling, saying that he had changed his ultimatum or telling my parents something to hurt me. In school when we passed in the hall he ignored me. The other kids who were in the school plays came up and asked, "What did you do to Roger? He's really hurt and angry. He says you'll never be a part of a drama production or be welcome in his classroom again." I didn't know what to say. I lost a lot of my friends because they were in the drama department and I was no longer welcome there.

Years after graduating and leaving the state I was in a large department store. I glanced up, and I thought I saw Roger. He was looking at me. I quickly turned away, hoping it wasn't really him or that he hadn't seen me. Prior to this moment I had imagined meeting him again. I had pictured myself being very forceful and confronting him loudly in front of other people. I envisioned him shrinking with humiliation and shame as I told everyone what he had done to me. But now, faced with the possibility of actually seeing him, I panicked. I now imagined him pointing his finger at me, calling me a pervert, and everyone in the store laughing or ridiculing me. I tried to console myself by thinking, I look so different now. My hair is different, and I wear glasses now. He won't be able to recognize me, even if that was him.

I looked up, and he was gone. I began wandering the store. I had to know if it was him. Suddenly, there he was. As he turned a corner, our eyes met. Two thoughts ran through my head: Don't hurt me, and I'm going to kill you. For what seemed like minutes, although it was only seconds, we stared at each other. His face flushed, and he turned, heading for the door. I just stood there. I didn't know what to do.

That encounter was several years ago, and I have not seen or heard from him since. As I write this I wonder what he thinks about what happened. Does he know what he did was abusive? What was done to him that he abused all those children that were entrusted to his care as a teacher? I have imagined him contacting me and making amends. For years I looked in phonebooks for his name and even called a Roger James or two. None of them were ever him. I don't know what I would have done if he had ever answered.

I still have scars from the sexual abuse. I get threatened when my wife is sexually aggressive. I rarely dance or do other things that call attention to my body. These two things are closely linked.

My wife loves to dance. She encourages me to dance with her, but I get frightened. If she continues to pressure me I start to get rageful and want to lash out. When she spends an evening dancing she becomes very aware of her body and wants to be sexual. When she comes on to me too strongly I get afraid and dissociate. I am still working on both of these problems. It makes me angry that I am burdened with this because of what was done to me.

Although I still have things I want to change about myself I have made great progress in healing from my past. I was in therapy (both individual and couples) for three years and continue to attend a Twelve-Step group. As a result of my efforts I have made no attempts to take my life for over ten years. I no longer think about suicide on a daily basis. I do not abuse others. I have stopped overusing drugs and food. I have started to take better care of my body. I am even liking it. I think of myself as a good-looking man for the first time in my life. My marriage is stable and full of fun. I have several close male and female friends. My career has improved. I have forgiven my parents for what they did and didn't do in the past.

When I began writing this story all my old defenses returned: the denial, rationalization, and minimization. The more I wrote, the more irritable I became, the less attractive life looked. This was the mood and outlook I used to have all the time. My life is very different now than it was before I addressed my history of sexual abuse. All that I went through to change has been well worth it. I am very thankful that I had the opportunity to recover from my abuse. I am grateful to the many people who patiently offered me their support when I needed it so much. Sometimes it was something simple, like saying, "I'm glad that you didn't kill yourself all those times you thought about it."

The final step in the Twelve-Step program suggests that we carry the message of recovery to others who still suffer. It is in this spirit that I have written my experiences. I sincerely hope that my story will aid you in healing from your abuse.

Questions to help you identify your thoughts and emotions:

How is your (your loved one's) story similar to Jim's?

How is your (your loved one's) story different from Jim's?

What emotions did you have reading Jim's story?

What was the most powerful section of the story for you?

What did you learn about yourself from reading this story?

16

Kent's Story

I do a great deal of writing both for a living and avocationally. Despite the fact that I usually have no trouble writing lots of things—from reports, articles, chapters, to entire books— this story is not an easy thing to write. This is something that involves me, and I have always found it hard to write about me. Perhaps the reason is that it has always been hard to find me amidst all of the things that I do. You will see why when you read my story.

One of the things which has been constant in my life is a struggle with various kinds of addictions. Toward the end of college I began to have trouble with drinking. When I was in graduate school I had trouble with smoking. When I quit smoking my weight went up. As a result I went on a weight reduction program and my workaholism increased. I entered private therapy, only to be sexually abused by my therapist. (He was eventually relieved of his position.) I also had a long period of sexual addiction and finally became involved in a Twelve-Step group called Sex Addicts Anonymous.[1]

All these addictions and the emotional confusion that I have had for much of my life might have been clues to other people that I had been abused. However, I was completely oblivious to the cause and worked on only the symptoms, as did the helping professionals I saw.

Beneath all of the various symptoms (whether it was hatred of my family or addictive behaviors) there was one thing that seemed to drive me: a childhood full of physical, emotional, and sexual abuse.

Before I discuss the abuse, I do want to preface it by saying that there were some positive features in my family. I did get food, shelter, and a chance to take vacations in the summer to many different places throughout the United States. In that way, it was a family like other people had. But there was always the pattern of abuse.

I did not seek therapy because of my history of abuse. I had decided that I needed to work on what I thought was the one unfinished piece of my life, my sexual identity. I had had a sexual experience with a man in a restroom and thought it was wonderful. Later I started to worry because I thought that I might get some venereal disease. So I went to a medical clinic. While I was talking to the doctor I began to cry when I told him about the experience. He sent me to a therapeutic clinic where a counselor asked me if I was having trouble with my "gay feelings." I forcibly told him I was not gay. He told me I had two choices: a lesbian/gay community clinic or a private therapist who was new in town but "very good." I was so paranoid that I chose the private therapist and paid him after each session in cash (no identifying checks, thank you). He had me read books on bisexuality and work on expression of feelings. After only nine sessions he dropped hints about how we might continue "being together." Well, I knew that this wasn't very bright, but he was the only bisexual person I knew. He had not taught me any coping skills for dealing with the gay life-style, except how to sneak into a certain gay bar through the side door. I figured that this was a good way of keeping my marriage together but still having a way of being connected with my true sexual identity.

Every four to five weeks we got together at his office. I fell head over heels in love with him, bought gifts for him, and generally fell into a one-way, semireciprocated affair. In between "sessions" I cruised the restrooms, for lack of a better way to relate to men emotionally. Without other gay role modeling, all I had was the visits once every few weeks and the restrooms. This, of course, was a frenzied and emotionally wrenching way of life. I finally went to another therapist and told him who I was dealing with. Later he figured out who I was telling him about and had my former therapist fired from his job.

Separating from my sexually abusive therapist was an emotionally traumatic experience. I had asked him to leave a group that
we were both members of. He protested, saying what a "good
friend" he had always been. I simply had to stay away from him
and from experiences which reminded me of him. If I did not, I
found myself in an emotionally intolerable situation.

I first became aware of the childhood abuse as a result of a letter
my sister's husband sent my father. I was also sent a copy of the
letter and was horrified to read that my father had sexually abused
my sister. I called her to find out if it was true and in the process
began to figure out that it had happened to me too. I wrote about
it in my journal:

> I remember this small apartment, that it was dark and I am afraid.
> We all slept in the same room. I don't want to be close to my dad.
> I have these feelings welling up in me which I don't know whether
> to trust; they seem so crazy. They suggest that he raped me anally,
> that I used to scream for him to stop, but he wouldn't. Finally, Mom
> would make him stop. This is why I hated my dad. I thought to
> myself, "Is this a fairy tale? Is this just because I read my brother-
> in-law's letter and I am too suggestible? No, I think it is true (or
> maybe it is not true . . .)."

I was sick in bed for two days after I remembered this. A few
days later I began to think that perhaps there was some truth to
what I had felt—but I had some difficulty when I tried to share it
with others. My lover, who works with abuse cases, thought I was
too suggestible. Similarly, when I talked with one of the fellows in
my gay father's group he asked me to "be sure that it had really
happened" before I told anybody about it. I would not have brought
it up unless I was pretty certain that something had in fact happened. But I wondered how I would ever know for sure. I even
tried to get my parents to take a polygraph or lie detector series.[2]
My boss was supportive and was extremely helpful in setting
boundaries with my father. Also, my Sex Addicts Anonymous group
was supportive because almost 50 percent of the members were
incest victims.[3] They suggested that I not contact my parents, and
hold my ground—I had told my parents that I would welcome
contact with them if they went to a therapist. I felt guilty about

confronting my dad when I found out he was going to the doctor for high blood pressure. But my sister reminded me that his blood pressure problem had existed for years.

Eventually, my father wrote me and asked me to return the copy of the letter my brother-in-law had sent about the abuse. Then a bit later he wrote to tell me he had canceled the magazine subscription he had given me for years. He sent this on a 3" × 5" notecard. This is the last I have ever heard from either him or my mother.

My aunt asked why I was bringing all this up. She asked what her role was supposed to be. She was sympathetic with my dad and his canceling my present. She didn't feel that any of the abuse had damaged me at all. She said my sister and I "should let sleeping dogs lie." I speculated that she was concealing what she knew about my dad and his sexual abuse patterns.

One day I was taking a walk when I had a flashback to when I was four or five years old and was being raped by my father. It was like I was detached from all of it, looking down on it from the ceiling, but was screaming for my mother to help.[4] She finally did by shouting my father's name and saying, "What if the neighbors hear this?"[5] I was grateful to my mother for stopping it. I remembered saying, "I'll be good, and I won't tell anybody." My father told me that I should not tell anybody because they would put him in a mental institution.

After I went through the flashback, I really felt paranoid at work, wondering if people knew about all of this and whether they would hold it against me. Surprising, isn't it, when I was really the victim and not the perpetrator. But during the time I was recalling the abuse the paranoia was certainly there, and it made my work life difficult to deal with.

I spent a lot of time trying to figure out if the flashback was really something that had happened to me or not. In the past when I was under stress I had experienced dreamlike hallucinations (which I learned is common in victims of incest). But this flashback had a different, and real, feeling to it. Rather than being something I remembered intellectually, it was something I *felt*. It was like the whole scene was being replayed in my head—with me feeling it— but also watching it like a play.[6]

I tried to understand why my father might have done something like this. I looked for ways to explain why he was under so much pressure. Later I got angry and pounded my pillow as I went to bed at night. It was good, I thought, that my lover was not around because he might wonder what the hell was wrong with me.

Finally, I went to my therapist to ask him if he thought I might really have been a victim of childhood sexual abuse. He thought I had—partly because flashbacks are pretty characteristic of sexual abuse situations and because of the dynamics in my family. After I talked with him, little things would come to mind suddenly during the day. Like how the incest did not just happen once; it happened at least four or five times. (Later I would remember that it happened even more.) Every day I would discover things which would simply make me nauseated. It was quite a strain. I talked a lot about it, which was hard on my partner to have to deal with, since he had to deal with lots of such cases at work. He was very supportive and helpful, though. He was very lonely during this and wished that I could be more "with him" while it was going on.[7]

Over the next few months I got involved in the effort to repeal the state's sodomy laws. This acted as therapy for me in some ways because I started having nightmares about the issue of anal sex. I started getting many issues disentangled. I now can say the word *"sodomy"* without going into a state of paralysis. To give you an example of what it was like, this is from my journal:

> I have always avoided the word *sodomy,* and now I am thinking that this is because of the incest experience. Sunday night I had a really bad nightmare, from which I awoke screaming. I was afraid that my father was going to sexually assault me. In the dream I was in this darkened room (with a bluish tinge, maybe from a Christmas tree) and I was so afriad that he would come and attack me. It is unusual for me to be able to consciously remember a dream, but it frightens me to think about it even when I am awake.

I am still afraid of that nightmare and the bluish light that I don't quite understand.

I shelved the incest issue for a couple of months by working on other things, at least until I talked to my sister on the phone again. I was pleased to hear about how well her therapy was going. In the conversation she made reference to my aunt, and this called up incidents from my childhood. In my journal I wrote:

I remember being in the sun, when I was nude (or seminude). I was about three or four years old. My aunt fondled me. I was amazed that I had almost total recall of that situation, in the form of two flashbacks. She would not stop doing it until my mother came along and asked her what was going on. I felt abandoned by my mother and betrayed by my aunt. I was so small, I was powerless to say anything myself. It was an impossible situation for a small child.[8]

All day I was a total mess, having woke up early, going through these flashbacks, realizing how intensely I disliked my parents—and realizing how I was tricked throughout my life by both my parents and my aunt. No wonder she defends my dad so much—because she is into this whole situation a lot. I wonder if she may have abused my dad (since my grandmother put her in charge of raising him). All of this has been so romanticized in my family, with me being her "favorite nephew" and the dutiful son, and my sister being "Dad's favorite."

Once again, the next day I went through having that awful experience of the flashbacks. In the evening, when my partner went out to dinner, I had an anxiety attack. I have the same problem that sent my sister into her therapy. She thought that she was my dad's "favorite girl," while I thought I was my aunt's "favorite nephew," when in fact I was her favorite *victim*

A lot of things get romanticized in my family. For example, my father always worshiped his mother, because his father had died in a tragic accident and she had to raise her poverty-stricken family on her own. But my grandmother too was diseased. My sister told me that when she was age ten our grandmother would reach under her panties, supposedly to determine if my sister was wearing a corset. My sister told me how repulsed she was at being violated this way[9]

After remembering what my aunt did to me I tried to decide if this abuse was as bad as the abuse with my father. *No* meant that it was not as big a deal to have my aunt fondle my penis as to have my dad rape me. *Yes* meant that any type of abuse is really pretty serious. A few months later I discovered that it really was serious because this incident has been the prototype for my sexual addiction—whenever I face a feeling of abandonment and betrayal, then I go to the gay beach and act out sexually. In essence, a lot of my psychological issues relate to the relationship with my parents and my aunt: it is pretty hard to *trust* a family like this; and since sex is supposed to be a shameful *secret* in my family, my life has been conditioned to ensure that same-sex preference is conditioned by shame. For years I had been afraid to "come out" as a gay man, my biggest fear being that I would hurt my father and that he would have a nervous breakdown, thereby having to go into a mental institution. Finally, at age forty-two I wrote him a letter and told him that I am gay.

My father was also very emotionally abusive to me, telling me that I "was never going to be a man." He was always picking on me, telling me that I "never did anything right." My sister tried to defend me, saying, "This is not right, this is not fair."

My sister and I lived in fear of physical punishment as well. When my sister was age sixteen my dad thought she had sassed him. He knocked her jaw out of place and said, "I have been nice to you, I almost killed Kent." She reported this event to her eighth-grade teacher, who did nothing about it.[10]

What I remember about what was done in terms of physical abuse to me began with a flashback, which I recorded in my journal:

> All that I can remember is that there was blood . . . It may have been in a shed, where he used to use a board to paddle me with. I do remember my mom saying, "You've hurt him." The feeling that I have is that of a very powerful person attacking me from all sides and I feel that I am terrorized, powerless, and shaking. Just remembering that feeling of terror actually makes me start crying. I am saying, "Dad, don't hit me." But he wouldn't stop. Now that I *do* remember that, I also remember that he used to beat me a lot, for little insignificant things, like making too much noise, or not making my bed, or not picking up my toys. It was just like his mother had raised him: "Spare the rod and spoil the child," she used to say.
>
> It is funny that I always thought that I could deal with the violence because that was a normal part of my life. It was the sexual abuse that was hard to deal with because it was kind of abnormal. I think, though, that both aspects drove me to try to escape my family—and contributed to my strong desire to succeed, so that I would never have to deal with my family and be dependent upon them again.

My father justified all of the abuse by saying, "I wanted to make a man out of you, son." In fact my father told me much later in life that he still thought the way he treated me was all right, because I had been raised to be such a success.[11]

Prior to becoming conscious of my repressed memories of incest I asked my parents to baby-sit my kids so my wife and I could go out for dinner. My mom expressed considerable reluctance to care for the children, who were fairly young at the time, because it had been "so long since she had taken care of kids." Now that I understand my family better I can see that she was afraid my dad might rape them if they didn't behave—just like he did to me, as a form of "discipline."[12]

I had seen my mom as the person who had not abused me and who protected me, but then I remembered the summer I went home from college. My parents had moved from my childhood home into a small apartment. I remember feeling uncomfortable with the place. One day, when only my mom and I were home, for some reason she called me into her bedroom. She was wearing a bra and a half-slip. By the way she tried to entice me into staying in the room I knew that there was something really unusual about the situation. I finally left the room and vowed never to be in the same room alone with her again. I have been uncomfortable with her ever since.[13]

When I told my ex-wife about the recollections of incest she told me about an odd situation she had encountered with my mother. The two of them were in my mom's bedroom talking about breast examinations (my ex-wife is a nurse), when suddenly my mom took off her blouse and bra and tried to get my ex-wife to do a breast examination on her. My former wife told her that she would describe how to do an exam, but would not perform it herself. My ex-wife was really uncomfortable with the situation and had a clear feeling that something was wrong. She never told me about it until I started to recall the incest. Until then I was never able to put this situation together with other incidents to get the whole family picture.

The realization of what my family was really like kept me depressed for months. Just about the time I was slowly coming out of it, my partner left for a month-long trip. I had trouble with my addictive sexual behavior again. I was going to the beach, the adult bookstores, and other places that had been out of bounds for my sex addiction program. These incidents became more and more self-abusive, till I finally gave up and called my therapist for help. He pointed out that I had in essence emotionally "shelved" the incest and this was not working. I went back to my Twelve-Step program more rigorously and began to write this story as one way to deal with the reality of what it is like to live in such a family. I read a book about incest and made notes about my life in it. The next morning I woke up, looked in the mirror, and started to cry because dealing with my life is sometimes too much to take.

I think the most important thing that has come out of my Twelve-Step group and my therapy is the sense of "when I am having problems and when I am not." The most difficult thing I have had to deal with in my life is to know that I am overstepping the bounds of good sense and doing things other people want me to do but which I do not necessarily want to do. I think this lack of clear self-identity is pretty characteristic of most abuse victims.

The connection with my incest victimization and my being abused by my first therapist is now clear to me. With the repressed sexual experience with my father lying under the surface, I was like an accident waiting to happen. When a therapist takes advantage of a person like this, I think they should be prevented from practicing therapy. In my mind there is only one thing worse than a sexually abusing therapist who has power over you—and that is a sexually abusive father who has power over you. In either case, it is dreadfully hard to escape, and you lose yourself in the process.

In both my Sex Addicts Anonymous group, as well as my current therapy, we work on boundaries. Essentially a boundary is a line that I do not cross unless I am prepared to harm myself. By carefully defining my boundaries, I can more easily keep myself out of situations which will shame me or cause me to be abused or physically harmed. Being gay in a society which intensely dislikes gays and lesbians is a continuing struggle. Almost as bad, and sometimes worse, is the sense of self-hatred that we often have about our homosexuality. My therapy and group have helped me to emerge from some of that shame and self-hatred and begin to be proud of myself and my accomplishments as a gay person.

Questions to help you identify your thoughts and emotions:

How is your (your loved one's) story similar to Kent's?

How is your (your loved one's) story different from Kent's?

What emotions did you have reading Kent's story?

What was the most powerful section of the story for you?

What did you learn about yourself from reading this story?

17

Kevin's Story

I WAS sexually abused by at least three people while I was growing up. As I write these words, doubt creeps in and I don't trust that you will believe me. The three people who abused me were my mother, brother, and a neighbor. There, I have put those words on paper. And my head is screaming at me with messages like, "Nobody will care about this stuff. You've had a good life, why are you dredging up the past? These things happen to everyone, and they don't seem to have trouble coping." As I write I will try to believe that something good will result from this disclosure.[1]

My family has a long history of shame about sexual matters, including my grandmother's birthing a child while not married. My father has admitted to me in a therapy session that he too had been sexually abused. A couple of cousins had abused him as a child, and a navy officer used his greater rank to force my father into being sexual when he was an adult. I can see why he would not want to see his son as an abuse victim, given he has kept his own history of abuse a painful secret.[2]

Each of my parents were in charge of hearing the confidences of their opposite sex parent. Both my mother and father were treated as if they were the spouse of that parent. Mom tells of her father always "getting a tongue-lashing from her mother for no good reason" and my mother trying to take care of her father by soothing him and reassuring him. When speaking of her family, my mother drifts off mentally, unable to complete sentences and forgetting where she is in the story.

A very few months after my parents were married and had my older brother, my mother was admitted to a hospital for psychiatric care. She was depressed, "nervous," and not functioning as an adult or parent. Immediately after my mom was discharged from the hospital, my brother started school and within three weeks my lonely mother conceived me. She didn't tell my father she intended to have another child. It seems to me she very badly wanted a baby to stop her loneliness.

At birth, my world included a disturbed, frightened mother, a scared and emotionally isolated father, and an angry, lonely brother. One of my earliest memories is having pneumonia at the age of two. I have a sense my early illness was a response to something. It could have been several things: my mother's pregnancy with my sister, another trip to the mental hospital, physical or sexual abuse; any or all are possible. In a way, it seems illness of this severe nature may have been either a way to act out a primal fear or a way to die.

As I got a little older my mother bonded with me very tightly, while my father was stern and separate. She confided in me as she would a spouse, telling me things she was afraid to tell her husband. I feared my father would certainly hate me for being so close to his wife. Yet I was told I was lucky to be so close; I was "special." But the "specialness" was definitely one-sided. She would confide in me, yet my concerns and feelings were dismissed: "There's nothing to be afraid of. Don't be angry with *me*, young man. Don't be sad, I hate to see you sad." I got the message loud and clear, to listen, but not to share myself. I also learned that anything I may have said to her would invariably come out in a family gathering as something cute or funny.

As part of her confiding in me, I was privy to information about my parents' sex life. She told me of their sexual problems and her frustration. Whenever my father was out of town on business, my sister and I would trade off sleeping with her. I believe this happened from the time I was an infant to the age of nine or ten. Although I have no memories of overt sexual activity, I get scared today when I think about the nights I spent in their bed with her. Again, I was taking my father's place and fearful of his anger.

For months while in grade school I went home for lunch to be with my mom. Neither my sister or brother did so, just me. This isolated me further from my peers by separating me from them at this social time. But I did get to feel "special." I also would stay home from school one out of every four days. I wasn't sick most of these days, but I was easily able to fake it because my mom wanted company.

She exposed her body to me on several occasions, wearing sheer nightgowns in front of me and keeping her bedroom door open while she dressed. I also saw her in the bathtub on several occasions. Once she called me into the bathroom while she was bathing to talk to me about something trivial. I was around five years old and obeyed my mother. She spoke to me to keep me there, slowly bathing herself, washing her arms and chest with a washcloth. She spoke to me for about five minutes, and I left with the feeling of attraction and revulsion.

When I was around six I came upon her when she was totally nude in her bedroom. Her door was right on the hallway that I regularly passed on the way to my room. Seeing me she started to dress slowly, looking at me and talking about something I don't remember. I felt as if her conversation was to keep me there, looking at the nude body she was dressing so excruciatingly slowly. I felt very embarrassed and wanted to run. It would have been rude to leave while she was talking to me, and I also felt stimulated and attracted seeing her nakedness. So simultaneously I felt shameful, scared, stimulated, and wanted to run. I know that this was an act of exposure because I can still remember her keeping me there and dressing so, so slowly. As I write today those same feelings happen and I know that it was real and it was a case of abusive sexual body exposure. These memories are very painful *not because I saw her body,* but because she actively placed her body in my view, to entice me, to use her power as my mother to get a "high" from exposing herself to me. I was at once attracted and revolted, thinking that something was wrong with *me.* She was my mother, why would she try to hurt me? It must be something wrong with me . . .

My father was very distant, working long hours and telling us he never believed a father should be buddies with his children. He demeaned me often by "teasing," saying, "It was just a joke," but doing mean things. One good example is the weekend he had football tickets, but only had two. And this time it would be Dad and my older brother who got to go. I was very disappointed, hurt, and angry that I couldn't go. Then on the day of the game he produced the third ticket which he had all along, surprising me with it. Now supposedly this gave me more of a thrill than if I'd gotten the ticket right away. But now that I am a parent I look back and see how mean this is. I was set up to feel the pain of disappointment. Then for the reaction: "How dumb of me to have been so disappointed. I should have known." But I didn't know and I was also robbed of the delicious anticipation of going to the game. What was so abusive about this was how I was led to discount my feelings. Dad would do things like this often, using his power to manipulate feelings. He also would pick on individual characteristics such as eating style, posture, and speech. He would always be smiling with an angry gleam in his eye. It felt as if he was trying to get back at me for something. But what? What had I done? Nothing of course; my goal was to be as inconspicuous as possible, not to be singled out for teasing. One way I found to distract him was to be funny and entertaining.

My father had pornography in a place that was accessible to me. He could have hidden it better, but he didn't. I used the pornography often to masturbate, and I am sure I did not replace it perfectly every time. In other words, I am sure he knew I used it yet said nothing. In fact he never mentioned sexuality directly, and it was my mother who sat my sister and me down to discuss sex when I was twelve. She asked if we had questions about sex, and I said no, I had been filled in during eighth-grade biology. My sister didn't ask any questions. Although my mom said she would be happy to discuss it, she was obviously quite relieved that we had not asked her any questions. The subject was never brought up again.[3]

My brother and I slept in the same bed for a couple of years when I was seven to nine years old. He was six years older. He said that because I was fat and had a large chest, he needed to put "chains" on my chest as a restraint. These chains were imaginary and, according to him, wrapped around my chest several times. He claimed he needed to change these chains periodically as they took such a strain in holding my chest. In "changing" these he fondled my chest from behind while we were lying down. I hated it and was angry at him for it. The abuse here was due both to his lies to me about why he did it and my lack of real choice, given his power, size, and threats of hurting me should I tell anyone. He said it was my fault, and I believed him. He would tease me too. He and my father conspired on several occasions to play cruel practical jokes on me.

So I had three abusive and shaming people in my life telling me I did not have a right to be me and express who I was. The message was that I was not of value and my job was to please others. I was a walking victim, ready to be further victimized.

When I was seven years old, a thirteen-year-old neighbor raped me on several occasions. He also forced me to masturbate him and perform oral sex on him. The threat of violence was there, if I were to try to end the abuse in any way. He abused me several times a week over several weeks in his basement and outside after dark. Our activities were obviously ignored by others because our neighborhood was one in which people were always around. He must have threatened others if they told. I am not sure of how I tried to tell my parents. The atmosphere at home was not one in which I trusted anyone to help me with this problem.

I learned not to be mentally present when afraid or hurt, and I believe I learned this before the neighbor's abuse. This ability served me well by protecting my emotions, my core, while being raped. While lying on the floor, he on top of me, I would look at a coconut carved in the shape of a pirate's head and just "space out." "This isn't happening to me" was the message I gave myself to numb the pain, protecting me from having to feel the fear, anger, shame, hurt, and hopelessness.

The abuse I suffered left a deep scar in my soul that I am just beginning to heal at age thirty-one. I was affected in many ways by being abused. I abused myself by eating compulsively, medicating the pain and pushing people away with my large size. Somewhere inside I believed if I just got big enough, no one could hurt me anymore. I also abused drugs in high school, again numbing the pain I felt.

Most of the healing and recovery I have achieved has revolved around trust. I was lied to by people. They told me to trust them, that everything would be okay. They were not worthy of my trust; they hurt me, and I was left not wanting to trust anyone again.

Trusting my own emotions and perceptions has been very difficult. I was trained not to trust my feelings. My father would tell me that my mother was back in the hospital but that everything was all right. Well, everything was *not* all right with me. I was hearing one thing but seeing and feeling another. My perceptions must have been wrong, I thought.

Trusting others to be close emotionally and sexually has been tough too. I learned sex was naughty, secretive, and something people did *to* rather than *with* each other. In my marriage I separated emotional closeness from sex and actually used sex to try to get some of the emotional closeness I needed. When I really needed to tell of the innermost parts of me, my hopes and fears, I was too scared to trust that she would still love me. So I opted for sexual closeness as a replacement, leaving me lonely and scared afterwards, still needing emotional closeness. I also masturbated compulsively to ease the emotional pain.

I sought professional help when my marriage became more and more unsatisfying. An extramarital affair had recently ended, leaving me with my loneliness, hopelessness, and fear. My wife, Lisa, and I had an unspoken rule that I was the sick one, the person with problems to solve in our marriage, so I went to a therapist to see how I could change to save our relationship.

My first counselor suggested I begin a process of recovery in group therapy, and within two weeks I was telling the parts I remembered of my painful story to a group of men struggling with similar problems. I also joined both Overeaters Anonymous for compulsive eating and Sex Addicts Anonymous for compulsive sexual behavior. By telling my story in all three groups I admitted my imperfection and admitted my life was out of control. My presence there was a further admission: that I could not get well alone. Every step I have taken, then and now, to live my new life I have taken with help and support.

The first group sessions were a struggle because I did not trust others and did not trust myself. I wanted to perform for that therapy group, to look good and not show my neediness. I had learned early in my life not to ask for help, and I now labored to ask for what I needed. Week after week I would merely report on what had gone wrong during the week and how I had solved the problem. I did build trust during those first few weeks and did get to the point where I could say those three difficult words: "I need help." Initially I was not sure what I needed help with and decided to listen to my dreams for an answer. I believed my dreams would tell me what I needed, if I could be open to the message.

One night I dreamed about my abusive neighbor and how he was still, twenty-two years later, holding me captive in that basement. I returned to the group, ready to "deal with the abuse." I had no idea what that meant but trusted I would get the assistance that I needed. Together, my therapist, the group, and I were able to "exorcise the demon" of shame inside of me by taking me back to my memories of the abuse.

The first assignment was to write about what Johnny did to me and how I felt about it. I did so and read my writing to the group. I feel fear as I think about how I sat there, reading about my repeated rapings and *did not feel a thing*. I felt *nothing*. It was as if I were reading a dictionary. The therapist suggested I go back in my mind to the abuse itself through hypnosis to find those hidden feelings.[4]

After some practice with the process of hypnosis, mind relaxation, and focus, we went back to my memories of that basement next door. I closed my eyes and descended a "flight of stairs" to a part of my mind that had been boarded up and guarded to protect me from the overwhelming feelings about being raped. As we went down those stairs hand in hand I knew I would not be alone with anything I found in those memories.

I imagined opening a door at the bottom of those stairs that led to Johnny's basement room. I felt I was seven years old again and was being raped. My awareness of the group therapy room lessened and that basement room was real. I cried, I yelled, I shoved him off of me, I screamed. I let out my revulsion, anger, desperation, and fear. My therapist stayed next to me, often holding and reassuring me, guiding me to freely express it all.

Suddenly, my lips locked together, out of my control, and would not part so that I could speak. My body was remembering something my conscious mind would not. My clenched lips reminded me that Johnny had forced me to perform oral sex on him.[5] I was able to part my lips enough to get that secret out, and as I did so my lips partially loosened. I told Johnny he could not be inside my body, and my lips relaxed even more. Then my legs started to go numb as I started to think about getting out of the basement to run for help. My numb and lifeless legs reminded me that I had no one to whom I could go to for help. The pain I felt then, about my aloneness with my terror and shame, was the worst feeling of all and perhaps the feeling I most needed to express. I believe that the abuse itself was not as horrible or destructive to me as keeping it inside all these years.

I was physically exhausted and emotionally spent when I opened my eyes to the looks of love and caring from the group members. I had trusted them with the deepest parts of me, and they had stayed to give me their support and nurturing.[6]

While in that "basement room" I was able to tell Johnny that he could not touch me anymore, that I was angry, and that I would no longer overeat to be big enough to push him away. To allow those messages to take hold in my life I wrote a letter to him.

Johnny

I see in the telephone book that you refer to yourself as "John," but I will call you Johnny and hope that this bothers you. My anger towards you is huge. That is why I am writing.

My name is still Kevin, Kevin Olson. I am sure you remember living next to me. I am also sure you remember raping me. That is why I am writing.

Your abuse of me has caused much pain in my life. You must hear/read and I must tell you what you did, how it has affected me, and what my choices are for the future.

What you did to me was rape me. You were thirteen and I was only seven. You were much larger and physically more powerful than I. You forced me. I remember clearly you making me go into your basement room. I laid on the floor while you rubbed your erect penis over my groin. Once your brother started down the stairs and you told him to leave you alone for a while. I'll bet he knew why—I'll bet you were raping him too.

While you were sexually abusing me I would try to pretend I wasn't there. I'd look up at that carved coconut head hanging on the wall and pretend I was somewhere else. Somewhere you couldn't hurt me.

You also made me masturbate you and give you oral sex by the trees in your backyard when it was dark. While everyone was playing hide and seek you'd make me go by the trees with you. Everyone knew to leave us alone . . . Did you threaten them or were you fucking them too?

I thought it was my fault. What did I do to make you want to do this? I thought I had done something wrong. I didn't Johnny. I didn't do anything wrong. You hurt me and I am pissed.

I had been slightly overweight before you abused me, but after the hurt you caused I ate much, much more. I figured if I ate enough I would be a much bigger boy—too big for you to hurt me anymore. You taught me that people are out to hurt me and I kept on eating. By being big and fat no one could get close enough to hurt me again. I have continued to eat myself to the point where I am a twenty-nine-year-old man whose face is attractive, but whose body is wrecked from constant compulsive eating and dieting. My twisted view of food, fat, and my body comes from your hurting me so badly and so deeply.

Food wasn't my only defense. My view of sexuality was twisted by you too. My sexual life has been compulsive, uncontrollable, abusive, and cold. One of the results of your work has been a string of unhappy relationships, including my crumbling marriage of six years. How do I tell my two-year-old son that the problems his mother and I have are rooted in my rape at the age of seven? You taught me that people will hurt me if allowed too close, and I have followed through by not letting my wife become close. We are near divorce.

I am sure people knew you were an abuser and did not stop you. My view of humanity has been damaged by seeing no one lift a finger to stop you. I see the human race as uncaring and hurtful.

With the assistance of a power greater than myself, I have reached out for help and found that I am not the rotten, shameful person your acts convinced me I was. I found I have choices and have already made some.

I will not eat for you anymore. You can no longer hurt me and I do not need to have fat to keep you away.

I will not be sexually abusive to myself or others. I deserve more and will have a healthy sex life.

I will have close and intimate relationships. I will allow people to be kind and share with me in a loving way, as I will share with them.

I will no longer allow you to be *any* part of my life.

Kevin Olson

The importance of writing that letter was to be honest with myself and others about what happened, how I felt about the abuse, how I had been affected by it, and what my options and choices were for the future. I read it aloud in a group therapy session and was surprised by how deeply the others were moved. I was reminded of how I minimize my struggles and the effect my sharing has on others.

I did not want a relationship with Johnny and therefore decided *not* to send the letter. In it I share many feelings I did not want him to hear. I did send him a short letter telling him I knew what he did to me, assumed he had hurt others, and told him to get help. I also sent him a brochure for Sex Addicts Anonymous.

In the following weeks I lost about thirty pounds. Food had pacified my inner need for nurturing since I was a child. The early human nurturing I needed was not given to me by my parents, and as I grew I did not know how to ask for it, nor did I believe I deserved it. In my recovery, as I allowed people into my life instead of actively pushing them away, I got the nurturing I needed and used food to fuel my body. My obsession with food lifted too, as I learned to trust people. Trust became a primary focus in my group therapy.

Identifying my feelings, trusting their validity, and acting on them took months to learn and practice. Much of the training ground for this work was in addressing the problems of my marriage.

In becoming involved with and eventually marrying Lisa I followed the pattern of my early life. When we met she was dating my best friend, Barry. As a child I had been my mother's confidant and now, as an adult, I became Lisa's. Both she and Barry began to inform me of the big problems in their relationship. I was listening to both of them, feeling that "specialness" and power I had felt with my parents. Before an "official" break-up between Barry and Lisa occurred, she and I were fully emotionally and sexually involved. We each kept it secret from Barry, each hoping the other would tell him. Within months we moved in together and were married eighteen months later. I looked to Lisa to give me the esteem I could not give myself and in doing so gave her much power.[7]

As I started to put together a recovery program from my abusive childhood, she pulled away more and more. For weeks we played a waiting game to see who would leave first. It seems as though we were fighting over who would emerge as victim and who as victimizer. I became convinced that I was not the "sick one," that each of us had a part in a marriage with very little closeness, shared feelings, or intimacy. I asked her to come to discuss the "shared responsibility" idea with my therapist. At my request he explained codependency and its symptoms to Lisa and me. As he spoke I heard example after example of how this illness manifests itself, and each time the example fit Lisa. She did not agree and was very upset by hearing all of this. My decision became clear: I could not continue a relationship with a person out of touch with reality. I told her I wanted a divorce and joint custody of our son.

Given the parental roles I learned, I don't know what kind of father I would be if I had not gotten help. I can look to my own parents as a probable prototype. Today my four-year-old son and I are very close, but fortunately I don't feel we have anything like the "closeness" I had with my mother. My role is to be available for my child, not the other way around. I have adults in my life to listen to my cares and worries, so my son is not my confidant. I hope I am letting him be just what he is, a four-year-old boy, not expecting him to perform as an adult for my convenience. The result so far is an assertive, loving, connected, and confident boy. I know my recovery has greatly affected his life.

My need for group therapy lessened as I was able to trust the appropriate people in my life. I had a model of functional relationships with others and also a higher power. Before leaving therapy I still needed to forgive my parents and decide what I wanted from my present relationship with them. I started with my father, probably because I didn't feel the need to protect him from my anger. In the group I talked about my feelings for Dad, the reality of our past relationship, and its effect on me. Getting these feelings out with others helped, but there were things I needed to tell him. I wanted a continuing relationship with him, but I wanted it to be one of honesty and openness. In order to release my shame I decided to tell him about being abused by our former neighbor. In a private therapy session I told of the abuse, how I lived with the pain and the effects of that, and how angry I was that he hadn't protected me.

He told me about his own childhood abuse, and as the session continued I saw him clearly for the first time in my life as a scared and lonely man who wanted the best for me, loved me, and was not capable of giving me what I had needed. I forgave him. I still keep some distance between us, but I feel neither better than nor less than my father, and I can communicate honestly with him.

The same cannot be said about my relationship with my mother. I still have more work to do regarding separation from and acceptance of her. As I turned my focus from Dad to Mom in my therapy group, I realized I had become emotionally involved in another love triangle with a good friend and his wife. She was very much like my mother, he like my dad, and I was very much involved with her. I did some work in therapy to separate from her, saying goodbye to her while staying friends with her husband. This action seemed a good model for my relationship with my mom. Yet I did not say goodbye to my mother and have yet to confront her or set clear boundaries between us. This hurts me in that I still hold on to much resentment, fear, anger, sadness, guilt, and shame around my relationship with her. My recovery is ongoing, and when I am ready to do this work I will.

The most important things I found in the last few years is that I am not alone and that I can trust others. I can trust my God too. I now know my abusive past wasn't my fault, that God and my friends love me, and that I never have to be alone with anything ever again.

The process of recovery has been a slow and painful one. As I peel back more memories and deal with present-day problems, I feel pain I wasn't willing to feel before. Recovery can be like when a child falls in the dirt and deeply scrapes his knee. Before the wound can heal all of the dirt and debris must be cleaned out. For me, recovery has been like taking a brush to that skinned knee and getting the dirt of shame, anger, fear, mistrust, and hopelessness out. And it has been worth it. I feel Kevin is a worthwhile, strong, and giving man. I lead an honest life, without the duality of my past. I can wake up and know that whatever greets me I can handle with help. I care about and care for my body and my soul, nurturing both with patience.

I want anyone who has been abused to know that you are not alone. It was not your fault, and you don't need to fix it all by yourself. You won't always feel like you are a bad person.

Questions to help you identify your thoughts and emotions:

How is your (your loved one's) story similar to Kevin's?

How is your (your loved one's) story different from Kevin's?

What emotions did you have reading Kevin's story?

What was the most powerful section of the story for you?

What did you learn about yourself from reading this story?

18

Richard and the Perfect Life

L OOKING at me one would never knew what happened. I was always popular, always smiles. I never had a bad day and was never in a bad mood. I was involved in extracurricular activities, my grades were good. I was accepted to one of the toughest colleges in the state. I graduated with two majors and one minor in four years. By all the signs, I was perfect. Perfectly dressed, perfectly poised, perfect at whatever I chose to try. I was a success. To my friends I was "the kid who had it all." There were ski vacations and trips to Europe, country club dances, yacht club picnics. Summers were filled with living in one of the most affluent suburbs of the city and everything that had to offer.

However, absolutely no one knew what was going on inside of me during that time. I did not have one intimate friend in the world. I was a stereotype, a role. It was something that had to be played day in and day out. It was to the point that I did not even realize that I was living that way. I went to school and was praised for doing well and punished for doing poorly. I became a mere performer.

To understand what happened to me you need to understand where I came from. The problem began long before I was born. My mother was a victim of incest. Her brothers and sister were all involved sexually with each other at one time or another.[1] I never knew this until I was twenty-one years old. Yet it affected me in so many ways. My mother took all her negative beliefs about sexuality and put them on me. She had been a victim of an extremely

damaging sexual experience. Her feelings on sex and sexuality came
down to me. It was as if the sins of the previous generation had to
be dumped on me. In my family sex was never talked about. My
mother made it very clear that it was something I was not supposed
to do. Good boys do not have sex. Continually I was praised for
my ability to have girls as friends, as opposed to girlfriends. The
message was clear. Thinking back I now realize that I was being
told that it is great that I was a eunuch ("a castrated man"[2]).

Secrets, I also learned about secrets. All my life I felt that things
had to be kept away from people. My mother harbored such a
large secret about her past, and she taught me that feelings were
not to be shared. They were not valid. Always put on a smile to
the world and never let anyone know that you are vulnerable. I
always believed that it was good to keep things inside.

Other things that I learned also affected me and what happened.
Touching was certainly out. I never remember being hugged by
anyone in the family after the age of nine. I also realize now that
showing someone that you cared about them was not done either.
People in my family were cold and distant when it came to anything
that had to do with emotions or sexuality. After childhood in my
family there was no nurturing at all. I felt as if that once you started
becoming something more than a child . . . I cannot even describe
what you become.

The summer I turned twelve I was sexually abused. This experience only magnified everything that I already believed about sex.
"Don't be sexual. Sex is bad. Sex is wrong. Nice boys *don't.*"

What happened was not dramatic, it was not something for a
made-for-TV movie. I was subtly and quietly raped by my best
friend all that summer in a tent in my own backyard. This was not
the adolescent mutual exploration that most boys experience. It
was rape. He was doing something to me that I did not want, and
it was something that I felt I had no say in. It seemed I was powerless to say no. He was older by one year and he was my best
friend and I trusted him. I played along with the initial exploration,
so I *looked* like a willing participant to what took place later.

My perpetrator did not even know what he was doing to me. I
went along with the taking off of our clothes and exploring each
other's genitals. Thinking back, it was him examining mine. Then
he would climb on top of me and pretend he was making love to

a girl. I remember asking him to stop once. But he didn't, and I did not insist, and he kept on going. All I remember him saying to the protest was, "Doesn't it feel good." I could not say how many times it happened. The summer lasted for three months, and it went on until school started in the fall.

What I felt at the time was nothing. I did not even have him stop coming over. Now I realize I was really being used. I know that I just went through it. I pretended to be willing. I would just lie there and hope that it would stop. I feel so stupid now. Why didn't I just scream *stop?* I still feel the shame of not being able to say *no!* I just let it happen and kept letting it happen. I got through it by not letting myself feel it. It just was not happening. It all goes back to my inability to feel things.

We were never friends again. In fact we did little that summer except sleep together. I moved away, and a few years later I went to visit him. In reference to that summer he said, "Remember the summer we slept in your tent?" Then he laughed. That was all that was ever spoken about that summer. I told no one. I could not tell my parents. Sex was not to be talked about, and this was same-gender sexual behavior as well. I felt I had broken every family rule. I had been sexual, and it had been with someone of the same sex. I felt that if I told my parents they would hate me. I had a hard enough time feeling that my parents cared about me. Emotionally I was not close to my parents. To them what I had done would push them away even further. So I put on "the mask." There was nothing wrong. My life became one of all smiles. They never could have seen that there was any pain in my life. I was too clever at twelve to let anyone know that things were not as they seemed. I was so ashamed of myself that I did nothing with my sexuality for several years. I am twenty-four years old and just beginning to realize that I am a sexual person.

After the abuse experience, puberty was horrifying to me. I tried to hide the fact that I was getting facial hair and that I had to shave. I refused to be seen in a bathing suit because I was so horribly modest that I did not want anyone to see my body. The school district I lived in had the barbaric attitude that boys could swim naked. I always had a "sore throat" and could not go in the pool. When I couldn't avoid going swimming I would think, I cannot let my modesty control my life. Then I just peeled off my clothes and dove into the pool as quickly as humanly possible but never enjoying it.

I dove into a million things. I was always staying after school for something. I knew everybody and everybody knew me. There was no time for anyone to notice that I had only one date all through junior and senior high school. There was no girlfriend, no love, and certainly no sex. In so many ways I was far beyond my peers. I was more responsible and always praised by my teachers for my leadership ability. I had to be better than all of them in so many ways just so I could feel like their equal. On the inside, emotionally and sexually, I was still twelve years old. I never felt I was allowed to grow past that stage.

In college things pretty much remained the same. I had one girlfriend briefly my sophomore year. I was so afraid every time we would make out. My heart would beat so fast that she once asked if she was causing me to have a heart attack. I told her it was only passion. I know now that it was the horrible fear I have of sex and my sexuality.

I became everyone's hero in college. The group mascot. The one everybody ran to when things went bad. That's how I protected myself from the pain of my life. I tried to fix everyone else. I became indispensable. Whenever someone broke up or lost a partner or slept with the wrong person, I knew about it and was there to help. Everyone trusted me so much, yet I trusted no one. Is it any wonder that I felt I could not share what was troubling me?

At times I would "forget" that I was "perfect" and my life "could not be any better" than it already was. What was I to complain about anyway? I notice the sarcasm in these remarks. That is only another way to mask the pain.

The day I graduated from college I lost a huge portion of my identity. The group was gone. I began to concentrate heavily on two friends who were very troubled. One had been raped that year, while the other had just announced to me his hidden sexuality.[3] I ended up in therapy to help these people. I went to help them, I stayed for myself.

What I learned about myself there could fill volumes. What I had to learn was that I was so shut down sexually that it was time to wake up. How many twenty-two-year-old men do you know that are still virgins? I had a tendency toward compulsive masturbation when my life was stressful or painful, something I still struggle with. When I masturbate at these times, the overwhelming sense of shame I have only makes me feel worse. It's as if I have to prove I am a bad person so I do the one thing that I know is self-abusive. I see it as self-abusive in the sense that I grew up believing that masturbation was bad. Anything which I did thinking it was bad would only make me feel worse about myself. If I am in a situation that I cannot feel the emotion, I just start to feel like a bad person. I then maturbate because "bad" people do that and then I can be the "bad" person I think I am.

My sexuality was totally unexplored. I had become homophobic because of my total inability to accept that part of myself. I had the inaccurate notion that if I had same-sex feelings at all I must be homosexual. This would be totally unacceptable in my family and would have put me on their "you are unlikeable" list. Since I did have same-sex feelings I just felt that I could not be sexual at all, because I certainly could not be homosexual. By rejecting that part of me that has a whole spectrum of sexual feelings, I rejected all of my sexuality.[4]

I had lost my adolescence, and it was time to take the steps to make that portion of my life happen. It was time to stop being a boy and become a man.

It sounded so easy at first. I was quite wrong. Life became much harder for me to deal with than it had ever been before. The first step of letting go of my defenses left me vulnerable. Before I could do anything I had to learn to trust. This proved to be almost impossible for me. I did not trust my therapist, my family, or the friends I had in school. It was hard for me to focus on all the things I did have. I had focused so hard on my inadequacies that I had nothing left. At the age of twenty-three I could not accept that I had no sexual experience with a woman. If I could not accept myself because of this one inadequacy, then how could I even begin to let anyone else accept me for who I was? I began to feel I had no peers. The students I worked with at my job seemed to have more experience with sex than I did.

These were only excuses to keep me away from dealing with the real problem. Staying isolated and a victim made it even more difficult to change things. I also used the excuse that I knew no one who had experienced the kind of abuse I had. It seemed so minor, yet so major in its effect on me. On the surface my abuse may not look that bad. What I need people to know is that just because it was not violent does not mean that the effect of it was not far-reaching. I see abuse as anything that is done to a person that he does not feel is in line with his values.

That is what happened to me. I had no sexual boundaries at the time of the rape. In order to live with the fear I had about my sexual identify I merely put up the thickest walls I possibly could. If I had only had someone to trust so I could have let them know what was happening to me, then perhaps I would not have had to live so many years feeling trapped by the shame and embarrassment I had over my sexuality.

Eleven years after the abuse happened I could finally tell people. Yet no one really seemed to take it seriously or to realize the pain it had put me through all of those years. But finally I allowed myself to begin to trust people. I had a few intimate friends and I began to tell one or two of them of the struggle I had gone through. I developed a good support system. I also got to know myself enough to figure out some career choices (and I applied to graduate school, which I am now attending). I could finally be more comfortable with my body. My old friends all mentioned how much I had changed. I had more self-confidence than before, I had a sincerity about myself that I had never known. Yet I was still held back. I could not let myself get involved romantically and sexually.

I was involved in a men's therapy group for a year. But no one in it had been sexually abused or had a history of it in their family. I felt stupid talking about being afraid of sex in a room full of men who seemed to have no trouble with it at all. I kept using them as my benchmark of where I should be sexually. That was a disaster. It made me feel even more inadequate. Here I was in a group of which I was supposed to be a contributing member and all I could think about was how they must see me as such a child. The recovery process seemed to hurt me more than help me. The idea of being thought of as totally inadequate as a man because of having no sexual experience with a woman only put my self-esteem more in the gutter than it already was. I could not accept that my sexuality was not all of who I was. It just seemed that I could find no one that had any compassion for the position I was in. I finally realized that the person who lacked compassion was *me*. In my struggle with my sexuality the most important person I needed to forgive was myself. If I did not, then I would be in the same place for the rest of my life. I had to stop seeing myself as different from everybody else. I had to stop being the victim I had learned to be. I began to take some control over my sexuality and make some decisions on my values. I started doing what I needed to do in order to become a sexual person. I realized that I have a whole range of sexual feeling, from homosexual to heterosexual. I have started to explore those feelings through dating and romantic relationships.

I have been sexual with people I care about and respect. I have felt good about the experience. In the past my fear and shame was so strong that I lost respect for myself and the other person if we even got close enough to have a sexual relationship. Rather than experience those feelings I kept out of any sort of intimate relationship. I am finally getting over my phobia of sex, and it is not nearly as frightening as had I believed. It seemed so natural to me. That is the only way to describe it. It was not painful or disgusting or even frightening. In fact, the first person I was sexual with as an adult told me that they never would have believed I had no sexual experience if I had not told them. This did great things for my self-esteem, especially in the area of sexual attractiveness.

I now see my ability to be involved with people as more of a trust issue than one of sexuality. I spent so much of my life not being involved, keeping a distance from people. The idea of being close with the possibility of being hurt kept me from going the full distance. Although I would invest so much in people, at times they would let me down and the pain would be devastating. I had to learn that people are not always there for you, and if they are not that does not mean they do not care. I also had to realize that self-esteem is in my hands, not in the hands of the people close to me. I can be a whole person whether they are there or not. That is the big difference now compared to the past.

I also learned to forgive my offender. If I cannot forgive him I could not have forgiven myself. He knew less about my feelings at the time than I did. I never said "stop." I never said "don't come back." I have to forgive him because he did not have the knowledge of what was going on inside of me. He had his part too and I forgive him: for his youth, his ignorance, and his curiosity to explore.

Another change for me is that I do not see myself as just playing a role. The things I do well are just as much a part of me as those which I am not so good at. The stereotype is gone, and I have finally become a person. I do not have to be perfect all the time, and I need to forgive myself when I do fail. The worst part is that I sometimes feel that I will never be cured. I sometimes think I will always have to fight the compulsive behavior and my lack of trust. When the going gets tough I always regress a little and have to take a step back and say, "It does not have to be this way. I was a victim once, but it does not have to keep plaguing me for the rest of my life."

Questions to help you identify your thoughts and emotions:

How is your (your loved one's) story similar to Richard's?

How is your (your loved one's) story different from Richard's?

What emotions did you have reading Richard's story?

What was the most powerful section of the story for you?

What did you learn about yourself from reading this story?

19

Tony's Story

I T has been three weeks since Mic asked me if I would be interested in having my story in his book. My first reaction was excitement and enthusiasm. However, over time I began to have mixed feelings about it. I began to feel not worthy of being in a book. I thought, Why is my story so different? and What makes me so special? As of my first night of writing I'm still not certain about the answer to Why me? But right now that's not important. What is important is that I want my story in this book, and if in some way, any way, it might help someone else who has been sexually abused, then it will be truly special.

My name is Tony. I am twenty-seven years old. I am employed as a construction worker. It's been nearly three years ago that I admitted myself into a chemical dependency treatment facility. I had been abusing drugs, alcohol, and myself. I was hurt financially, physically, mentally, spiritually, and emotionally. The last year before treatment, I had been trying to escape the pain I felt after finding my friend dead after he committed suicide. I knew I had to get help or in a short time I would be dead too.

While in treatment I chose not to deal "directly" with my sexual abuse. I did discuss it briefly with my counselor. This was the first time in ten years that I had ever told anyone about being sexually abused. Little did I know then that this was only the beginning.

My chemical dependency counselor referred me to a therapist who specializes in treating men who as children were sexually abused. During our first visit together I told him about my self-consciousness, fits of rage, overwhelming mood swings, severe depression, sexual hang-ups, low self-worth, thoughts of suicide, and inability to communicate in platonic and intimate relationships. He suggested that I join a weekly therapy group with five to seven other men. This idea was very scary to me, so I chose not to enter the group. I thought I would be capable of handling my problems on my own.

So for six weeks I went about my business, only to find myself becoming more overwhelmed with emotions that were starting to get out of control. I would have fits of laughter followed by fits of crying. I would break out in goose bumps, and my body would shake uncontrollably. But most of all, my depression worsened. I went two weeks with a gun on my dresser in my bedroom. Every day, several times a day, I would look into my mirror, holding the gun to my head, wanting so bad to end all the pain.

Fortunately, my girlfriend found the gun and confronted me with my Alcoholics Anonymous sponsor.[1] It was then I decided to go back to the therapist and reluctantly, though with some relief, joined the men's group.

The first day at the group was very frightening. There I was, all alone, in all of this pain, in a room with five guys that I had never seen in my life. After listening to some of the guys talk, it was my turn. I told them the reason that I was joining the group was because I was sexually abused as an adolescent and that I was a bullet away from committing suicide. My first responsibility after that first meeting was to dispose of the gun. Which I did.[2]

After a couple of weeks in the group I started to feel comfortable with the therapist and the other guys in the group. It was very hard for me to talk in any detail about my sexual abuse, so it was suggested that I write as much down as my emotions would allow and then bring it in to the group and read it. This turned out to be a very long but productive process. What you are about to read is the actual writing that I shared in my group.[3]

First Session

I started working at the ranch when I was twelve years old after my two older brothers had been working there for some time.[4] I would always want to ride out to the ranch with my mom or dad when they went to pick them up or drop them off. I had some sort of fascination with the ranch. It was so big and interesting.

It seems like Frank took me under his wing ever since the first time I met him.[5] I don't know if it was because of my age or what, but he was always treating me differently than the other guys. When I first started working there I had little "duties," like feeding the cats and dogs, going out to pick up the mail, little things like that. He would take me with him if he had to run errands, have me help him in the shop or office. At first I liked all of the attention that Frank gave me, but after a while I started to get some shit from the other guys who worked out there. They would call me names like "the little blow boy," "kiss-ass," and others, all basically saying the same thing.

As I think back now, there were so many things that Frank did.[6] I remember him coming into the bathroom when I would be taking showers or baths. He would slide the shower doors open and jokingly throw cold water on me or he would "have to talk" to me about something. I always felt so uncomfortable. There was never a lock on the door. (To this day I can't go to the bathroom in front of people. I always, I mean *always*, lock the door.)

When I first started staying there I slept in a room along with three other guys. I liked that. We would stay up all night, laughing, joking, and fooling around. But by the time I was thirteen he had me in a different room, by myself.[7] I remember Frank coming in to wake me up in the morning. He would always be sort of rough or he would sprinkle cologne or water on me to get me up.

Frank was always overly physically aggressive with me, always holding me down and touching me all over my body. We used to wrestle on the floor at night, usually after he had his two to four highballs. Occasionally he would let us drink too. He was always getting so close to me. His face would be right up tight against mine, and his body would always be covering me so that I couldn't move. I used to hate it when he got so close to me, but I could never tell him because I was too afraid.

Second Session

As I left off last week I was describing the beginning and how I started to work at the ranch, how I met Frank and how he immediately took me under his wing.

As I begin to write, I've been feeling like never before. I'm really scared. I've never done anything like this before. After all of the hours, days, weeks, and years of trying to forget about what happened I now find myself trying to recall, in detail, what happened . . . (pause, three deep breaths).[8]

When I was roughly thirteen I remember Frank getting physically close to me. He would treat any cuts or bruises. He would squeeze my zits, cut my toenails, anything of that nature.[9] I can remember him having me come into his room to watch TV or play cribbage. He would always want to give me back rubs with his hand massager or he would want me to give him a back rub. He was always in his underwear. I used to get embarrassed to see him like that. Whenever I didn't want to go into his room, he would get very cold and nasty. The following day he would act real pissed off at me. There were mornings when he wouldn't even wake me up. He would just let me sleep and then be very pissed off at me when I got up late.[10]

I think that the sexual abuse started then. His "back rubs" would consist of rubbing and touching my whole body from my head to my toes. He would always take my pajamas off and rub my crotch and butt. I fucking hated it. I don't think that he was kissing me at this time, but it eventually led to that. I'm having a tough time writing right now. I feel like a fucking time bomb, ready to go off. I just can't believe that all of this went on. How could it? How could he? I was just a boy. I was just a fucking kid. I hate his fucking guts right now.[11] I remember him always pulling down his underwear over his buttocks, taking my hand and pushing it down to his butt. He always pushed me. He always forced me, and I could never say no, because I always felt like such a bad person when I didn't do what he wanted me to do.[12] He always made me feel like I did something wrong because I didn't want to be with him or touch him.

Third Session

I don't want to write. I feel pain and sadness just knowing that I am going to think about the past. It really makes me realize how hard all of this has been and how hard I am working.

At one time, for a period of three or four months, Frank had me sleeping in the same bedroom as him. He said that the other rooms were too crowded and that he had plenty of space in his room for another bed. I believe that I left off last time with Frank and the back rubs. I remember him now pulling his and my underwear off completely. He used to kind of play with my genitals and ask me questions like, "Does it get hard?" or "Do you play with it?" He used to tell me that someday I would have hair on my testicles and pubic area. He asked me if I knew how to jack off (which at the time I didn't). Do you know how fucking sick and fucking disgusted I get whenever I think of the fact that Frank showed me how to jack off? And he did it to me, so many fucking times. And he made me do it to him. I want to kill him.

Eventually it led to him sucking on my penis, and he would kiss me on my mouth, French-kissing me. I used to just fucking close my eyes and just fucking lay there. He had to know, man, he *had to fucking know* that I hated what he was doing to me. I can't even cry while I'm writing this. I feel really numb. I don't know why. What the fuck is wrong with me?[13]

Fourth Session[14]

It was bad enough what Frank was doing to me, but then that fucker started making me do things to him. He would lay there while I was rubbing his back and then he would pull down his underwear over his butt and push my hands onto his butt so that I would rub it.[15] After a while he would have me rubbing his balls and penis. I just can't fucking believe it. I hate him right now. I'll never forget how he felt and how I hated to do that to him. Nobody will ever know how much I hated touching that bastard.[16] He would also lay on top of me and hump himself on my legs or on my face until he would come. He used to hold his penis so that he wouldn't come on me. I used to fucking think that he was nice because he wouldn't get any come on me.[17]

It eventually led to me jacking him off. I'm getting sick to my stomach. That fucker! I could kill him right now. I want to stop writing but I know what comes next. He used to push my head down, and he would make me suck his cock and balls. I'll never forget him pushing me down. I don't know how I'll ever read this to the group. God, grant me strength.

Fifth Session[18]

I want to start today by telling everybody that for some reason this part of my abuse has always been the most difficult for me to face. However, after going through all of the other abuse in detail I'm beginning to see that this part is really no "worse" or "different" than anything else that happened. Nevertheless, this is very difficult and very painful for me to do.

After a long time of being sexually touched, physically and orally, over every part of my body, and me being forced to do the same to Frank, he started doing things with my rear end. He started by just touching me there with his fingers. Then he would shove his fingers into my butt. He would do this when he was sucking on my penis and when he was humping on my body. He would also get me in the "69'" position, and he would put his tongue and his fingers inside of me. He basically did just about anything that you could imagine. Needless to say, he was making me do all of the same type of things to him. I'll never forget him telling me that he would do anything for me, that he would "even eat my shit."

He tried to have intercourse with me anally quite a few times. I would always fight against it and complain about it hurting me to try to make him stop.[19] It must have worked because I don't remember him fucking me anally very often. It did happen, though, more than once, and most likely a lot more if I wouldn't have complained so much.

How can I care for that man? How can I feel sorry for him? He fucked me. He forced me to do all those things to him. He forced me to suck on his cock. He forced me to play with his balls. That fucker forced me to stick my tongue and my fingers up his fucking ass. Why the fuck do I feel sorry for that low-life fucking child-abuser? He fucked me, goddamn it. Do I fucking realize that? That the bastard *fucked* me. He ruined my life. I never knew what it was like to grow up halfway fucking normal. How could he do that to me? Why did he do that to me?

All I ever wanted to do was to try to make him happy, and he fucking used me. I hate him. I want to hurt him right now.[20] He is going to pay for this. I don't care if it looks like a payoff, he is going to pay for this for the rest of his rotten fucking life. I lived in a fucking nightmare for fourteen years. Now it's his turn. I want to make him suffer. I want him to fucking crawl.[21] Goddamn it. Why wasn't there anybody there to help me? Why couldn't I reach out and tell someone? I hate everybody for not helping me. I hate me for letting this happen. I just fucking hate everything.[22] My life sucks right now. This shit sucks. Fuck everybody and fuck everything. I can't do shit. I can't even look in the mirror at myself because I get embarrassed. I feel so ugly and so alone. I'm never happy with how I look or how I feel. I can't remember what it feels like to want to get out of bed. I hate getting up in the morning. The only part of the day I enjoy is when I go to sleep because then everything feels okay. I don't feel the pain then, and that is why I want to die so badly. I'm so tired of living in pain. I'm so sad and so lonely, but I feel so inadequate to go out and do anything about it.[23] I fucking quit.

Needless to say, after writing down and reliving what happened to me, I had a lot of emotions to deal with. So week after week I discussed things in group with the guys. I received a great deal of beneficial feedback from them, all of which I tried to use in my life.

Eventually I decided that I wanted to confront Frank with my therapist. My goal was to finally ask him why he abused me, what he was thinking, how he justified it, and to inform him on what it was like for me to be abused and how painful and traumatic it was for me. I wanted to tell him how badly it screwed me up. I wanted an apology, and I wanted back the power and control that I had given him. So after a few weeks of preparation I had Frank come in.[24] I was nervous at first, but after a while I felt completely in control and very confident. I felt like I did a great job. I feel like I overcame one of the biggest fears of my life. After I went home I wrote:

Tuesday, 10:04. Tired, relaxed, sad, happy, drained, rested. The big session—over. How did I do? I did great. I was strong, confident, direct, considerate, clear, blunt, honest. In retrospect I feel like I covered everything I wanted to. I try not to think about Frank and how he is doing, but I can't help but think of him. I feel like all the work that I've been doing is finally paying off. It certainly helped me tonight. I want to write more, but I'm tired and I need to sleep and rethink about what all has happened. I'm very proud of myself. I can honestly say that I did the most difficult and inconceivable thing ever.[25]

After the session I didn't see Frank for a few weeks, but now I see him quite regularly. We talk about the abuse, and I share with him if I'm having a hard time with it. He has been very supportive of me. He asks what he can do to help, and I think he genuinely feels remorse over what he did.[26] I think he truly wants to help me. I know he does. I still feel anger towards him at times, but I also still love him.[27] He has done a lot of good things for me too. I believe that our relationship has taken on a lot of new meaning after I talked openly to him about him abusing me. He is also in the process of getting therapy to deal with his problem.

Up to this point I've dealt with my feelings about myself and Frank, but now things seem to be directed towards my family and how they played a role in everything that happened to me. I never used to blame my family, mainly my parents, but now I'm starting to see things from a different perspective. I'm noticing things in my family that I've never really looked at before, and its starting to generate feelings of anger in me. I used to think that my parents were not involved in anything that happened to me, that they raised me the best way they knew how, and although that may be true, it still doesn't justify the fact that they didn't do anything for me or that they couldn't tell by my actions that something was going on with me. So what I did was basically the same thing I did with Frank; I wrote a letter and read it in the group.

Mom and Dad,

What to say to you? I've had quite a struggle trying to relate to you my thoughts and, more importantly, my feelings (how I *really* feel inside). I'm confused. For so long I've thought of people as either good or bad, and it's not until lately that I've begun to realize that there are good people and they do bad things or use bad judgment.[28]

I've been very hurt and very angry at you lately. Perhaps I've brought a lot of it on myself. I'm not really sure. I know that I've always acted very independent, like I didn't need you or your love, but I did. I needed it so much. I need to know that you care and that you love me, but you don't show me very well. I get angry with you, especially you, Dad. You treat my friends and my co-workers with more respect and concern for their lives than you do me. Do you realize that I am almost twenty-seven years old and I can't remember you telling me that you love me? Is that so God-damn hard for you to say, or is it that you just don't love me? You always have to be so fucking strong, so tough, so insensitive. Some-times I wonder if you feel anything at all. The only time you even showed me a little bit of love was when Taylor died. You rushed out to the ranch because you thought it was me that committed suicide. I really thought that you cared about me then, but what the fuck did you do when you found out it wasn't me; did I get any compassion or love or anything? Fuck, no, all I got was a "Oh, this ain't nothing. I've seen lots worse." Well, fuck you Dad. Fuck you, it was something. It was important. He was my friend.[29] I was hurt. I needed you then. I needed you so much, but you were there, never. Your work and your own life were the only fucking thing that you ever cared about. Sometimes I think that the only differ-ence between the mind-fuck you did on me and what Frank did to me was that Frank got a real fuck, lots of real fucks in too. I fucking hate you both.

I can bust my ass for you at work and I hardly get any credit, but as soon as anybody else does anything they are just the greatest guys in the world. Why, why do you pick others over me? Why do you treat me like I'm *less?* I'm not. I'm just as fucking capable as they are, but I didn't grow up the way you wanted. Is that it? I have earrings. I let my hair grow. I got into drugs and alcohol. I did crazy things. Is that it? I didn't conform to your ways. I went my own way. Is that why you treat me like you do?[30] Well, some-day you're gonna fucking miss me, you asshole. You're going to miss my earrings, my smile, my laugh, and me. Someday I'm gonna be gone. Maybe then you will fucking wake up and realize that I wasn't such a bad kid, that I did good things, that I had a brain, that I was worth something.

Do you have an inkling as to why I act like I do or do the things I do? Do you have any idea? Do you fucking know what it's like to suck on some guy's cock or to be fucked by another guy? Do you fucking have any idea?[31] Yes, Dad, your son, your boy, was fucked, over and over again, and you didn't know, did you? You, who thought he knew everything, you didn't know. Perhaps you did know and didn't do anything about it. Maybe some people would have thought that you failed as a father. Well, Dad, you did fucking fail, you flunked. You've never been there emotionally for me, and I needed that. I still need it, now more than ever. I hate you right now. I'm so angry and so hurt. Why can't you just once show me that you care about me and that *I'm okay?*

And then there is you, Mother. You always told me that I should find something else other than the ranch, but I didn't listen. Tell me, did you have any idea? I could always talk to you easier than Dad, but you've always protected and defended him, your care-taker. Maybe that's where I get it from. Why is it that I have a hard time getting angry with you? Maybe because you showed me love more than anyone else. You took the time to listen to me. You've accepted me as the person that I am. Quite possibly it's for all those reasons that I have a hard time believing that maybe you knew about Frank and me. I loved you, respected you, admired you, and don't want to think that you could do that to me. I'm feeling very drained and *sad.*

I am now in the process of trying to prepare myself for a session with my parents. I don't know if I will ever actually do it or not, but I'm finding that by doing all the necessary preparation, it helps me greatly in trying to deal with what's been going on. I have also written a letter to my friend Taylor after his suicide. This helped me uncover a lot of emotions and helped me deal with his death.

In conclusion, my life has changed dramatically. I've done a lot of work, and it is paying off in many different ways. I still have my share of bad days. Most people would never believe it, but what took place so many years ago in my life still affects me. At times I have trouble believing it. It gets to be very hard and de-pressing, but I keep on pushing and communicating with people that have helped me to reach this point in my recovery. I'm not nearly as far along as I would like to be, but at least I can get out of bed, face the world, and not come home to a loaded gun on my dresser.

On this last day of writing for this story my telephone rang. A new member of Alcoholics Anonymous, twenty-five years old, wants me to become his sponsor. He is facing three to five years hard time in prison for sexually abusing his two kids. Where and when does it end?

Questions to help you identify your thoughts and emotions:

How is your (your loved one's) story similar to Tony's?

How is your (your loved one's) story different from Tony's?

What emotions did you have reading Tony's story?

What was the most powerful section of the story for you?

What did you learn about yourself from reading this story?

20

Resources

The following organizations specialize in addressing issues related to abuse.

Adults Molested as Children United is a mutual-help group that is an outgrowth of Parents United. The address is: P.O. Box 952, San Jose, CA 95108; (408) 280-5055.

The American Professional Society on the Abuse of Children is an organization that seeks to bring together the professional disciplines for promoting improvements in the area of identification, assessment, and treatment of child victims, offenders, and family members. Write c/o University of Chicago, 969 E. 60th St., Chicago, IL 60637; (213) 836-2471.

The *Child Help National Child Abuse Hotline* provides twenty-four-hour crisis counseling, referrals, and information from professional counselors. Write to: P.O. Box 630, Hollywood, CA 90028; (800) 422-4453.

The *Henry Kempe National Center for the Prevention and Treatment of Child Abuse and Neglect* reports that their treatment services are for children, but that they have written materials that could be of use for adults. Address: 1205 Oneida Street, Denver, CO 80220; (303) 321-3963.

The *Incest Recovery Association* is a nonprofit organization dedicated to providing information and treatment for victims of incest. Address: 6200 North Central Expressway, Suite 209, Dallas, TX 75206; (214) 373-6607.

The *Incest Survivor Information Exchange* publishes a quarterly newsletter with a theme related to sexual abuse. The mailing list is kept confidential. Address: P.O. Box 3399, New Haven, CT 06515; (203) 389-5166.

The *Incest Survivors Resource Network International* was founded and is operated by incest survivors from a variety of professions. It is a Quaker-affiliated educational resource that functions mainly through participation in committees and conferences of international and national organizations. Address: P.O. Box 911, Hicksville, NY 11802; (516) 935-3031. Contacts: Erik A. Eriksson, Anne-Marie Eriksson.

The *National Organization for Victim Assistance (NOVA)* addresses victims and covictims of crime of all types. They organize public campaigns to protest victimization. Address: 717 D Street NW, Suite 200, Washington, DC 20004; (202) 393-NOVA.

The *National Resource Center on Child Sexual Abuse* is an information, training, and technical assistance center that is part of the National Children's Advocacy Center. Address: 11141 Georgia Ave., Suite 310, Wheaton, MD 20902; (301) 949-5000, (800) KIDS-006.

Prevention, Leadership, Education, and Assistance (PLEA) describes itself as a nonprofit organization for nonoffending adult male survivors of childhood sexual, physical, or emotional abuse. It is also open to prosurvivors such as partners, friends, family members, clergy, and "all other individuals who care for or about the male survivor." Address: P.O. Box 291182, Los Angeles, CA 90029; (213) 254-9962.

Safer Society Press publishes materials related to abuse. Address: 3049 East Genesee Street, Syracuse, NY 13224.

Survivors of Incest Anonymous (SIA) is a mutual-help group, guided by the Twelve Steps and Traditions of AA, and is made up of men and women eighteen years of age or older. They have a list of twenty questions to help individuals determine whether SIA might be useful, and a "First Step Inventory" to help in identifying how sexual abuse has affected one's life. SIA was started in St. Cloud, Minnesota, in 1981, and there are meetings in various states. Address: P.O. Box 21817, Baltimore, MD 21222; (301) 282-3400 (answered twenty-four hours a day).

VOICES in Action, Inc. VOICES stands for Victims of Incest Can Emerge Survivors. VOICES can be reached at P.O. Box 148309, Chicago, IL 60614; (312) 327-1500. This group organizes conferences, publishes a newsletter, and offers a "Survival Kit," which includes a bibliography and information on how to choose a therapist and how to start a self-help group. They also have "special interest groups," which confidentially correspond by letter or phone and hold meetings at the conferences. These special interest groups are made up of people who

Experience "dissociated childlike states"

Were abused by a family member other than a parent

Are/were involved in self-abuse

Had several perpetrators

Are/were members of a religious community

Are single

Have addictive personalities or are involved in Twelve-Step programs

Were abused by authority figures (religious leaders, teachers, therapists, and so forth)

Are victims of posttraumatic stress syndrome

Recently confronted their family about the abuse

Are college students

Were in mental institutions as young children or adolescents

Are working for legislative change

Are lesbians

Treat surviving victims

Carry physiological ailments because of the abuse

Are/were anorexic and/or bulemic

Have developed multiple personalities

Are recovering from amnesia

Are/were depressed and/or suicidal

Were abused by their mothers

Were abused by both parents

Were abused with emotional incest

Were raped as adults

Want to have children but are afraid to

Are parents

Are adult children of alcoholics

Experience problems fulfilling their sexuality because of the abuse

Are going through a sexual identity crisis

Are having difficulty communicating with their mothers

Were abused by their stepfathers

Are Jewish

Were abused by one or more siblings

There are also groups for partners/spouses of survivors, survivors whose spouse/partner is having a difficult time as a result of knowing about the abuse, researchers studying the effects of abuse on survivors, mothers of survivors, and those whose abuse involved

Animals

Satanic rituals

Pornography

Sadistic perpetrators

Many sexual abuse survivors become adults who have compulsive sexual patterns and/or get involved in relationships with people who do. The following reading materials and mutual-help groups address these issues.

Co-dependents to Sex Addiction (Co-SA). Address: P.O. Box 14537, Minneapolis, MN 55414; (612) 537-6904. For people who are in or have been in a relationship with a sex addict.

Sex Addicts Anonymous (SAA). P.O. Box 3038, Minneapolis, MN 55403; (612) 871-1520. For people who are sexually compulsive.

Sex and Love Addicts Anonymous (SLAA). The Augustine Fellowship, P.O. Box 88, New Town Branch, Boston, MA 02258. For people who are sexually compulsive or obsessive about romantic relationships.

Adult Children of Sex Addicts (ACSA) P.O. Box 8084, Lake Street Station, 110 E. 31st St., Minneapolis, MN 55408. For people who were raised in sexually addictive or dysfunctional families. The membership of this group has developed the following list of characteristics:

1. Many of us were given inappropriate, harmful, inaccurate, or useless information about sex, and were not given appropriate, helpful, accurate, or useful information about sex.

2. Many of us experience confusion, discomfort, or terror in the face of sexuality (even appropriate sexuality), often leaving us unable to act in appropriate or healthy ways.

3. Many of us feel shame about our bodies, our sexuality, and sexuality generally.

4. Many of us grew up in families that had unhealthy boundaries around sexuality. Sex tended to be viewed in extremes: sex was all-important, everything; or sex was dirty, disgusting, or naughty.

5. Many of us grew up in families in which gender-disrestpectful remarks were made about us, about others, or about sexuality.

6. As adults, we often experienced difficulties in establishing intimate (including sexual) relationships with others.

7. As adults, many of us experienced shame or perceived ourselves as disloyal when we thought, felt, or acted in ways that challenged sexual rules (covert or overt) learned in our families of origin.

8. As adults, many of us reacted to perceived abandonment by engaging in or avoiding sexual behavior. (Created and copyrighted by the membership of Twin Cities ACSA, 1988. Used with permission.)

The First Step Workbook for People in Relationships with Sex Addicts: A Recovery Workbook. (Mic Hunter and Jem.) This workbook helps readers go through their lives and look at the experiences that helped form their self-identity and led to forming relationships with sex addicts. It also acts as a First-Step guide for people in Twelve-Step groups in looking at the effect that being with sex addicts has had on their lives. Available from CompCare Publications, 2415 Annapolis lane, Minneapolis, MN 55441; (800) 328-3330.

Hope and Recovery: A 12 Step Guide to Healing from Compulsive Sexual Behavior. This book contains chapters on the Twelve Steps and Traditions, sponsorship, abstinence and sobriety, the slogans, slips/relapses, starting or finding a group, as well as eighteen stories of female and male recovering sex addicts and the story of a female codependent to sex addiction. Portions are also available on audiotape. Available from CompCare Publications (address given above).

Out of the Shadows: Understanding Sexual Addiction. (Patrick Carnes.) This book describes the addiction cycle, levels of addiction, the belief systems of the addict and the coaddict. Available from CompCare Publications (address given above).

Sex and Love Addicts Anonymous. This book contains chapters on the Twelve Steps, withdrawal, starting a group, and living with a sex and love addict. Available from The Augustine Fellowship, P.O. Box 88, New Town Branch, Boston, MA 02258.

What Everyone Needs to Know about Sex Addiction and Codependency. This pamphlet introduces the concepts of sex addiction and codependency and contains the stories of a married couple. Available from CompCare Publications (address given above).

What is Sex Addiction? (Mic Hunter.) This flier provides a basic introduction to the concept of sex addiction. Available from Hazeldon Foundation Educational Materials, Box 176, Center City, MN 55012-0176; (800) 328-9000.

Appendix: Questionnaire

Dear Reader,
  I would like to hear your reactions to this book. Please answer the following questions, add your comments, and send it to me in care of Lexington Books, 125 Spring Street, Lexington, MA 02173. Thank you.

Mic Hunter

1. Your age: _____ years

2. Your sex: Male _____ Female _____

3. Your race/ethnic background: (check *one* only)
   __ Asian, Asian-American, Pacific Islander
   __ Black or African-American
   __ Hispanic
   __ North American Indian or Alaska Native
   __ White or Caucasian
   __ Other (please specify: _____)

4. Your *highest* educational level: (check *one* only)
   __ Elementary school   __ Some college
   __ Some high school   __ College graduate
   __ High school graduate   __ Some graduate school
   __ GED   __ Graduate degree
   __ Vocational/technical   __ More than one graduate
   school   degree

5. The general nature of your current or most recent employment: (check *one* only)

— Agriculture
— Business
— Homemaker
— Military
— Office/clerical
— Professional

— Retired
— Semi-skilled labor
— Skilled labor
— Full-time student
— Unemployed
— Other

6. Approximate income: $_____ per year

7. Current marital status:

— Never married — Married — Separated — Divorced

8. Sexual preference: (check the *one* that best describes you)

— Bisexual — Heterosexual — Homosexual
          (other sex)   (same sex)

9. Which of these mutual-help groups do you attend? (check *as many* as apply)

— Alcoholics Anonymous
— Al-anon
— Bulimics Anonymous
— Co-SA
— Emotions Anonymous
— Families Anonymous
— Gamblers Anonymous
— Narcotics Anonymous
— Adult Children of Alcoholics
— VOICES in Action, Inc.
— Overeaters Anonymous
— Other (please specify) _____

— Parents Anonymous
— Pills Anonymous
— Sexual Abuse Anonymous
— Sexaholics Anonymous
— Shoplifters Anonymous
— Spenders Anonymous
— Sex and Love Addicts Anonymous
— Adult Children of Sex Addicts
— PLEA

10. Do you (or have you) attend(ed) counseling or therapy to address your issues related to sexual abuse?   No __   Yes __
If yes, please check all that apply:
Individual sessions __   Couple's sessions __
Family sessions __   Group sessions __

11. Did you read this book because you or someone you know was sexually abused?

Myself ___ Another ___ Both ___

12. If you were abused, who abused you? (please check all that apply)
Father ___ Mother ___ Stepfather ___ Stepmother ___
Sibling(s) ___ Other family member(s) ___ Foster-parent ___
Guardian ___ Clergy ___ Teacher ___ Coach ___
Employer ___ Therapist/counselor ___ Physician ___
Family friend(s) ___ Stranger(s) ___

13. At what age did the abuse begin? ___ years old

14. How long did it last? (please check only one)
One time ___ Several times ___ Less than a year ___
Onc year ___ Two to three years ___
More than three years ___

15. Are you employed in a profession that treats sexual abuse victims? If so, what is your title and setting?

16. How did you hear about this book?

17. What do you find *most* helpful about this book?

18. What do you find *least* helpful?

19. What questions would you like to see added to future editions?

Comments:

Notes

1. Understanding Sexual Abuse

1. Rape is one of the most underreported crimes. In eleven states, in the eyes of the legal system, a male can't be raped because the laws are gender-specific—that is, worded in a manner that excludes males. Males make up 12–15 percent of all rape cases. R. Kempe and C. Kempe, *The Common Secret: Sexual Abuse of Children and Adolescents* (New York: Freeman, 1984); P. Sarrel and W. Masters, "Sexual Molestation of Men by Women," *Archives of Sexual Behavior* 11:2 (April 1982):117–31.
2. David Walters, *Physical and Sexual Abuse of Children: Causes and Treatment* (Bloomington: Indiana University Press, 1975), p. 29.
3. Judith Lewis Herman, *Father-Daughter Incest* (Cambridge: Harvard University Press, 1981), p. 70.
4. As you read the recovery stories in Part II of this book, you will see that violence is rarely required.
5. Walters, *Physical and Sexual Abuse of Children*, p. 29.
6. Kempe and Kempe, *The Common Secret*.
7. D. Finkelhor, *Child Sexual Abuse: New Theory and Research* (New York: Free Press, 1984), p. 107.
8. Notice that although I ask him about his emotions in the present, he responds concerning his sensations in the past.
9. See Daniel's and Kevin's stories.
10. Kempe and Kempe, *The Common Secret*, p. 50.
11. Although I am not denying the concept of the Oedipus complex, I think it can be inappropriately applied.
12. Kempe and Kempe, *The Common Secret*, p. 49.
13. Examples of this type of abuse can be found in the stories of Al, Allen, Jim, Kent, Kevin, Richard, and Sonny (see part II of this book).
14. Examples of this type of abuse can be found in this book in the stories of Greg and Kevin.

15. Examples of this type of abuse can be found in Jim's story.
16. Examples of this type of abuse can be found in Greg's story.
17. See Henry's story.
18. Examples of this type of abuse can be found in the stories of Greg, Jim, and Kevin.
19. Examples of this type of abuse can be found in Greg's story.
20. Readers are invited to write to me and to describe additional types of abuse, which can be included in future editions.
21. J. Crewdson, *By Silence Betrayed: Sexual Abuse of Children in America* (Boston: Little, Brown, 1988).
22. A.W. Burgess, C.R. Hartmann, M.P. McCausland, and P. Powers, "Response Patterns in Children and Adolescents Exploited through Sex Rings and Pornography," *American Journal of Psychiatry* 141:5 (1984): 656–62.
23. Finkelhor, *Child Sexual Abuse.*
24. Walters, *Physical and Sexual Abuse of Children,* page 131.
25. Kempe and Kempe, *The Common Secret;* Burgess et al., "Response Patterns."
26. American Psychiatric Association, *Diagnostic and Statistical Manual of Mental Disorders,* 3d ed., rev. (Washington, D.C.: A.P.A., 1987), p. 282. Italics added.
27. P. Roth, *Portnoy's Complaint* (New York: Bantam, 1967), pp.46–47.
28. C. Courtois, *Healing the Incest Wound: Adult Survivors in Therapy* (New York: Norton, 1988).
29. See Henry's story, where the father justified the sexual abuse as a "lesson."
30. *Diagnostic and Statistical Manual,* 3d ed., 1987.
31. Kempe and Kempe, *The Common Secret.*
32. Walters, *Physical and Sexual Abuse of Children.*
33. Gail Berry, "Incest: Some Clinical Variations on a Classical Theme," *Journal of the Academy of Psychoanalysis* 3:2 (1975).
34. The preceding entries are from Minnesota Program for Victims of Sexual Assault, *Biennial Report: Fiscal Years 1985-1986* (St. Paul: Minnesota Department of Corrections, 1987).

2. The Frequency of Sexual Abuse

1. When I started seeking a publishing company for this book, I thought I would have no trouble finding one that would be eager to release it. My co-workers had assured me that there was a great need for such a book, and it was clear to me that my clients needed written materials to aid them in their recovery. Much to my surprise I had two dozen publishers reject my proposal. In most cases they told me that they did not believe there were enough boys who had been sexually abused to make it worthwhile to publish a book on the topic.
2. R.H. Bixter, "The Incest Controversy," *Psychological Reports* 49:267-283 (1981).
3. A. Kohn, "Shattered Innocence," *Psychology Today* 21:2 (1987).

4. S.K. Weinberg, *Incest Behavior* (New York: Citadel, 1955).
5. K. Meiselman, *Incest: A Psychological Study of Causes and Effects with Treatment Recommendations* (San Francisco: Jossey-Bass, 1978).
6. Bixler, "The Incest Controversy."
7. D. Finkelhor, *Child Sexual Abuse: New Theory and Research* (New York: Free Press, 1984).
8. Eugene Porter, *Treating the Young Male Victims of Sexual Assault: Issues and Intervention Strategies* (Syracuse, N.Y.: Safer Society Press, 1986).
9. A. Kinsey, W. Pomeroy, and C. Martin, *Sexual Behavior in the Human Male* (Philadelphia: Saunders, 1948).
10. S. Newlund, "Rate of Abuse Reports in '84 is State Record," *Minneapolis Star Tribune*, March 27, 1986.
11. D. Hedin, *Preliminary Analysis of High School, College, Prison, Juvenile Corrections and Adult Populations* (Minneapolis: WCCO Television/University of Minnesota, 1984).
12. A. Bell and M. Weinberg, *Preliminary Data: Childhood and Adolescent Sexuality San Francisco Study* (Bloomington, Ind.: Institute for Sex Research, n.d.) mimeo; D. Finkelhor *Sexually Victimized Children* (New York: Free Press, 1979). G. Fritz, K. Stoll, and N. Wagner, "A Comparison of Males and Females Who Were Sexually Molested as Children," *Journal of Sex and Marital Therapy* 7 (1981): 54–59; G. Kercher and M. McShane, "The Prevalence of Child Sexual Abuse Victimization in an Adult Sample of Texas Residents," Sam Houston State University, Huntsville, Tex., 1983.
13. Finkelhor, *Child Sexual Abuse.*
14. Committee on Sexual Offences against Children and Youths, *Sexual Offences against Children: Report of the Committee on Sexual Offences against Children and Youths* (Ottawa: Canadian Government Publishing Centre, 1984).
15. D. Besharow, "Doing Something about Child Abuse," *Harvard Journal of Law and Public Policy* 8 (1985): 539–89.
16. W. Friedrich, A. Urquiza, and R. Beilke, "Behavioral Problems in Sexually Abused Young Children," *Journal of Pediatric Psychology* 11 (1986): 45–57.
17. Ironically, there is evidence that Freud himself was a childhood sexual abuse victim (see A. Elms, "Was Freud Molested?" *Psychology Today* [Aug. 1986]). He referred to his father as a "pervert" and wrote that at age two his governess was his "teacher in sexual matters" (see J. Masson, ed., *The Complete Letters of Sigmund Freud to Wilhelm Fliess, 1887–1904* [Cambridge: Harvard University Press, 1985]).
18. J. Peters, "Children Who Are Victims of Sexual Assault and the Psychology of Offenders," *American Journal of Psychotherapy* 30 (1976): 407–8.
19. R. Gardner, *The Parental Alienation Syndrome and the Differentiation between Fabricated and Genuine Child Sex Abuse* (Cresskill, N.J.: Creative Therapeutics, 1987), p. 274.
20. Meiselman, *Incest*, p. 70.
21. C. Dietz and J. Craft, "Family Dynamics of Incest: A New Perspective," *Social Casework* 61:10 (1980): 602–9.

22. As Meiselman puts it: Once the incest admission is received, many therapists seem uncomfortable with it and may convey to the patient, purposefully or not, the sense that the issue should not be brought up again. . . . It appears that any relationship between premature incest disclosure and psychosis is a very weak one and does not justify the therapist's being especially wary of allowing the patient to describe the incest experiences. Another source of concern mentioned frequently by therapists is that the patient may use the incest revelation as a diversionary tactic to escape the responsibility of dealing with problems in their present life situations. If so, then the therapist would be justified in de-emphasizing the importance of the incest incident and avoiding further discussion of it. In avoiding discussion of incest, however, the therapist takes the risk of leaving patients with the feeling that they have been "cut off" and that an event that still seems very important to them had been minimized. Therapists should therefore carefully explore their motivation for avoiding a discussion of incest before jeopardizing the patient-therapist relationship; in particular, they should ask whether their own discomfort with the topic of incest may not be at the root of their unwillingness to discuss it with a patient. (Meiselman, *Incest*, pp. 346–47.)

23. Sonny, Jim, Al, Greg, Kent, and Allen all mention that they entered therapy without knowing that they had been sexually abused (see part II of this book).

24. See Allen's story as an example.

25. P. Huyghe, "Voices, Glances, Flashbacks: Our First Memories," *Psychology Today* 19:9 (Sept. 1985).

26. C. Rogers and T. Terry, "Clinical Intervention with Boy Victims of Sexual Abuse," in *Victims of Sexual Aggression,* edited by I.R. Stewart and J.G. Greer (New York: Van Nostrand Reinhold, 1984).

27. Older man to younger man is not necessarily abusive, but man to boy is (R.B. Adams, personal communication, 1989).

28. Rogers and Terry, "Clinical Intervention."

29. David Walters, *Physical and Sexual Abuse of Children: Causes and Treatment* (Bloomington: Indiana University Press, 1975), pp. 7, 116.

30. Rogers and Terry, "Clinical Intervention."

31. Greg, Jim, Al, Daniel, Kent, Kevin, and Sonny all describe abuse by females.

32. M. Margolis, "A Case of Mother–Adolescent Son Incest: A Follow-up Study," *Psychoanalytic Quarterly* 53:3 (July 1984): 355–85.

33. W. Arroyo, S. Eth, and R. Pynoos, "Sexual Assault of a Mother by Her Preadolescent Son," *American Journal of Psychiatry* 141:9 (1984): 1107–8.

34. MCA, *Private Lessons,* Universal City, Calif., 1981, videotape; MCA, *Homework,* Universal City, Calif., 1982, videotape.

35. In a society where adults are given more permission to neglect and abuse children than they are given to nurture them, child protection services can serve as a method of lessening our guilt. By their existence we can pretend that we are doing something about the widespread mistreatment of children. Child protection workers are given a mandate to protect children, but then are given inadequate resources and are met with societal outrage when they "don't respect the sanctity of the family" by removing a child from a dangerous home. What can be more "profamily" than defending the physical,

mental, and emotional health of a child? We live in a culture that still believes parents have more of a right to mistreat their children than children have a right to safety (M. Hunter and R.B. Adams, personal communications, 1989).

36. Walters, *Physical and Sexual Abuse of Children,* p. 127.
37. P. Sarrel and W. Masters, "Sexual Molestation of Men by Women," *Archives of Sexual Behavior* 11:2 (April 1982): 117–31.
38. Walters, *Physical and Sexual Abuse of Children,* p. 127.
39. A. Van Buren, "Boy's Early Sex Life Disturbing to Mother," *Star Tribune,* July 6, 1986. Copyright Universal Press Syndicate, 1986, used with permission.
40. J. McKechnie, ed., *Webster's New Universal Unabridged Dictionary,* 2d ed. (Cleveland: Simon and Schuster, 1983).
41. E. Sagarin, "Incest: Problems of Definition and Frequency," *Journal of Sex Research* 13:1 (1977): 126–35.
42. Finkelhor, *Child Sexual Abuse.*
43. C. Courtois, *Healing the Incest Wound: Adult Survivors in Therapy* (New York: Norton, 1988), p. 116.
44. D. Finkelhor, "Implications for Theory, Research and Practice," in *The Educator's Guide to Preventing Child Sexual Abuse,* edited by M. Nelson and K. Clark (Santa Cruz, Calif.: Network Publications, 1986), pp. 107–8.
45. A. Yorukoglu and J. Kemph, "Children Not Severely Damaged by Incest with a Parent," *Journal of the American Academy of Child Psychiatry* 5 (1966): 482–85.
46. If any reader knows the identity of this boy, I would be very interested in having him contact me and in learning how his life has gone since this article was written.
47. Finkelhor, *Child Sexual Abuse.*
48. Ibid., p. 91.
49. Ruth Mathews, "Typologies of Female Sexual Offenders," 1987.
50. Courtois, *Healing the Incest Wound.*
51. J.L. Herman, *Father-Daughter Incest* (Cambridge, Mass.: Harvard University Press, 1981), p. 20.
52. A. Groth, "The Incest Offender," in *Handbook of Clinical Intervention in Child Sexual Abuse,* edited by S. Sgroi (Lexington, Mass.: Lexington Books, 1982), p. 231.
53. Mathews, "Typologies of Female Sexual Offenders."
54. Sarrel and Masters, "Sexual Molestation of Men by Women."
55. M. Nasjleti, "Suffering in Silence: The Male Incest Victim," *Child Welfare* 49:5 (1980): 269–75.
56. M. Gendel and M. Hunter, personal discussion, 1988.

3. Factors Affecting the Impact of Childhood Sexual Abuse

1. When research articles report on children who experienced sexual abuse and suffered no lasting effects, it is important to look at the details of the data.

For example, according to one study, 81 percent of the males reported that they believed that they suffered no lasting emotional damage from their experience (see J.T. Landis, "Experiences of 500 Children with Adult Sexual Deviation," *Psychiatric Quarterly Supplement* 30 [1956]: 91–109). However, two-thirds of these males did not know the abuser, and half of the cases involved no physical contact. In another study, 65 percent of the male subjects stated that their sexual abuse had a "significant impact on their lives" (see R. Johnson and D. Schrier, "Sexual Victimization of Boys: Experience at an Adolescent Medicine Clinic," *Journal of Adolescent Health Care* 6:5 [1985]: 372–76). Fifty-three percent of another group of sexual abuse victims reported that there was nothing in their lives that had more impact on them than being abused (see D. Zuckerman, "The Hurt That Keeps on Hurting," *Psychology Today* 18:11 [Nov. 1984]).

2. Common is not the same as natural. Common means it happens frequently. Natural means that is occurs in nature. But sexual abuse is very rare in other animals. See also R. Janoff-Bulman and I. Frieze, "Theoretical Perspective for Understanding Reactions to Victimization," *Journal of Social Issues* 39 (1983): 1–180.

3. A. Brown and D. Finkelhor, "Impact of Child Sexual Abuse: A Review of the Research," *Psychological Bulletin* 99:1 (Jan. 1986): 66–77; C. Courtois, *Healing the Incest Wound: Adult Survivors in Therapy* (New York: Norton, 1988); C. Courtois and D. Watts, "Counseling Adult Women Who Experienced Incest in Childhood or Adolescence," *Personnel and Guidance Journal* 60:5 (Jan. 1982): 275–79; W. Friedrich, A. Urquiza, and R. Beilke, "Behavioral Problems in Sexually Abused Young Children," *Journal of Pediatric Psychology* 11 (1986): 45–57; J. Herman and E. Schatzow, "Recovery and Verification of Memories of Childhood Sexual Trauma," *Psychoanalytic Psychology* 4 (1987): 1–4; P. Mrazek and D. Mrazek, "The Effects of Child Abuse: Methodological Considerations," in *Sexually Abused Children and Their Families,* edited by P. Mrazek and C. Kempe (Oxford, New York: Pergamon, 1981); D. Russell, *The Secret Trauma: Incest in the Lives of Girls and Women* (New York: Basic Books, 1986); C.P. Walsh, "The Self-concept and Sex-role Orientation of Adult Females in Therapy with and without Incest History," Ph.D. diss., University of Florida, Gainesville, 1986.

4. The majority of the personal stories involve nonviolent abuse. Sonny, Kevin, and Kent describe being assaulted as part of their history.

5. J. Hassol, Norfolk County Rape Unit workshop presentation, Dedham, Mass., 1978, as reported in L. Anderson, "Notes on the Linkage between the Sexually Abused Child and the Suicidal Adolescent," *Journal of Adolescence* 4:2 (June 1981): 147–62.

6. K. Meiselman, *Incest: A Psychological Study of Causes and Effects with Treatment Recommendations* (San Francisco: Jossey-Bass, 1978).

7. Zuckerman, "The Hurt That Keeps on Hurting."

8. A. Kohn, "Shattered Innocence," *Psychology Today* 21:2 (1987).

9. N. Ellerstein and J. Canavan, "Sexual Abuse of Boys," *American Journal of Diseases of Children* 134:3 (March 1980): 255–57.

10. A. DeJong, G. Emmett, and A. Hervada, "Sexual Abuse of Children," *Journal of Diseases of Children* 136 (Feb. 1982): 129–34.

11. D. Finkelhor, *Sexually Victimized Children* (New York: Free Press, 1979).

12. Courtois, *Healing the Incest Wound;* Walsh, "Self-concept and Sex-role Orientation."

13. Russell, *The Secret Trauma.*

14. Ibid.

15. Greg, Jim, Al, Kent, Kevin, Henry, and Sonny all describe abuse from more than one person.

16. All of the authors of the personal stories were abused by someone they knew.

17. R. Summit, "The Child Sexual Abuse Accommodation Syndrome," *Child Abuse and Neglect* 7:2 (1983): 182. As Kempe and Kempe point out, only one-third of those who sexually abuse children are nonparental perpetrators; the other two-thirds are biological parents and nonrelated parental figures (see R. Kempe and C. Kempe, *The Common Secret: Sexual Abuse of Children and Adolescents* [New York: Freeman, 1984], p.16). Groth reported that in the cases he studied, 29 percent of the offenders were males unknown to the victim (see N. Groth, "Sexual Trauma in the Life Histories of Rapists and Child Molesters," *Victimology: An International Journal* 4 [1979]). Petrovich and Templer found in their 1984 study that women offenders who were strangers to the boy victim accounted for 5 percent of their cases (see M. Petrovich and D. Templer, "Heterosexual Molestation of Children Who Later Become Rapists," *Psychological Reports* 54 [1984]:810). Again, the majority of the abusers were people the victim knew or was related to.

18. Meiselman, *Incest.*

19. M. Symonds, "The 'Second Injury' to Victims," *Evaluation and Change* (1980): 36–38.

20. Anderson, "Notes on the Linkage"; Boy Scouts of America, *Child Abuse: Let's Talk about It* (Irving, Tex.: B.S.A., 1986); Courtois, *Healing the Incest Wound;* M. de Young, "Incest Victims and Offenders: Myths and Realities," *Journal of Psychosocial Nursing and Mental Health Services* 9(1)(1981): 61–71; Kempe and Kempe, *The Common Secret;* J. Peters, "Children Who Are Victims of Sexual Assault and the Psychology of Offenders," *American Journal of Psychotherapy* 30 (1976): 398–421.

21. Courtois, *The Common Secret.*

22. See Al's and Kent's stories.

23. American Humane Association, 1978, as reported in D. Finkelhor, *Child Sexual Abuse: New Theory and Research* (New York: Free Press, 1984).

24. G. Awad, "Father-Son Incest: A Case Report," *Journal of Nervous and Mental Diseases* 162 (1976): 135–39.

25. See Henry's story, where he describes choosing boys who were lonely to molest.

26. Anderson, "Notes on the Linkage."

27. Courtois, *The Common Secret.*

28. Ibid.; Summit, "Child Sexual Abuse Accommodation."

29. Peters, "Children Who Are Victims."

30. C. Rogers and T. Terry, "Clinical Intervention with Boy Victims of Sexual Abuse," in *Victims of Sexual Aggression,* edited by I.R. Stewart and I.G. Greer (New York: Van Nostrand Reinhold, 1984).
31. Finkelhor, *Child Sexual Abuse.*
32. Landis, "Experiences of 500 Children."
33. David Walters, *Physical and Sexual Abuse of Children: Causes and Treatment* (Bloomington: Indiana University Press, 1975).
34. Kempe and Kempe, *The Common Secret.*
35. Walters, *Physical and Sexual Abuse of Children.*

4. Life Areas Affected by Childhood Sexual Abuse

1. J. Crewdson, *By Silence Betrayed: Sexual Abuse of Children in America* (Boston: Little, Brown, 1988).
2. N. Ellerstein and J. Canavan, "Sexual Abuse of Boys," *American Journal of Diseases of Children* 134:3 (March 1980): 255–57.
3. R. Kempe and C. Kempe, *The Common Secret: Sexual Abuse of Children and Adolescents* (New York: Freeman, 1984).
4. K. Swink and A. Leveille, "From Victim to Survivor: A New Look at the Issues and Recovery Process for Adult Incest Survivors." *Women and Therapy* 5 (Summer/Fall 1986): 119–41.
5. Daniel's story mentions drug abuse; Richard identifies compulsive sexual behavior as a problem; Allen reports compulsive eating and being overweight; Kevin, Sonny and Greg report compulsive eating, being overweight, and compulsive sexual behavior; Kent reports several compulsive behaviors, including sex; and Tony is recovering from chemical dependency.
6. A. Kohn, "Shattered Innocence," *Psychology Today* 21:2 (1987).
7. A. Reber, *A Dictionary of Psychology* (New York: Viking Press, 1985).
8. Kohn, "Shattered Innocence."
9. See Al's and Jim's stories for examples.
10. E. Bass and L. Thornton, eds., *I Never Told Anyone: Writing for Women Survivors of Child Sexual Abuse* (New York: Harper and Row, 1983).
11. Swink and Leveille, "From Victim to Survivor."
12. M. Barry and A. Johnson, "The Incest Barrier," *Psychoanalytic Quarterly* 27 (1958): 485–500; D. Finkelhor, "What's Wrong with Sex between Adults and Children?" *American Journal of Orthopsychiatry* 49:4 (Oct. 1979); D. Finkelhor, *Child Sexual Abuse: New Theory and Research* (New York: Free Press, 1984); J.L. Herman, *Father-Daughter Incest* (Cambridge, Mass.: Harvard University Press, 1981).
13. Barry and Johnson, "The Incest Barrier." The same holds true for a mature homosexual love relationship.
14. Herman, *Father-Daughter Incest.*

15. T. Sandfort, "Sex in Pedophiliac Relationships: An Empirical Investigation among a Nonrepresentative Group of Boys," *Journal of Sex Research* 20:2 (May 1984): 123–42.

16. On occasion I have had people argue this point with me by constructing scenarios in which the child is ultimately responsible for the sexual contact. The enormous effort these people expend to formulate such situations only reinforces my belief that children are blameless for sexual contact with adults. Once we have taken effective steps to reduce the frequency of the obvious cases of child sexual abuse, then we can afford to expend our energy debating the fine distinctions and the "what ifs."

17. Ellerstein and Canavan, "Sexual Abuse of Boys."

18. Finkelhor, *Child Sexual Abuse.*

19. See Jim's story.

20. Kohn, "Shattered Innocence."

21. American Psychiatric Association, *Diagnostic and Statistical Manual of Mental Disorders,* 3d ed., rev. (Washington, D.C.: A.P.A., 1987). An automaton is a robot, or someone who behaves in a mechanical manner. Some people say this state is like being on "automatic pilot."

22. See Al's, Allen's and Greg's stories.

23. APA, *Diagnostic and Statistical Manual,* 3d ed.

24. V. Saltman and R. Solomon, "Incest and Multiple Personality," *Psychological Reports* 50 (1982): 1127–41. Saltman and Solomon reviewed 125 articles on MPD and found that a majority of the articles described people with incest in their backgrounds. Another researcher reported a history of childhood sexual abuse in three-fourths of the multiple personality disorder cases he studied (see R. Schultz, address at the Second International Conference on Multiple Personality/Dissociative States, [Chicago, Ill., 1986]).

25. Saltman and Solomon, "Incest and Multiple Personality."

26. R. Silver, C. Boon, and M. Stones, "Searching for Meaning in Misfortune: Making Sense of Incest," *Journal of Social Issues* 39:2 (1983): 81–102.

27. In the 1960s experiments were done in which dogs were given electric shock that they could neither avoid nor escape. They developed what the researchers termed "learned helplessness" such that even when the circumstances were modified so the dogs could escape, they showed a much poorer escape response than did dogs who had never acquired helplessness (J. Overmeir and M. Seligman, "Effects of Inescapable Shock upon Subsequent Escape and Avoidance Learning," *Journal of Comparative and Physiological Psychology* [1967] 23–33; M. Seligman and S. Maier, "Failure to Escape Traumatic Shock," *Journal of Experimental Psychology* 74 [1967]: 1–9). I conceptualize the victim mentality as a form of learned helplessness.

28. R. Janoff-Bulman and I. Frieze, "Theoretical Perspective for Understanding Reactions to Victimization," *Journal of Social Issues* 39 (1983): 1–18.

29. Swink and Leveille, "From Victim to Survivor."

30. APA, *Diagnostic and Statistical Manual,* 3d ed., pp. 347, 349, 353, 354.

31. I am not suggesting that child sexual abuse is the only reason one develops such personality disorders.

32. APA, *Diagnostic and Statistical Manual,* 3d ed., p. 232.
33. Herman, *Father-Daughter Inest.*
34. APA, *Diagnostic and Statistical Manual,* 3d ed., p. 250.
35. See Tony's story.
36. S.K. Weinberg, *Incest Behavior* (New York: Citadel, 1955.
37. K. Meiselman, *Incest: A Psychosocial Study of Causes and Effects with Treatment Recommendations* (San Francisco: Jossey-Bass, 1978). Meiselman points out that when a historical and global view is taken, it is clear that although sexual contact between adults and children takes place, most cultures do not view it as appropriate behavior:

> The taboo on nuclear family incest *is* more or less universal. The exceptions that are so frequently listed often serve to distract the reader from apprehending the truly remarkable degree of regularity with which nuclear family incest is prohibited. Of the thousands of cultural groupings that we have knowledge of, both past and present, only a few have been shown to permit nuclear family incest of any kind, and these groups have stopped far short of allowing intrafamilial promiscuity. Incestuous marriages have almost always been restricted to brother-sister marriages within a privileged group, and incest during magical rites has been condoned in a few societies that hold to strict incest rules most of the time. Murdock (1949) surveyed 250 primitive societies that had been thoroughly studied by anthropologists and reported that *all* of them banned nuclear family incest.

38. N. Lukianowicz, "Incest I: Paternal Incest; Incest II: Other Types of Incest," *British Journal of Psychiatry* 120 (1972): 310–13; I. Kaufman, A. Peck, and C. Tagiuri, "The Family Constellation and Overt Incestuous Relationships between Father and Daughter," *American Journal of Orthopsychiatry* 24 (1954).
39. P. Gebhard, *Sex Offenders: An Analysis of Types* (New York: Harper and Row, 1965).
40. Meiselman, *Incest,* p.111.
41. Reber, *A Dictionary of Psychology.*
42. Ibid.
43. APA, *Diagnostic and Statistical Manual,* 3d ed.
44. A. Reber, *A Dictionary of Psychology.* See Al's Story.
45. G. Kaufman, *Shame: The Power of Caring* (Cambridge, Mass.: Schenkman, 1980); M. Fossum and M. Mason, *Facing Shame* (New York: Norton, 1986).
46. Meiselman, *Incest.*
47. J. McKechnie, ed., *Webster's New Universal Unabridged Dictionary,* 2d ed. (Cleveland: Simon and Schuster, 1983).
48. R. B. Adams, personal communication, 1989.
49. See Henry's story, in which Henry describes the self-abuse of his penis, particularly his foreskin.
50. C. Courtois, *Healing the Incest Wound: Adult Survivors in Therapy* (New York: Norton, 1988); M. de Young, "Self-injurious behavior in incest Vic-

tims: A research note," *Child Welfare* 61 (8) (Nov/Dec, 1982) 577–84.; A. Favazza, *Bodies under Siege: Self-mutilation in Culture and Psychiatry* (Baltimore: Johns Hopkins University Press, 1987).

51. See Tony's story.
52. Herman, *Father-Daughter Incest.*
53. J. Briere and M. Runtz, "Suicidal Thoughts and Behaviors in Former Sexual Abuse Victims," *Canadian Journal of Behavioral Science* 18 (1986): 413–23.
54. Herman, *Father-Daughter Incest.*
55. See K. Swink and A. Leveille, "From Victim to Survivor: A New Look at the Issues and Recovery Process for Adult Incest Survivors," *Women and Therapy* 5 (Summer/Fall 1986): 119–41. Even this figure is probably low for the reasons discussed earlier.
56. Silver, Boon, and Stones, "Searching for Meaning."
57. R. Johnson and D. Shrier, "Sexual Victimization of Boys: Experience at an Adolescent Medicine Clinic," *Journal of Adolescent Health Care* 6:5 (1985): 372–76.
58. APA, *Diagnostic and Statistical Manual,* 3d ed.; S.H. Kaplan, *The New Sex Therapy: Active Treatment of Sexual Dysfunctions* (New York: Brunner/Mazel, 1974); A. Reber, *A Dictionary of Psychology.*
59. Courtois, *Healing the Incest Wound.*
60. The Kinsey Institute reported that 9 percent of a sample of men who had been imprisoned for rape had been sexual with their sisters, aunts, or mothers (see Gebhard, *Sex Offenders).* Another study reported that 44 percent of the men referred to a sex offender treatment group had been sexually abused as boys (S. Carlson, "The Development of a Therapy Model for Sex Offenders," unpublished position paper for St. Mary's College Graduate Program, Minneapolis, 1983). In their study of eighty-three incarcerated men who were convicted of raping women, Petrovich and Templer found that 59 percent of them had been molested as children by women (see M. Petrovich and D. Templer, "Heterosexual Molestation of Children Who Later Become Rapists," *Psychosocial Reports* 54 [1984]: 810). In 77 percent of these cases there was more than one occasion of abuse; the abuse took place when the child was between the ages of four and sixteen, with the average age being about ten. In 82 percent of the cases there was sexual intercourse. The offenders were neighbors, mothers, grandmothers, strangers, baby-sitters, aunts, teachers, friends of the family, a sister, a foster mother, and a probation officer. Some therapists believe that all sex offenders have been sexually abused as children and do not report it because of their denial and repression (R.B. Adams, personal communication, 1989).
61. M. Hunter, "The Membership Demographics of the Self-help Group Sex Addicts Annonymous," master's thesis, University of Wisconsin, Superior, 1984.
62. M. de Young, "Counterphobic Behavior in Multiply Molested Children," *Child Welfare* 63:4 (July/Aug. 1984): 333–39.
63. One weakness with the use of the term *phobia* is that often phobias are thought to be *irrational* fears, and it is in fact highly rational to be afraid of a situation that replicates a traumatic experience.

64. Finkelhor, *Child Sexual Abuse.*
65. APA, *Diagnostic and Statistical Manual,* 3d ed.
66. See Henry's story.
67. M. Jakubiak and S. Murphy, "Incest Survivors in Women's Communities," *Human Development* 8 (1987): 1381–85.
68. Courtois, *Healing the Incest Wound.*

5. Recovery Issues

1. Although the problem of sexual abuse has been around a long time, the study of it is relatively new, and there is a lack of data concerning treatment approaches. For example, in the index of one book on child sexual abuse, the index lists under the topic of treatment: "agency cooperation," "community response," and "(treatment) of offenders" (see D. Finkelhor, *Child Sexual Abuse: New Theory and Research* [New York: Free Press, 1984]). Out of 239 pages of text, a total of six pages (2.5 percent) are concerned with treatment. In Meiselman's book on incest, thirty pages (8.5 percent) address treatment (see K. Meiselman, *Incest: A Psychological Study of Causes and Effects with Treatment Recommendations* [San Francisco: Jossey-Bass, 1978]). Many of the therapists who supervised me when I was an intern learned how to treat sexual abuse victims from their clients and/or through informal discussions with other therapists. Although neither of these methods is very scientific or efficient, this approach, unfortunately, is the best we have.
2. Finkelhor, *Child Sexual Abuse.*
3. *Webster's Third New International Dictionary* (Springfield, Mass.: Merriam, 1971).
4. McKechnie, ed., *Webster's New Universal Unabridged Dictionary,* 2d ed. (Cleveland: Simon and Schuster, 1983).
5. C. Barnhart and J. Stein, eds., *The American College Dictionary* (New York: Random House, 1962).
6. Janoff-Bulman and I. Frieze, "Theoretical Perspective for Understanding Reactions to Victimization," *Journal of Social Issues* 39 (1983):1-18; R. Bulman and C. Wortman, "Attributions of Blame and Coping in the 'Real World': Severe Accident Victims React to Their Lot," *Journal of Personality and Social Psychology* 35 (1977): 351-63.
7. K. Swink and A. Leveille, "From Victim to Survivor: A New Look at the Issues and Recovery Process for Adult Incest Survivors," *Women and Therapy* 5 (Summer/Fall 1986): 119-41; C. Courtois, *Healing the Incest Wound: Adult Survivors in Therapy* (New York: Norton, 1988).
8. The First Step in Alcoholics Anonymous is this: "We admitted that we were powerless over alcohol—that our lives had become unmanageable" (Alcoholics Anonymous, *Twelve Steps and Twelve Traditions* [New York: AA World Services, 1953]). Some groups addressing sexual abuse have adapted this for their purposes to read, "We admitted that we were powerless over

sexual abuse (or compulsive sexual behavior)—that our lives had become unmanageable."

9. Step Eight, AA, *Twelve Steps.*

10. See M. Hunter, *The Twelve Steps and Shame,* for more details on how Twelve-Step groups can be useful in healing shame.

11. Swink and Leveille, "From Victim to Survivor."

12. M. Symonds, "The 'Second Injury' to Victims," *Evaluation and Change* (1980): 36–38.

13. E. Kubler-Ross, *On Death and Dying* (New York: Macmillan, 1969).

14. See Al's and Allen's stories.

15. See Kevin's and Tony's stories.

16. M. Lew, *Victims No Longer: Men Recovering from Incest and Other Sexual Child Abuse* (New York: Nevraumont, 1988), p. 300.

17. Swink and Leveille, "From Victim to Survivor."

18. McKechnie, *Webster's Unabridged Dictionary.*

19. When putting a letter in the mailbox, make sure you don't put any identifying information on or in it. I called the postal service and was told that envelopes that are not deliverable are opened to see whether there is any information within to help make delivery possible. If you are going to put a letter in a mailbox, write on the envelope "Not Mail—Destroy."

20. Women tend to become sad prior to getting angry. Men frequently have a more difficult time finding sadness.

21. E. Bass and L. Davis, *The Courage to Heal: A Guide for Women Survivors of Child Sexual Abuse* (New York: Harper and Row, 1988).

22. Symonds, "The 'Second Injury.' "

23. Swink and Leveille, "From Victim to Survivor."

24. A. Meissner, instructor, Intensive post-graduate training program, Gestalt Institute of the Twin Cities (I attended Ms. Meissner's class in October of 1988).

25. T. Fitzgibbons, "The Cognitive and Emotive Uses of Forgiveness in the Treatment of Anger," *Psychotherapy* 23 (1986): 629–33.

26. Ibid.

27. Swink and Leveille, "From Victim to Survivor."

28. C. Adams-Tucker, "A Socioclinical Overview of 28 Sex-abused Children," *Child Abuse and Neglect* 5:3 (1981): 361–67.

29. Swink and Leveille, "From Victim to Survivor."

30. You may want to send your family members a copy of this book or other material on sexual abuse as part of the process of telling them. Always remember that regardless of how respectfully you tell the secret, you cannot control another's response.

31. The Twelfth Step is "Having had a spiritual awakening as a result of these steps, we tried to carry this message to others, and to practice these principles in all our affairs." (Al-Anon, *Living with an Alcoholic with the Help of Al-Anon* [New York: Al-Anon Family Group Headquarters, 1978]).

6. Healing the Affected Areas of Your Life

1. E. Gil, *Outgrowing the Pain: A Book for and about Adults Abused as Children* (Walnut Creek, Calif.: Launch Press, 1983).
2. P. Gebhard, *Sex Offenders: An Analysis of Types* (New York: Harper & Row, 1965); S.K. Weinberg, *Incest Behavior* (New York: Citadel, 1955).
3. M. Symonds, "The 'Second Injury' to Victims," *Evaluation and Change* (1980): 36–38.
4. K. Meiselman, *Incest: A Psychological Study of Causes and Effects with Treatment Recommendations* (San Francisco: Jossey-Bass, 1978), p. 345.
5. K. Swink and A. Leveille, "From Victim to Survivor: A New Look at the Issues and Recovery Process for Adult Incest Survivors," *Women and Therapy* 5 (Summer/Fall 1986): 119–41.
6. A. Kohn, "Shattered Innocence," *Psychology Today* 21:2 (1987).
7. W. Goodman, personal communication, 1986.
8. Alcoholics Anonymous, *Twelve Steps and Twelve Traditions* (New York: AA World Services, 1953); M. Hunter *The Twelve Steps and Shame* (Center City, Minn.: Mazeldon Educational Materials, 1988).
9. AA, *Twelve Steps.*
10. AA, *Alcoholics Anonymous* (New York: AA World Services, 1939).
11. Narcotics Anonymous, *Narcotics Anonymous* (Los Angeles: C.A.R.E.N.A. Publishing, 1982).
12. See Katherine's and Greg's stories.
13. For information on sexuality and spirituality, see J. Nelson, *Embodiment: An Approach to Sexuality and Christian Theology* (New York: Pilgrim Press, 1978).
14. D. Gelinas, "The Persisting Negative Effects of Incest," *Psychiatry* 46 (1983): 313–32.
15. Considering the frequency of sexual abuse in our society, any therapist who has worked with more than a handful of people has worked with a sexual abuse victim; whether he or she focused on that issue in the therapy is another story. See C. Courtois and D. Watts, "Counseling Adult Women Who Experienced Incest in Childhood or Adolescence," *Personnel and Guidance Journal* (1982): 275–79.
16. See Katherine's story.
17. Allen, Greg, and Kevin all fathered children who lived with them, and they did not sexually abuse them. Only one of the men, Henry, abused any children.

7. Greg's Story: The Son They Never Had

1. Notice that although Greg had been writing in the past tense, as he began to write about the abuse experience he started to use the present tense. This tense

change is common when victims talk about their abuse. Dissociation is a nearly universal response to sexual abuse, and victims regularly drift in and out of trance states when discussing or, in this case, writing about abuse. Greg is describing his experience with a formal hypnotic trance, but during his therapy he regularly went into a trance spontaneously and regressed without the use of hypnotic ritual.

2. Here Greg is exhibiting a classic symptom of abuse—his memory of the experience is highly depersonalized. The sexual abuse is being done to someone who looks like him, but the "real Greg" is in the impossible position of hovering up in the corner of the ceiling, out of harm's way. These bizarre distortions help to cushion the victim against the full impact of what happened. For example, Greg is unable to see what is happening because Grandpa's body is blocking his view. Although these images lessen the trauma of recalling the abuse, their unusual nature can cause the victim to wonder whether he is insane or to have difficulty in trusting his memory.

8. Katherine's Story

1. Many partners of sexual abuse victims are relieved finally to have a term to help them understand the dynamics in their relationship.

2. You can see that Katherine too has a victim mentality. She blames herself for all of the difficulties in the marriage. It is understandable that two incest victims would become a couple, since they both have the same type of family rules and view of the world.

3. Co-SA is a mutual-help group based on the adapted Twelve Steps of Alcoholics Anonymous and is for the partners of sexually compulsive people (see chapter 20).

4. Katherine was used to this type of treatment since her stepfather repeatedly told her that she did not measure up.

5. Once Katherine's denial about her own sexual abuse lessened, she too had similar experiences when they were sexual. She would suddenly begin crying and trying to "protect" herself.

6. One of Katherine's struggles in her therapy was to accept her body. She became anxious whenever she wore colorful, fashionable clothing or dresses: she was afraid to wear anything that might call attention to herself or her body. So, she worked with the other group members to practice dressing differently and being comfortable with this change.

7. Katherine was shocked the first time someone suggested that what her stepfather was doing was abusive. She rationalized that the lack of physical touch meant that no real abuse had taken place. Once she came to accept this behavior as abusive, her fear level about life in general greatly lessened. Once her fear decreased, she began to notice her anger at her stepfather, mother, and husband. She used this anger to set appropriate limits with them.

8. As Katherine said when she first joined the group, she was unable to speak. Whenever the group's attention was on her, she would sob and be frozen with

fear. She grew into an active and assertive member of the group, whose opinions were highly valued by the other group members. She became assertive with her husband, in-laws, and family. She obtained employment with higher pay and more responsibility. At one point she discovered that one of her children was being mistreated in day care. She and her husband believed their child and took appropriate action to protect the child, breaking the chain of abuse and neglect. Katherine and Greg protected their child in a way that their own parents had not protected them.

9. The Story of Sonny Hall

1. Sonny's depression may not have lifted because neither he nor his first therapist was addressing what could have been a major cause of his depressed mood—his history of abuse.
2. When these sudden floods of sensations, images, and emotions come, they can be terribly frightening. It is important when addressing your history of sexual abuse that you have an active support system in place. This group should be made up of people who know what you are dealing with and are willing to get late-night phone calls. Keep them up to date so you don't have to explain what you are experiencing when you are in the middle of a flashback.

10. Ruth's Story: Falling Together

1. This illustrates why it is important for partners to have access to a group of their own. Ruth needed a safe place to vent her emotions. Sonny was too angry with women and too preoccupied with his pain to be very supportive of her.

11. Al's Story

1. Victimized people often wonder if they are reporting a memory or merely a fantasy. I think that having physical reactions to the thoughts is a clear clue that what the person is describing actually took place and is not a figment of his imagination.
2. You will notice that when Al is describing events he includes many details about the setting in which the event took place. He does this because he was taught that recalling these details helps him to retrieve other, more painful memories and helps him to trust his recall better.
3. As Al writes about this occurrence, his use of past and present tense changes. It is as if part of the time he is reexperiencing the incident and at other times he is merely reporting a past event. This frequently happens when people describe their abuse.

4. Here is an example of the neglect that is usually associated with sexual abuse. This child has just been sexually assaulted in his own home, by a relative. He is dazed, dissociated, and perhaps physically injured, yet no family member takes notice of his condition. He is ignored, his trauma overlooked. This neglect can be more abusive than the actual assault.

5. Recently Al received a letter from his mother stating that she "came from an incestuous family."

6. It is common for abuse victims to report their memory of a traumatic event as an out-of-body experience.

7. Notice how Al validates his own abuse by reminding himself that others have been abused or have symptoms of abuse.

8. Al is describing a dissociative response or negative hallucination.

9. You can see from this list of symptoms why it is not surprising that many sexual abuse victims think they are "crazy." Unfortunately, many professionals also see victims as insane, so they treat only the symptoms and never address the underlying cause.

12. Allen's Story

1. Allen's fear that he was "going crazy" is a common one for those who have been sexually abused. Since the memories often come back in fragments, or as he calls them, "slides," they are more difficult to focus on than are normal thoughts, and they therefore seem "crazy." In addition, he is describing how many of his memories came back as physical sensations, such as feeling fingers around his throat or his rectum contracting. These sensations are frightening since they seem to come from nowhere and the person experiencing them has a sense of being out of control.

2. Notice how up to this point Allen has been writing in the first person. He has a pattern of speaking in the second person when he is discussing a particularly painful experience.

3. For more information on how Twelve-Steps groups help in the healing process see Hunter, *The Twelve Steps and Shame* (Hazelden Foundation, 1988).

13. Daniel's Story

1. This type of less overt sexual abuse is often overlooked by therapists and by those who experienced it. There is a role reversal taking place: rather than his needing her, she is needing him. Daniel is being used by his mother. He is being placed in a role that is not his to fill; he is a boy and her son, yet she treats him as a man, an equal, and in a romantic fashion. It is no wonder that he begins to view her as sexual object.

2. I'm sure that she did know and merely did not speak about it.

3. Many people would not see this as abusive. They would focus on Daniel's excitement as a sign that it was not abuse and would overlook his fear or even find it funny. However, many of these same people, when faced with the case of a girl being treated the same way by a man twice her age, her mother's lover, would then see the situation as abusive.

4. I think it is more likely that *he* didn't know what he wanted. I think it is clear what she wants.

5. Again, if you are having trouble seeing Daniel as a victim, imagine your reaction to a sixteen-year-old girl having her first sexual experience with her stepfather who is twice her age.

6. It is common for victims to begin actively seeking out sex. This behavior is seen by some as evidence that the child was not negatively affected by the sexual contact with an adult. I believe that this shows a lack of understanding of victim/abuse dynamics.

7. Daniel's father is neglecting him by not protecting him.

8. Regardless of who is the "winner," she is abusing him by setting him up as his father's rival.

9. As you can see, contrary to the stereotype, Daniel is not looking back fondly at the woman who "taught him about sex," "turned a boy into a man," nor thinking how "lucky he was to score at that age." He is angry about the way he was used by an adult for her sexual gratification.

10. Many abuse victims end up in disrespectful adult relationships. Daniel's relationship with this woman has echos of his relationships with his mother and his stepmother: it is based on sex, he is not the only male she is being sexual with, and he has a sense of powerlessness.

11. Daniel's disclosure of incest is met with two common responses. His therapist takes it "seriously" yet does not see it as serious enough to be a focus of the therapy. Daniel's wife, on the other hand, blames him for the sexual contact. Perhaps Daniel divorced the wrong woman. Maybe it was his stepmother he needed to "divorce."

12. Even if he had done things to encourage and invite the sexual contact, it is the responsibility of the adults to set limits. Children and teenagers encourage adults to do many irresponsible things, like spend money on them inappropriately, let them smoke, or stay home from school to avoid tests, but it is the duty of the parent or guardian to be responsible.

13. This statement sums up the issue of sexual abuse. It is not the contact that is hurtful, it is the meaning of the contact that is significant.

14. Considering how common sexual abuse is in our society one could argue that what happened to Daniel and the other men in this book is "normal." Perhaps it would be useful to replace the word *normal* with *healthy:* "I have had a difficult time believing that my feelings are *healthy.* What wasn't *healthy* was the depriving and ignoring of my needs as a child. What wasn't *healthy* was the meeting of these needs by a mother who used me as a surrogate husband to meet her emotional needs and a stepmother who used me as a sexual object. I have to keep telling myself that my feelings and needs for love and affection are *healthy,* and I can have them met in healthy ways."

14. Henry's Story

1. You may notice that Henry's story has a "flavor" to it different from the other stories. This may be because Henry has to recover not only from his childhood sexual abuse but also from his offender mentality. Your reaction to his story may be different from that which you had to the other stories.
2. It is common for a victimized child who was set up to touch an adult sexually to believe that the adult is unaware of what is taking place, that the child is "getting away" with something. Often the adult will pretend to be asleep.
3. You will see that during Henry's childhood years his emphasis is on relationship while the older person's focus is sex. When he became an adult, his concentration shifted from relationship to sex. When a victimized person realizes that the relationship was not special to the abuser, he will experience a great sense of betrayal, with feelings of hurt and anger. The victimized person often says, "How could I have been so foolish to believe that he [she] really cared about me?"
4. Henry's body shame is not eliminated merely by seeing that there are many others like him. He still believes that he is somehow defective. When people wonder if they are "normal," they usually are wondering if they are acceptable.
5. This is the beginning of a long pattern of setting others up to abuse them sexually.
6. Henry's father is acting as if he is not aware that his son is being sexual with the dog, just as he led Henry to believe that he was not aware that Henry was touching his penis. This pretending that "nothing unusual is happening" is common in sexually abusive families. It leads children to question their view of reality, and they often wonder "what is *really* happening?"
7. It is common for victimized persons to neglect or abuse their sexual organs or any part of their body that represents the abuse.
8. Henry is caught up in a cycle. He feels ashamed and turns to sex for momentary relief, but he then feels ashamed of the sexual acts he has taken part in. When sex is the only way a person knows to nurture himself, he is likely to develop a sexually compulsive life-style.
9. Ironically, Henry's father justifies the rape of his son by claiming it is a lesson to teach him to be gentle with the calf.
10. Again, as is so common, Henry's father justifies his sexually abusive acts by calling them a lesson, giving the impression that he is doing his fatherly duty. He also pairs the abuse with some action that Henry does or doesn't perform so that it appears that Henry brought on the sex.
11. The lesson from all sexual abuse is shame.
12. Notice how Henry uses the word *let* as he described the situation. Just as when he was a child in his father's bed he now believes that he is being given a special treat by being "allowed" to touch his father's penis, the same penis that he is orally and anally assaulted with. Offenders and others who do not understand the nature of the victim mentality would point to Henry's fasci-

nation with his father's penis as proof that Henry is not being abused but rather wants to be sexual with his father.

13. In spite of being sexually assaulted by his father and sexually abused by his brother, Henry still saw his family as being close.

14. Henry recalls the charge as "indecent assault." He was found guilty and placed on one year of probation, which was dropped after three months. He received a pardon after one year. He was not required to obtain any form of treatment.

15. It is rare for boys who are sexually victimized over a long period of time to come from families where they received a great deal of attention and warmth. The boys Henry was setting up were lonely, and this loneliness made them easy targets for his presexual conditioning. They tolerated the sexual abuse in order to have a relationship with him, just as Henry had done with his offenders when he was a child.

16. One of the differences between being sexual with men and with boys is that Henry is inherently more powerful when he is being sexual with a child. Having sex with a peer puts him in a more vulnerable situation and is therefore more frightening.

17. Althought this doctor tells Henry that he won't be able to help him, he continues to charge Henry for another six months of sessions. This is another example of how Henry was mistreated by male authority figures and doesn't realize it. There may also have been a voyeuristic aspect to the doctor's desire to continue to meet with Henry.

18. Henry reported that he owned both adult and child pornography. His collection included fifty videotapes and movies, one hundred books, and more than two hundred photographs of him with others.

15. Jim's Story

1. Most of my clients contact me for problems other than sexual abuse. The presenting complaints may be depression, chemical abuse, poor school or work performance, or lack of intimacy or other relationship issues.

2. Jim has already identified several symptoms of sexual abuse: inability to identify or express emotions, a sense of being different from other people, thoughts of being "crazy," and an inability to recall large portions of his life.

3. Jim's father's absence played a significant role in setting Jim up to be starved for attention, particularly from a male. Later in his story you will see how Jim is willing to tolerate abuse in order to obtain a relationship with a male authority figure.

4. All of these experiences that Jim describes are examples of covert sexual abuse. The women are hiding the sexual nature of their actions. In addition, except for the last case, the women had more power than Jim: by being in the presence of his father, by being a paid caregiver chosen by his parents, by being significantly older, or by being his mother.

5. Just as many female rape victims have been told they should have "lain back and enjoyed it," many male victims of sexual maltreatment are told that not only were they not abused but they were in fact fortunate. This leads many boys to feel ashamed about feeling ashamed over something they "should" have enjoyed.

6. This is an other example of covert sexual abuse. This teacher is being sexual with these boys under the pretense of coaching their acting.

7. As you read on, notice how Jim does not trust his emotions. When he is afraid or nervous he will find reasons to explain away his emotions.

8. Although there is nothing inherently wrong with this action, it turns out to be the beginning of the covert presexual conditioning that child abusers often use to manipulate children.

9. Jim is being manipulated more and more to think of himself not only as "special" but also as different from other students. This will lead him to become more isolated from his peers and more dependent on Mr. James for attention and companionship.

10. This is all part of the covert presexual conditioning process. While in therapy Jim confused his willingness to go to his teacher's house to run an errand with asking to be abused. He said such things as "It's my fault for going over there in the first place."

11. The covert presexual conditioning is continuing. Slowly Jim is being manipulated to spend progressively more time with his teacher and to think of himself as a peer rather than a student.

12. Jim's parents do not seem to notice the unusual nature of Jim's relationship with his teacher. Jim was very angry with his parents for not noticing and taking action to protect him.

13. The issue is not whether he is homosexual or heterosexual, but rather, does he sexually abuse children. These are separate issues.

14. As you read this section, notice how the level of sexual explicitness is slowly increased. Roger never comes out and says, "I want pictures of you so I can masturbate to them." Instead, he slowly asks more and more of Jim.

15. This is an excellent example of the mental and emotional abuse components found in sexual abuse cases. Jim is being taught not to trust his assessment of the situation or his emotional response to it.

16. Again, Jim's parents do not question the nature of the relationship and the unusual request of Jim's schoolteacher to take their son alone to a distant city and pay his expenses.

17. The relationship is getting more sexual, but the covert nature of it is still intact. Roger does not ask for permission to be sexual and ignores Jim's resistance to his advances.

18. The implication is that the relationship is contingent on its being sexual. In other words, "Either you be sexual with me or the nice things I have been doing for you will stop."

19. Jim is confusing enjoying spending time with another man and being homosexual. He is also confusing the issue of homosexuality and sexual abuse. Even if Jim were gay, he is still being sexually abused since he is not in a peer

relationship. Roger is older and has money, a position of authority, and the stamp of approval from Jim's parents.

20. Again, it is important to point out that this is not a peer relationship. It is not two boys or young men discussing their developing sexuality. This is a form of voyeurism on Roger's part.

21. Jim would experience these symptoms as an adult when recalling the abuse. These sensations were part of what convinced him that he indeed had been abused.

22. Sex is tough enough for parents to talk about with their children, but the topic of sexual abuse is even more difficult. It is clear that Jim's mother suspected that something inappropriate was taking place, but her discomfort, her own history of sexually abusing Jim, and Jim's shame made it unlikely that Jim would turn to her for help. When Jim invited his mother and father into a therapy session and told them about how he had been abused by Roger, they both said that they had "worried that something like that was taking place" but were afraid to inquire too much for fear that their worst fears were true. When asked to be specific they reported that this worst fear was that Jim was homosexual. They said that they were relieved to learn that it had "only been sexual abuse." So their homophobia prevented them from taking action to protect their son.

---

16. Kent's Story

1. See chapter 20 to learn how to get in contact with this Twelve-Step group and to find books on the topic.

2. You can see how difficult it would be for Kent to believe his emotions and sense of what happened when everyone around him is discouraging him from trusting himself.

3. My research showed that 37.1 percent of the male and 65.2 percent of the female members of SAA reported that they had been sexually abused as children. As I have said earlier, I think male sexual abuse is greatly underidentified. In my clinical practice I find that easily 90 percent of the people I work with who are sexually compulsive were sexually abused as children (Hunter 1984).

4. Kent's memory is from the impossible vantage point of viewing himself from the ceiling. Although it is common for trauma victims to recall the event as an out-of-body experience, this makes it more difficult for such victims to trust the memory.

5. Notice how Kent's mother ignores his abuse by focusing on what the neighbors will think of the screaming. She does not make it clear that what is taking place is abusive, comfort him, or protect him.

6. A flashback is different from a regular memory in that the person experiences it as if it were actually occurring. In addition, flashbacks are often spontaneous and intrusive, constituting therefore very powerful and frightening events.

7. It is common for victims to feel guilty for seeming to be a burden to others.

8. It is clear why Kent's aunt was not interested in his learning more about how he was abused by his father, since she also had abused Kent and was protecting the family secret. My hypothesis is that both Kent's aunt and father were sexually abused when they were children.

9. Here is further evidence of the likelihood that Kent's father and aunt were also abused. It is common to find three generations or more of sexual abuse in one family.

10. As I wrote earlier, one of the factors determining how deeply a victimized person will be affected is how people around him or her respond to the abuse. This is an example of how the victim mentality is developed in children. The child reports her abuse to an authority figure and is ignored. Kent's sister learned that she is helpless to stop the abuse and that she is not considered important enough to have someone protect her. Even when Kent was an adult, those around him did not want to believe that he had been abused.

11. Here is an example of the double messages commonly found in sexually abusive families. Kent's father tells him that he'll never be a man and also that he was raping Kent in order to make a man out of him.

12. Abusive families often justify emotional, physical, and sexual abuse as a form of education or discipline, or they somehow label it as necessary and even desirable for a child to experience. When the child objects, the parents often label him as ungrateful for not appreciating their efforts to raise him properly.

13. Here is a time when Kent trusted his view of a situation. All he needed to know to take action was that "there was something really unusual about the situation." He didn't need further "proof"; his emotional reaction was enough for him.

17. Kevin's Story

1. Kevin is very fortunate because he has what most victims can only hope for: an eyewitness. Following the writing of his story, he had a therapy session with one of his siblings who confirmed everything he wrote. It was a very powerful moment for him to hear "I believe because I was there and I saw you being sexually abused."

2. Many people who were sexually abused assume that nobody else in their family has a similar history. However, they often find that there are several others who also have been abused and have kept it a secret from the rest of the family.

3. It is common in families where there is sexual abuse for the children to receive either no information or inaccurate information about sexuality.

4. As Kevin mentioned earlier, when he was being abused he was "spaced out," or emotionally numb. The first time he described the abuse to the group he spoke in a very detached manner. In order to heal he needed to experience the emotions associated with the abuse in the safe environment of the group.

5. Some "memories" of abuse come as physical sensations rather than as mental images.

6. Perhaps the most powerful aspect of that session for Kevin was the acceptance that he received from the other group members.
7. Notice how the dynamics of this relationship Kevin had with his mother. There is the secretness, the specialness, the sexual overtones.

18. Richard and the Perfect Life

1. As you have seen in several of the other stories, it is common for parents of sexually abused boys to be sexual abuse victims themselves. Rather than making the parents more aware of sexual abuse issues and more protective of the child, it often has the opposite effect: the parents overlook anything in the child's life that might remind them of their own sexual abuse.
2. C. Barnhart and J. Stein, eds., *The American College Dictionary* (New York: Random House, 1967).
3. His homosexuality.
4. "All or nothing"— extremes in thinking are common in dysfunctional families.

19. Tony's Story

1. A sponsor is a person within a Twelve-Step mutual-help group who acts as a guide for another recovering person.
2. Originally Tony agreed to leave the gun with me, the group's therapist. However, this seemed too threatening, and he gave it to his girlfriend instead. Considering that he was sexually abused by a male authority figure, it makes sense that Tony would have difficulty trusting a therapist with a valuable possession that is also a symbol of his power over life and death.
3. Although the sessions are numbered here, they do not indicate how much time was involved; only a portion of the sessions directly related to sexual abuse is included. Further, Tony would often take "breaks" in which he would use his group time to discuss topics other than sexual abuse. This allowed him to be in charge of the pace at which he disclosed to the group and of the level of emotions he experienced. This sense of being in charge of himself, what he told to whom and when, was an important part of his healing process.
4. Since writing his story, Tony has learned from questioning Frank that Frank also sexually abused Tony's brothers.
5. Frank is the owner of the ranch, so in addition to being an adult he is in the powerful position of being able to decide whether Tony would continue to remain on the ranch.
6. Tony is describing the covert presexual conditioning process that people who are planning to abuse a child often use to groom the child prior to any actual sexual contact.

7. One common dynamic of the presexual conditioning is the use of isolation and treating the child as "special" or different from others.

8. Therapy can be a very frightening process. The client is being asked to do the very opposite of what he has done for years in order to survive: to become aware of his emotions and memories, to trust others, and to talk openly about the abuse and its effects. It takes great courage to begin sexual abuse therapy.

9. Frank is getting Tony used to being physical with him. First came the "wrestling" and the "joking around" during Tony's showers; now, further, less public touch is taking place.

10. Tony is being punished for not doing what Frank wants him to do. Tony has been masterfully set up by Frank. Tony is isolated from the others boys, dependent on Frank to awaken him, and he spends most of his free time being Frank's special boy. You will see later that this process leads Tony to feel guilty and ashamed whenever he refuses Frank's desires.

11. One of the effects of Tony's sexual abuse is that he sexualizes anger: he uses a sexual term, *fucking*, whenever he is angry. This makes sense since as a youngster his first sexual experiences were paired with his being angry.

12. The earlier programming has paid off for Frank.

13. Tony is being hard on himself for the common symptom of emotional numbness when describing abusive experiences. As he proceeds in his recovery, this numbness is replaced by the ability to be empathic with others and to identify and express his emotions appropriately.

14. This session took place one year from Tony's original assessment session.

15. As you see, a great deal of repetition takes place when Tony is telling his story to the group. This redescribing of events numerous times allows him to accept them at a deeper level.

16. Victimized persons often believe that no one can grasp the intensity of their pain or truly understand what they went through. Groups help to reduce this sense of isolation and of being different.

17. Victims often look for signs of concern or goodness in those who are abusing them.

18. One month later.

19. In spite of Tony's protests, Frank reported that he thought that Tony enjoyed the sexual contact.

20. Tony's use of the phrase *right now* is important. Some part of him is aware that even though he is expressing hatred right now, he also has great affection for Frank.

21. Tony's desire for revenge is understandable and common at this stage of recovery.

22. It is common for the victim's anger and rage to be global and to be directed at everyone and everything.

23. Tony suffered with symptoms of depression throughout the early stages of his recovery.

24. Tony role-played what he would say and how he would respond to various things that Frank might say. The group helped him to identify ways in which

his victim mentality might make it less likely that he would get what he wanted out of the session.

25. Tony did not use the same language in the session with Frank he used in his writing, which he read in group. This is one of the advantages of writing: the victim can write whatever comes to mind, and he need not censor himself. This allows easier identification of emotions. In the session, Frank tried several methods of avoiding responsibility for the sexual abuse, including not remembering, minimizing, and rationalizing. Tony had role played each of these defenses and so was prepared to confront Frank each time he attempted to avoid taking responsibility for his actions. For example, when Frank stated that he didn't recall whether any sexual abuse had taken place, Tony replied, "I clearly remember it happening. I know what happened, and I live with the effects of it every day."

26. Unfortunately, although Frank states that he wants to help Tony, Frank was unwilling to get help for himself. Frank agreed in the session with Tony to get sex offender treatment for himself, but he never followed through. As you may have guessed, Tony was not Frank's only victim. Frank acknowledged that he had abused numerous boys in the same manner over many years.

27. Many people find it hard to believe that a victim can have love for the person(s) who abused him. In Tony's case, Frank was the closest thing to a father he had while growing up, and abusive attention was better than no attention at all.

28. It is this "all or nothing" thinking that made it difficult for Tony to hold his parents responsible for not protecting him or noticing the effects of the abuse and getting him some help. He was afraid that if he held his parents responsible for their actions that this meant that they were bad people and he couldn't love them. He struggled to learn that you can hate someone's behavior and still love the person. Again, writing is a method of exploring one's thoughts and emotions without the risk of saying something to someone that might cause harm rather than healing.

29. Tony's friend Taylor committed suicide on the ranch, and Tony found him.

30. Just as Tony repeatedly asked himself questions about the way Frank treated him, he also tried to understand what he had done that would cause his father to treat him the way he did.

31. Again, when Tony becomes angry he expresses it in a sexualized manner. Many survivors, at some time in their recovery, choose to eliminate the word *fuck* from their vocabulary as a way to break the connection between sex and anger.

Bibliography

Adams, P. and G. Roddey. "Language Patterns of Opponents to a Child Protection Program." *Child Psychiatry and Human Development* 11:3 (Spring 1981): 135–57.

Adams, R.B. Personal communication, 1989.

Adams-Tucker, C. "A Socioclinical Overview of 28 Sex-abused Children." *Child Abuse and Neglect* 5:3 (1981): 361–67.

———. "Proximate Effects of Sexual Abuse Childhood. A Report on 28 Children." *American Journal of Psychiatry* 139:10 (Oct. 1983): 1252–56.

———. "Defense Mechanisms Used by Sexually Abused Children." *Children Today* 34 (Jan.– Feb. 1985): 9–12.

Ageton, S. *Facts about Sexual Assault: A research Report for Adults Who Work with Teenagers*. Rockville, Md.: Department of Health and Human Services, 1985.

Al-Anon. *Living with an Alcoholic with the Help of Al-Anon*. New York: Al-Anon Family Group Headquarters, 1978.

Alcoholics Anonymous. *Alcoholics Anonymous*. New York: AA World Services, 1939.

———. *Twelve Steps and Twelve Traditions*. New York: AA World Services, 1953.

American Humane Association. *Highlights of the Official Child Neglect and Abuse Report, 1984*. Denver: American Association for Protecting Children, 1986.

American Psychiatric Association. *Diagnostic and Statistical Manual of Mental Disorders*. 3rd ed. Washington, D.C.: A.P.A., 1980.

———. *Diagnostic and Statistical Manual of Mental Disorders*. 3rd ed. rev. Washington, D.C.: A.P.A., 1987.

Anderson, L. "Notes on the Linkage between the Sexually Abused Child and the Suicidal Adolescent." *Journal of Adolescence*. 4:2 (June 1981): 147–62.

Anderson, L., and G. Shafer. "The Character-Disordered Family: A Community Treatment Model for Family Sexual Abuse." *American Journal of Orthopsychiatry* 49:3 (July 1979): 436–45.

Arroyo, W., S. Eth, and R. Pynoos. "Sexual Assault of a Mother by Her Preadolescent Son." *American Journal of Psychiatry* 141: 9 (Sept. 1984): 1107–8.

Awad, G. "Father-Son Incest: A Case Report." *Journal of Nervous and Mental Diseases* 162 (1976): 135–139.

Bagley, C. "Incest Behavior and the Incest Taboo." *Social Problems* 16: 4 (Spring 1969): 505–19.

Barnhart, C., and J. Stein, eds. *The American College Dictionary*. New York: Random House, 1962.

Barry, M., and A. Johnson. "The Incest Barrier." *Psychoanalytic Quarterly* 27 (1958): 485–500.

Barton, B., and A. Marshall. "Pivotal Partings: Forced Termination with a Sexually Abused Boy." *Clinical Social Work Journal* 14:2 (Summer 1986): 139–49.

Bass, E., and L. Davis. *The Courage to Heal: A Guide for Women Survivors of Child Sexual Abuse*. New York: Harper and Row, 1988.

Bass, E., and L. Thornton, eds. *I Never Told Anyone: Writing for Women Survivors of Child Sexual Abuse*. New York: Harper and Row, 1983.

Bear, E., and P. Dimock. *Adults Molested as Children: A Survivor Manual for Women and Men*. Orwell, Vt.: Safer Society Press, 1988.

Bell, A., and M. Weinberg. "Preliminary Data: Childhood and Adolescent Sexuality San Francisco Study." Bloomington, Ind.: Institute of Sex Research, n.d. Mimeo.

Bender, L., and A. Blau, "The Reaction of Children to Sexual Relations with Adults." *American Journal of Orthopsychiatry* 7 (1937): 500–18.

Bender, L., and A. Grugett. "A Follow-up Report on Children Who Had Atypical Sexual Experiences." *American Journal of Orthopsychiatry* 22 (1952): 825–37.

Benward, J., and J. Gerber. *Incest as a Causative Factor in Anti-social Behavior: An Exploratory Study*. New York: Odyssey Institute, 1975.

Bergeron, A. "La pédophile comme source d'éducation sexuelle." Paper presented at the International Symposium on Childhood and Sexuality. Montreal, Sept. 7–9, 1979.

Berry, Gail. "Incest: Some Clinical Variations on a Classical Theme." *Journal of the American Academy of Psychoanalysis*. 3:2 (1975): 151–61.

Besharow, D. "Doing Something about Child Abuse." *Harvard Journal of Law and Public Policy* 8 (1985): 539–89.

Bieber, I. *Homosexuality: A Psychoanalytical Study*. New York: Vintage, 1962.

Bixler, R.H. "Primate Mother-Son 'Incest.' " *Psychological Reports* 48 (1981): 531–36.

———. "The Incest Controversy." *Psychological Reports* 49 (1981): 267–83.

———. "The Multiple Meanings of Incest." *Journal of Sex Research*. 19:2 (May 1983): 197–201.

Boy Scouts of America. *Child Abuse: Let's Talk about It*. Irving, Tex.: B.S.A., 1986.

Brant, R., and V. Tisza, "The Sexually Misused Child." *American Journal of Orthopsychiatry* 47:1 (Jan. 1987): 80–90.

Briere, J., and M. Runtz. "Suicidal Thoughts and Behaviors in Former Sexual Abuse Victims." *Canadian Journal of Behavioral Science* 18 (1986): 413–23.

Brown, A., and D. Finkelhor. "Impact of Child Sexual Abuse: A Review of the Research." *Psychological Bulletin* 99:1 (Jan. 1986): 66–77.

Brown, S. "Clinical Illustrations of the Sexual Misuse of Girls." *Child Welfare* 58: 7 (July/Aug. 1979): 435–42.

Browning, D., and B. Boatman. "Incest: Children at Risk." *American Journal of Psychiatry* (Jan. 1977).

Bulman, R., and C. Wortman. "Attributions of Blame and Coping in the 'Real World': Severe Accident Victims React to Their Lot." *Journal of Personality and Social Psychology* 35 (1977): 351–63.

Burgess, A. "Intra-familial Sexual Abuse." *Nursing Care of Victims of Family Violence,* edited by J. Campbell and J. Humpreys. Reston, Va.: Reston Publishing, 1984.

Burgess, A, ed. *Child Pornography and Sex Rings.* Lexington, Mass.: Lexington Books, 1984.

Burgess, A., H. Davidson, A. Groth, K. MacFarlane, and S. Sgroi. "Responding Panel: The Sexual Victimology of Youth." In *Proceedings of the First National Conference on Child Sexual Victimization.* Washington, D.C.: Children's Hospital National Medical Center, 1979.

Burgess, A., A. Groth, L. Homstrom, and S. Sgroi. *Sexual Assault of Children and Adolescents.* Lexington, Mass.: Lexington Books, 1978.

Burgess, A., and L. Homstrom. "Rape Trauma Syndrome." *American Journal of Psychiatry* 131 (1974): 981–86.

———. "Adaptive Strategies and Recovery from Rape." *American Journal of Psychiatry* 136 (1979) 1278–82.

———. "Sexual Trauma of Children and Adolescents." *Nursing Clinics of North America* 26:4 (Nov. 1979).

Burgess, A.W., C.R. Hartman, M.P. McCausland, and P. Powers. "Response Patterns in Children and Adolescents Exploited through Sex Rings and Pornography." *American Journal of Psychiatry* 141:5 (May 1984): 656–62.

Butler, S. *Conspiracy of Silence: The Trauma of Incest.* San Francisco: New Glide, 1978.

Carlson, S. "The Development of a Therapy Model for Sex Offenders." Unpublished position paper for St. Mary's College Graduate Program. Minneapolis, 1983.

Carmen, E., P. Rieker, and T. Mills. "Victims of Violence and Psychiatric Illness." *American Journal of Psychiatry* 143 (1984): 378–83.

Cohen, J. "Theories of Narcissism and Trauma." *American Journal of Psychotherapy* 35:1 (Jan. 1981): 93–100.

Cohen, T. "The Incestuous Family Revisited." *Social Casework* 64 (March 1983): 154–61.

Cohen, Y. "The Dissappearance of the Incest Taboo." *Human Nature* 6 (1978): 72–78.

Collins, J., W. Hamlin, M. Minor, and A. Kanasel. "Incest and Child Sexual Abuse." *Journal of the National Medical Association* 74:6 (June 1982): 513–17.

Committee on Sexual Offences against Children and Youths. *Sexual Offences against Children: Report of the Committee on Sexual Offences against Children and Youths.* Ottawa: Canadian Government Publishing Centre, 1984.

Conran, M. "Incestuous Failure: Studies of Transference Phenomena with Young Psychotic Patients and Their Mothers." *International Journal of Psychoanalysis* 57:4 (1976): 477–81.

Constanine, L. "Effects of Early Sexual Experiences: A Review and Synthesis of Research." In *Children and Sex: New Findings, New Perspectives,* edited by L. Constantine and F. Martinson. Boston: Little, Brown, 1981.

Conte, J., and L. Berliner. "Sexual Abuse of Children: Implication for Practice." *Social Casework* 62:10 (Dec. 1981): 601–7.

Cotton, D., and A. Groth. "Inmate Rape: Prevention and Intervention." *Journal of Prison and Jail Health* 2 (1982): 47–57.

Courtois, C. "Victims of Rape and Incest." *Counseling Psychologist* 8:1 (1979).

———. *Healing the Incest Wound: Adult Survivors in Therapy.* New York: Norton, 1988.

Courtois, C., and D. Watts. "Counseling Adult Women Who Experienced Incest in Childhood or Adolescence." *Personnel and Guidance Journal* 60:5(1982): 275—79.

Crewdson, J. *By Silence Betrayed: Sexual Abuse of Children in America.* Boston: Little, Brown, 1988.

Crigler, P. "Incest in the Military Family. In *The Military Family,* edited by F. Kaslow and R. Ridenour. New York: Gilford, 1984.

Daugherty, M. "The crime of incest against the Minor Child and the States' Statutory Responses." *Journal of Family Law* Vol 17 (1978).

Davies, R. "Incest: Some Neuropsychiatric Findings." *International Journal of Psychology in Medicine.* Vol 9:(2) (1978).

Deed, M. "Clinical Conflicts in the Child Sex Abuse Arena." *Readings: A Journal of Reviews and Commentary in Mental Health* 3:4 (Dec. 1988): 11–15.

DeFrancis, V. *Protecting the Child Victim of Sex Crimes Committed by Adults, Final Report.* Denver: The American Humane Association, Children's Division, 1969.

Deisher, R., V. Eisner, and S. Sulzbacher. "The Young Male Prostitute." *Pediatrics* 43:6 (June 1969): 936–41.

DeJong, A. "Epidemiologic Factors in Sexual Abuse of Boys." *American Journal of Diseases of Children* 134:255 (1980).

———. "The Sexually Abused Child: A Comparison of Male and Female Victims." *Child Abuse and Neglect* 9:4 (1985): 576–86.

DeJong, A., G. Emmett, and A. Hervada. "Sexual Abuse of Children. " *Journal of Diseases of Children* 136 (Feb. 1982): 129–34.

———. "Epidemiological Factors in Sexual Abuse of Boys." *American Journal of Diseases of Children* 136:11 (Nov. 1982): 990–93.

Delson, N., and M. Clark. "Group Therapy with Sexually Molested Children." *Child Welfare* 60:3 (March 1981): 175–82.

Demott, B. "The Pro-incest Lobby." *Psychology Today* 13 (1980): 11–16.

DePanfilis, Diane. *Literature Review of Sexual Abuse.* Washington, D.C.: U.S. Dept. of Health and Human Services, Office of Human Development Services, National Center on Child Abuse and Neglect, Aug. 1986.

de Young, M. "Case Reports: The Sexual Exploitation of Incest Victims by Helping Professionals." *Victimology: An International Journal* 6:1–4 (1981): 92–100.

———. "Promises, Threats and Lies: Keeping Incest Secret." *Journal of Humanics* 9:1 (May 1981): 61–71.

———. "Siblings of Oedipus: Brothers and Sisters of Incest Victims." *Child Welfare* 60:8 (Sept./Oct. 1981): 561–68.

———. "Incest Victims and Offenders: Myths and Realities." *Journal of Psychosocial Nursing and Mental Health Services* 19:10 (Oct. 1981): 37–39.

———. "Innocent Seducer or Innocently Seduced? The Role of the Child Incest Victim." *Journal of Clinical Child Psychology* 11:1 (Spring 1982): 56–60.

———. "Self-injurious Behavior in Incest Victims: A Research Note." *Child Welfare* 61:8 (Nov./Dec. 1982): 577–84.

———. "Counterphobic Behavior in Multiply Molested Children." *Child Welfare* 63:4 (July/Aug. 1984): 333–39.

———. *Incest: An Annotated Bibliography.* London: McFarland, 1985.

Dietz, C., and J. Craft. "Family Dynamics of Incest: A New Perspective." *Social Casework* 61:10 (1980): 602–9.

Dixon, K., E. Arnold, and K. Calestro. "Father-Son Incest: Underreported Psychiatric Problem?" *American Journal of Psychology* 135:7 (July 1978).

Donaldson, M., and R. Gardner. "Diagnosis and Treatment of Traumatic Stress among Women after Childhood Incest." In *Trauma and its Wake: The Study of Post-Traumatic Stress Disorder,* edited by C. Figley. New York: Brunner Mazel, 1985.

Doueck. "Adolescent Maltreatment." *Journal of Interpersonal Violence* 2:2 (1987): 139–53.

Edwards, D., and E. Gil. *Breaking the Cycle: Assessment and Treatment of Child Abuse and Neglect.* Santa Monica, Calif.: Association for Advanced Training in the Behavioral Sciences, 1987.

Elkind, J., A. Berson, and D. Edwin. "Current Realities Haunting Advocates of Abused Children." *Social Casework* (Nov. 1977).

Ellerstein, N., J. Canavan, and M. Williams. "Sexual Abuse of Boys." *American Journal of Disturbed Children* 134 (March 1980): 255-257.

Elms, A. "Was Freud Molested?" *Psychology Today* (Aug. 1986).

Elwell, M. "Sexually Assaulted Children and Their Families." *Social Casework* 60:4 (April 1979): 227–35.

Erikson, E. *Identify: Youth and Crisis.* New York: Norton, 1968.

Eth, S., and R. Pynoos, eds. *Post-Traumatic Stress Disorder in Children.* Washington D.C.: American Psychiatric Press, 1985.

Farber, E., J. Showers, C. Johnson, J. Joseph, and L. Oshins. "The Sexual Abuse of Children: A Comparison of Male and Female Victims." *Journal of Clinical Child Psychology* 13:3 (1984): 294–97.

Favazza, A. *Bodies under Siege: Self-mutilation in Culture and Psychiatry.* Baltimore: Johns Hopkins University Press, 1987.

Ferenczi, S. "Confusion of Tongues between Adults and the Child." *International Journal of Psychoanalysis* 30 (1949): 225–30.

Finch, S. "Sexual Abuse by Mothers." *Medical Aspects of Human Sexuality* 7:1 (Jan,1973): 191.

Finkelhor, D. *Sexually Victimized Children.* New York: Free Press, 1979.

———. "What's Wrong with Sex between Adults and Children?" *American Journal of Orthopsychiatry* 49:4 (Oct.1979).

———. "Sex among Siblings: A Survey of Prevalence, Variety and Effects." *Archives of Sexual Behavior* 9:3 (June 1980): 171–94.

———. *Child Sexual Abuse: New Theory and Research.* New York: Free Press, 1984.

———. "Implications for Theory, Research and Practice." In *The Educator's Guide to Preventing Child Sexual Abuse,* edited by M. Nelson and K. Clark. Santa Cruz, Calif.: Network Publications, 1986.

Finkelhor, D., and S. Araji. *"Explanation of Pedophilia—A Four Factor Model."* New Hampshire University Family Violence Program, Durham, July 1983.

Finkelhor, D., and A. Brown. "The Impact of Child Sexual Abuse: A Conceptualization." *American Journal of Orthopsychiatry* 55:4 (Oct. 1985): 530–41.

Fitzgibbons, T. "The Cognitive and Emotive Uses of Forgiveness in the Treatment of Anger." *Psychotherapy* 23 (1986): 629–33.

Flannery, R. "From Victim to Survivor: A Stress Management Approach to the Treatment of Learned Helplessness." In *Psychological Trauma,* edited by B. van der Kolk. Washington, D. C.: American Psychiatric Press, 1987.

Fossum, M., and M. Mason. *Facing Shame.* New York: Norton, 1986.

Fox, J. "Sibling Incest." *British Journal of Sociology* 13 (1962): 128–50.

Frances, V., and A. Frances. "The Incest Taboo and Family Structure." *Family Process* 15:2 (June 1976): 235–44.

Friedrich, W., A. Urquiza, and R. Beilke. "Behavioral Problems in Sexually Abused Young Children." *Journal of Pediatric Psychology* 11 (1986): 45–57.

Friedman, W., and R. Reams. "Course of Psychological Symptoms in Sexually abused Young Children." *Psychotherapy* 24:2 (Summer 1987): 160–70.

Fritz, G., K. Stoll, and N. Wagner. "A Comparison of Males and Females Who Were Sexually Molested as Children." *Journal of Sex and Marital Therapy* 7 (1981): 54–59.

Frude, N. "The Sexual Nature of Sexual Abuse: A Review of the Literature." *Child Abuse and Neglect* 6:2 (1982): 211–23.

Furniss, T., L. Bingley-Miller, and A. Bentovim. "Therapeutic Approach to Sexual Abuse." *Archives of Disease in Childhood* 59:9 (1984): 865–87.

Gardner, R. *The Parental Alienation Syndrome and the Differentiation between Fabricated and Genuine Child Sex Abuse.* Cresskill, N.J.: Creative Therapeutics, 1987.

Garrison. "Psychological Maltreatment of Children." *American Psychologist* 42:2 (Feb. 1987): 157–59.

Gebhard, P. *Sex Offenders: An Analysis of Types.* New York: Harper and Row, 1965.

Geiser, R. *Hidden Victims.* Boston: Beacon, 1979.

———. "Incest and Psychological Violence." *International Journal of Family Psychiatry* 2:3–4 (1981): 291–300.

Geiser, R., and S. Norbert. "Sexual Disturbance in Young Children." *Maternal Child Nursing* (May/June 1976).

Gelinas, D. "The Persisting Negative Effects of Incest." *Psychiatry* 46 (1983): 313–32.

Gelles, R. "Violence toward Children in the United States." *American Journal of Orthopsychiatry* (Oct. 1978).

Gendel, M., and M. Hunter. Personal discussion, 1988.

Gentry, C. "Incestuous Abuse of Children: The Need for an Objective View." *Child Welfare* 57 (June 1978): 355–64.

Giaretto, H. *Integrated Treatment of Child Sexual Abuse.* Palo Alto, Calif: Science and Behavior Books, 1982.

Gibbens, T., K. Soothiel, and C. Way. "Sibling and Parent Child Incest Offenders." *British Journal of Criminology* 18:1 (Jan. 1978).

Gil, E. *Outgrowing the Pain: A Book For and About Adults Abused as Children.* Walnut Creek, Calif.: Launch Press, 1983.

Glueck, B. "Early Sexual Experiences and Schizophrenia." In *Advances in Sex Research,* edited by H. Beigel. New York: Harper and Row, 1963.

Godin, A. and M. Hallez. "Paternal Images and Divine Paternity." In *From Religious Experience to Religious Attitude,* edited by A. Godin. Chicago: Loyola University Press, 1965.

Gold, E. "Long-term Effects of Sexual Victimization in Childhood: An Attributional Approach." *Journal of Consulting and Clinical Psychology* 54 (1986): 47–75.

Goldstein, S. "Sexual Exploitation of Children: Ignorance vs. Innocence." *Journal of California Law Enforcement* 14:3 (Jan. 1980): 113–19.

Goodman, W. Personal communication, 1986.

Goodwin, J., M. Simons, and R. Bergman. "Hysterical Seizures: A Sequel to Incest." *American Journal of Orthopsychiatry* 49:4 (Oct. 1979).

Green, A. "Filicidal Impulses as an Anniversary Reaction to Childhood Incest."

———. "Dimensions of Psychological Trauma in Abused Children." *Journal of the American Academy of Child Psychiatry* 22 (1983): 231–37.

Greenberg, M., and B. van der Kolk. "Retrieval and Integration of Traumatic Memories with 'the Painting Cure.'" In *Psychological Trauma,* Washington, D.C.: American Psychiatric Press, 1987.

Greenberg, N. "The Epidemiology of Childhood Sexual Abuse." *Pediatric Annals* 8:5 (May 1979).

Gross, M. "Incestuous Rape: A Cause for Hysterical Seizures in Adolescent Girls." *American Journal of Orthopsychiatry* 19:4 (Oct. 1979).

Groth, A. "The Adolescent Sexual Offender and His Prey." *International Journal of Offender Therapy and Comparative Criminology* 21:3 (1977): 249–54.

————. *Men Who Rape: The Psychology of the Offender.* New York: Plenum Press, 1979.

————. "The Incest Offender." *Handbook of Clinical Intervention in Child Sexual Abuse,* edited by S. Sgroi. Lexington, Mass.: Lexington Books, 1982.

Groth, A., and W. Burgess. "Male Rape: Offenders and Victims." *American Journal of Psychiatry* 137:7 (1980): 806–10.

Groth, N. "Patterns of Sexual Assault against Children and Adolescents." In *Sexual Assault of Children and Adolescents,* edited by A. Burgess. Lexington, Mass: Lexington Books, 1978.

————. "Sexual Trauma in the Life Histories of Rapists and Child Molesters." *Victimology: An International Journal* 4 (1979).

————. Personal communications, as reported in Finkelhor, 1984.

Gruber, K. "The Child Victim's Role in Sexual Assault by Adults." *Child Welfare* 40:5 (May 1981): 305–11.

Gutheil, T., and N. Avery. "Multiple Overt Incest as Family against Loss." *Family Process* 16 (March 1977): 105–16.

Guyon, R. *Ethics of Sexual Acts.* New York: Blue Ribbon, 1941.

Hall, J., D. Orr, and W. Winter. "Children of Incest: When to Suspect and How to Evaluate?" *American Journal of Disturbed Children* 132 (Oct. 1978).

Harris, C. *When the Silence Is Broken: A Guide for Men Who Love and Live with Women Who Were Sexually Abused as Children.* Dallas: Victim's Recovery Association, 1988.

Hartman, M., S. Finn, and G. Leon. "Sexual Abuse Experience in a Clinical Population: Comparisons of Familial and Nonfamilial Abuse." *Psychotherapy* 24:2 (Summer 1987): 154–59.

Hassol, J. Norfolk County Rape Unit workshop presentation. Dedham, Mass., 1978. As reported in Anderson, L. "Notes on the Linkage between the Sexually Abused Child and the Suicidal Adolescent." *Journal of Adolescence* 4:2 (June 1981): 147–62.

Hedin, D. *Preliminary Analysis of High School, College, Prison, Juvenile Corrections and Adult Populations.* Minneapolis: WCCO Television/University of Minnesota Study, 1984.

Heims, L., and I. Kaufman. "Variations on a Theme of Incest." *American Journal of Orthopsychiatry* 33 (1963): 311–12.

Henderson, D. "Incest: A Synthesis of Data." *Canadian Psychiatric Association Journal* 17:4 (1972): 229–313.

————. "Incest." In *Textbook of Psychiatry* 2d ed., edited by H. Kaplan and B. Sadock. Baltimore: Williams and Wilkins, 1975.

Herjanic, B. "Sexual Abuse of Children." *Journal of the American Medical Association* 239:4 (Jan. 1978).

Herman J. L. *Father-Daughter Incest.* Cambridge Mass.: Harvard University Press, 1981.

Herman, J., and E. Schatzow. "Recovery and Verification of Memories of Childhood Sexual Trauma." *Psychoanalytic Psychology* 4 (1987): 1–4.

Hersch, P. "Coming of Age on City Streets." *Psychology Today* 22:1 (Jan. 1988): 28–37.

Hersko, Marvin. "Incest: A Three Way Process." *Journal of Social Therapy* 7 (1966): 22–31.

Horowitz, M. *Stress Response Syndromes* 2d ed. Northvale, N.J.: Aronson, 1986.

Horoyd, J., and A. Brodsky. "Physical Contact with Patients." *American Psychologist* 32 (1977): 843–47.

Howard, H. "Incest—The Revenge Motive." *Delaware State Medical Journal* 31 (1959): 223–25.

Hunter, M. "The Membership Demographics of the Self-help Group Sex Addicts Anonymous." Master's thesis, University of Wisconsin, Superior, 1984.

———. *The Twelve Steps and Shame.* Center City, Minn.: Hazelden Educational Materials, 1988.

———. *What is Sex Addiction?* Center City, Minn.: Hazelden Educational Materials, 1988.

———, and R.B. Adams. Personal discussion, 1989.

———, and Jem. *The First Step for People in Relationships with Sex Addicts.* Minneapolis.: CompCare Publications, 1989.

Huyghe, P. "Voices, Glances, Flashbacks: Our First Memories." *Psychology Today* 19:9 (Sept. 1985).

Ingram, M. "Participating Victims: A Study of Sexual Offenses with Boys." In *Children and Sex: New Findings, New Perspectives,* edited by L. Constantive and F. Martison. Boston: Little, Brown, 1981.

Jakubiak, M., and S. Murphy. "Incest Survivors in Women's Communities." *Human Development* (1987): 19–25.

James, J., and J. Meyerding. "Early Sexual Experiences and Prostitution." *American Journal of Psychiatry* 134:12 (Dec. 1977): 1381–85.

Janas, C. "Family Violence and Child Sexual Abuse." *Medical Hypoanalysis* 4:2 (April 1983): 68–76.

Janoff-Bulman, R. "Characterological versus Behavioral Self-blame: Inquiries into Depression and Rape." *Journal of Personality and Social Psychology* 37 (1979): 1798–1809.

Janoff-Bulman, R. and I. Frieze. "Theoretical Perspective for Understanding Reactions to Victimization." *Journal of Social Issues* 39 (1983): 1–18.

Johnson, M. "The Sexually Mistreated Child: Diagnostic Evaluation." *Child Abuse and Neglect* 3 (1979): 943–51.

Johnson, R., and D. Shrier. "Sexual Victimization of Boys: Experience at an Adolescent Medicine Clinic." *Journal of Adolescent Health Care* 6:5 (1985): 372–76.

Joy, S. "Retrospective Presentations of Incest: Treatment Strategies for Use with Adult Women." *Journal of Counseling and Development* 65 (1987): 317–19.

Justice, B., and R. Justice. *The Broken Taboo.* New York: Human Sciences Press, 1979.

Kahn, M., and M. Sexton. "Sexual Abuse of Young Children." *Clinical Pediatrics* 22 (1983): 369–72.

Kaplan, S.H. *The New Sex Therapy: Active Treatment of Sexual Dysfunctions.* New York: Brunner/Mazel, 1974.

Kaufman, A., P. Divasto, and R. Jackson. "Male Rape Victims: Noninstitutionalized Assault." *American Journal of Psychiatry* 137 (1980): 835–38.

Kaufman, G. *Shame: The Power of Caring.* Cambridge, Mass.: Schenkman, 1980.

Kaufman, I., A. Peck, and C. Taguiri. "The Family Constellation and Overt Incestuous Relationships between Father and Daughter." *American Journal of Orthopsychiatry* 24 (1954).

Kempe, R., and C. Kempe. *The Common Secret: Sexual Abuse of Children and Adolescents.* New York: Freeman, 1984.

Kercher, G., and M. McShane. "The Prevalence of Child Sexual Abuse Victimization in an Adult Sample of Texas Residents." Sam Houston State University, Huntsville, Tex., 1983. Mimeo.

Kinsey, A., W. Pomeroy, and C. Martin. *Sexual Behavior in the Human Male.* Philadelphia: Saunders, 1948.

Kohn, A. "Shattered Innocence." *Psychology Today* 21:2 (1987).

Krieger, M., A. Rosenfeld, A. Gordon, and M. Bennett. "Problems in the Psychotherapy of Children with Histories of Incest." *American Journal of Psychotherapy* 34 (1980): 81–88.

Krupnick, J., and M. Horowitz. "Stress Response Syndromes." *Archives of General Psychiatry* 38 (1981).

Krystal, H. "Psychoanalytic Views on Human Emotional Damage." In *Post-Traumatic Stress Disorder: Psychological and Biological Sequelae,* edited by B. van der Kolk. Washington, D.C.: American Psychiatric Press, 1984.

Kubler-Ross, E. *On Death and Dying.* New York: Macmillan, 1969.

Lamb, S. "Treating Sexually Abused Children: Issues of Blame and Responsibility." *American Journal of Orthopsychiatry* 56 (1986): 303–7.

Landis, J.T. "Experiences of 500 Children with Adult Sexual Deviation." *Psychiatric Quarterly Supplement* 30 (1956): 91–109.

Langley, D., M. Schwartz, and R. Fairbairn. "Father-Son Incest." *Comprehensive Psychiatry* 9:3 (May 1968): 218–26.

Layman, W. "Psuedo Incest." *Comprehensive Psychiatry* 12:4 (July/Aug. 1972): 385–89.

Lehfeldt, H. "Unusual 'Sex Crime.'/" *Journal of Sex Education* 4 (1952): 176.

Lester, D. "Incest." *Journal of Sex Research* 8:4 (1972): 268–85.

Lew, M. *Victims No Longer: Men Recovering from Incest and Other Sexual Child Abuse.* New York: Nevraumont, 1988.

Lewis, M., and P. Sarrel. "Some Psychological Aspects of Seduction, Incest and Rape in Childhood." *Journal of the American Academy of Child Psychiatry* 8 (1969): 606–19.

Libow, J., and D. Doty. "An Exploratory Approach to Self-blame and Self-derogation by Rape Victims." *American Journal of Orthopsychiatry* 49:4 (Oct. 1979).

Lister, E. "Forced Silence: A Neglected Dimension of Trauma." *American Journal of Psychiatry* 139 (1982): 872–76.

Lloyd, R. *Tap Dancing for Big Mom.* St. Paul, Minn.: New Rivers Press, 1985.

Lukianowicz, N. "Incest I: Paternal Incest; Incest II: Other Types of Incest." *British Journal of Psychiatry* 120 (1972): 310–13.

MacFarlane, K., and J. Bulkley. "Treating Child Sexual Abuse: An Overview of Current Program Models." *Journal of Social Work and Human Sexuality* 1:1–2 (Fall/Winter): 69–91.

MacFarlane, K., and J. Korbin. "Confronting the Incest Secret Long After the Fact: A Family Study of Multiple Victimization with Strategies for Intervention." *Child Abuse and Neglect* 7 (1983): 225–40.

MacFarlane, K., and J. Waterman. *Sexual Abuse of Young Children: Evaluation and Treatment.* New York: Gilford Press, 1986.

Maltz, W., and B. Holman. *Incest and Sexuality: A Guide to Understanding and Healing.* Lexington, Mass.: Lexington Books, 1987.

Margolis, M. "A Case of Mother-Adolescent Son Incest: A Follow-up Study." *Psychoanalytic Quarterly* 53:3 (July 1984): 355–85.

Masson, J. *The Assault on Truth: Freud's Suppression of the Seduction Theory.* New York: Farrar, Straus and Giroux, 1984.

Masson, J., ed. *The Complete Letters of Sigmund Freud to Wilhelm Fliess: 1887–1904.* Cambridge: Harvard University Press, 1985.

Masters, R., ed. *Patterns of Incest.* New York: Julian Press, 1963.

Mathews, R. "Typologies of Female Sexual Offenders." Unpublished, federal copyright 1987.

Mayer, A. *Incest: A Treatment Manual for Therapy with Victims, Spouses and Offenders.* Holmes Beach, Fla.: Learning Publications, 1983.

MCA. *Private Lessons.* Universal City, Calif., 1981 (videotape).

MCA. *Homework.* Universal City, Calif., 1982 (videotape).

McCaghy, C. "Drinking and Deviance Disavowal: The Case of Child Molesters." *Social Problems* 16 (1968): 43–49.

———. "Child Molesting." *Sexual Behavior* 1 (1971).

McCarty, L. "Mother-Child Incest: Characteristics of the Offender." *Child Welfare* 65 (1986): 447–58.

McCaussland, M. "Sexual Development and Sexual Abuse: Emergencies in Adolescents." *Pediatric Clinic of North America* 26:4 (Nov. 1979).

McKechnie, J., ed. *Webster's New Universal Unabridged Dictionary,* 2d ed. Cleveland: Simon and Schuster, 1983.

Meek, J., A. Askari, and A. Belman. "Prepubertal Gonorrhea." *Journal of Urology* 122 (Oct. 1979): 532–34.

Meiselman, K. *Incest: A Psychological Study of Causes and Effects with Treatment Recommendations.* San Francisco: Jossey-Bass, 1978.

———. "Personality Characteristics of Incest History Psychotherapy." *Archives of Sexual Behavior* 8:3 (1980): 195–97.

Melnar, G., and P. Cameron. "Incest Syndromes." *Canadian Psychiatric Association Journal* 20:5 (1975): 373.

Miller, N. "Male Rape." *Boston Phoenix,* Nov. 1983, p. 12

Minnesota Program for Victims of Sexual Assault. *Biennial Report: Fiscal Years 1985–1986.* St. Paul: Minnesota Department of Corrections, 1987.

Molnar, G., and P. Cameron. "Incest Syndromes: Observations in a General Hospital Psychiatric Unit." *Canadian Psychiatric Association Journal* 20 (1975).

Mrazek, P. "Sexual Abuse of Children." *Journal of Child Psychology and Psychiatry* 2:1 (Jan. 1980): 91–95.

Mrazek, P., and D. Mrazek. "The Effects of Child Abuse: Methodological Considerations." In *Sexually Abused Children and Their Families*, edited by P. Mrazek and C. Kempe. Pergamon Press, 1981.

Murdock, G. *Social Structure*. New York: Macmillan, 1949.

Narcotics Anonymous. *Narcotics Anonymous*. Los Angeles: C.A.R.E.N.A. Publishing, 1982.

Nasjleti, M. "Suffering in Silence: The Male Incest Victim." *Child Welfare* 49:5 (May 1980): 269–75.

Nelson, J. *Embodiment: An Approach to Sexuality and Christian Theology*. New York: Pilgrim Press, 1978.

Neu, J. "What Is Wrong with Incest?" *Inquiry* 19 (1976).

Newberger, E. "Child Abuse and Neglect: Towards a Firmer Foundation for Practice and Policy." *American Journal of Orthopsychiatry* (July 1977).

———. "The Medicalization and Legalization of Child Abuse." *American Journal of Orthopsychiatry* (Oct. 1978).

Newlund, S. "Rate of Abuse Reports in '84 Is State Record." *Minneapolis Star Tribune,* March 27, 1986.

Newton, D. "Homosexual Behavior and Child Molestation: A Review of the Evidence." *Adolescence* 13 (1978): 29–43.

Nielsen, T. "Sexual Abuse of Boys: Current Perspectives." *Personnel and Guidance Journal* 62 (Nov. 1983).

O'Hare, J., and K. Taylor. "The Reality of Incest." *Women and Therapy* 2:2–2 (Summer-Fall 1983): 215–29.

Overmeir, J., and M. Seligman. "Effects of Inescapable Shock upon Subsequent Escape and Avoidance Learning." *Journal of Comparative and Physiological Psychology* 63 (1967): 23–33.

Pagels. E. *The Gnostic Gospels*. New York: Random House, 1979.

Parker, D. "The Precultural Basis of the Incest Taboo: Toward a Biosocial Theory." *American Anthropologist* 78 (1976).

Peters, J. "Children Who Are Victims of Sexual Assault and the Psychology of Offenders." *American Journal of Psychotherapy* 30 (1976): 398–421.

Petrovich, M., and D. Templer. "Heterosexual Molestation of Children Who Later Become Rapists." *Psychological Reports* 54 (1984): 810.

Peirce, R., and L. Pierce. "The Sexually Abused Child: A Comparison of Male and Female Victims." *Child Abuse and Neglect* 9 (1985): 191–99.

Pittman, F. "Incest." *Current Psychiatric Therapies* 17 (1977).

Polier, J. "Professional Abuse of Children: Responsibility for the Delivery of Services." *American Journal of Orthopsychiatry* 435 (1975): 357–62.

Porter, Eugene. *Treating the Young Male Victims of Sexual Assault: Issues and Intervention Strategies*. Syracuse, N.Y.: Safer Society Press, 1986.

Rader, R., R. Kellner, D. Laws, and W. Winslow. "Drinking, Alcoholism and the Mentally Disordered Sex Offender." *Bulletin of the American Academy of Psychiatry and Law* 6 (1978): 296–300.

Raphling, D., B. Carpenter, and A. Davis. "Incest: A Geneological Study." *Archives of General Psychiatry* 16:4 (1967).

Raybin, J. "Homosexual Incest." *Journal of Nervous and Mental Disease* 148 (1969): 105–10.

Reber, A. *A Dictionary of Psychology*. New York: Viking Press, 1985.

Renshaw, D., and R. Renshaw. "Incest." *Journal of Sex Education and Therapy* 3 (1977).

Rhinehart, J. "Genesis of Overt Incest." *Comprehensive Psychiatry* 2:6 (Dec. 1961): 333–49.

Rieker, P., and E. Carmen. "The Victim-to-Patient Process: The Disconfirmation and Transformation of Abuse." *American Journal of Orthopsychiatry* 56 (1986): 360–70.

Riemer, S. "A Research Note on Incest." *American Journal of Sociology* 45 (1940): 566–75.

Riordan, R., and M. Beggs. "Counselors and Self-help Groups." *Journal of Counseling and Development* 65 (April 1987): 427–29.

Rist, K. "Incest: Theoretical and Clinical Views." *American Journal of Orthopsychiatry* 49:4 (Oct. 1979).

Robinson, H., D. Sherrod, and C. Malcarney. "Review of Child Molestation and Alleged Rape Cases." *American Journal of Obstetrics and Gynecology* 110 (1971): 405–6.

Rogers, C., and T. Terry. "Clinical Intervention with Boy Victims of Sexual Abuse." In *Victims of Sexual Aggression*, edited by I. Stewart and G. Greer. New York: Van Nostrand Reinhold, 1984.

Rosenberg, M. "New Directions for Research on the Psychological Maltreatment of Children." *American Psychologist* 42:2 (Feb. 1987): 166–71.

Rosenfeld, A. "Sexual Misuse and the Family." *Victimology: An International Journal* 2:2 (Summer 1977): 226–35.

———. "Endogamic Incest and the Victim-Perpetrator Model." *American Journal of the Disabled Child* 133 (April 1979).

———. "The Clinical Management of Incest and Sexual Abuse of Children." *JAMA* 242:16 (Oct. 1979).

Rosenfeld, A., C. Nadelson, and M. Krieger. "Incest and Sexual Abuse of Children." *Journal of the American Academy of Child Psychiatry* 16 (1977): 327–39.

———. "Fantasy and Reality in Patients' Reports of Incest." *Journal of Clinical Psychiatry* 40:4 (April 1979): 159–64.

Rossman, P. *Sexual Experience between Men and Boys: Exploring the Pederast Underground*. New York: Association Press, 1976.

Roth, P. *Portnoy's Complaint*. New York: Bantam Books, 1967.

Ruch, L., and S. Chandler. "The Crisis Impact of Sexual Assualt on Three Victim Groups: Adult Rape Victims, Child Rape Victims and Incest Victims." *Journal of Social Service Research* 5:1–2 (1982): 83–100.

Rush, F. "Freud and the Sexual Abuse of Children." *Chrysalis* 1 (1977): 31–45.

———. *The Best Kept Secret*. Englewood Cliffs, N.J.: Prentice Hall, 1980.

Russell, A., and C. Trainor. *Trends in Child Abuse and Neglect: A National Perspective*. Denver: American Humane Association, 1984.

Russell, D. *The Secret Trauma: Incest in the Lives of Girls and Women*. New York: Basic Books, 1986.

Sagarin, E. "Incest: Problems of Definition and Frequency." *Journal of Sex Research* 13:1 (1977): 126–35.

Salter, A. *Treating Child Sex Offenders and Victims: A Practical Guide*. Beverly Hills, Calif.: Sage, 1988.

Saltman, V., and R. Solomon. "Incest and Multiple Personality." *Psychological Reports* 50 (1982): 1127–41.

Sandfort, T. "Pedophile Relationships in the Netherlands: Alternative Lifestyle for Children?" *Alternative Lifestyles* 5:3 (Spring 1983): 164–83.

———. "Sex in Pedophiliac Relationships: An Empirical Investigation among a Nonrepresentative Group of Boys." *Journal of Sex Research* 20:2 (May 1984): 123–42.

Santiago, L. *The Children of Oedipus: Brother-Sister Incest in Psychiatry, Literature, History and Mythology*. Roslyn Heights, N.Y.: Libra, 1973.

Sarrel, L., and P. Sarrel. *Sexual Unfolding: Sexual Development and Sex Therapies in Late Adolescence*. Boston: Little, Brown, 1979.

———. "Incest: Why Is It Our Last Taboo?" *Redbook* (Nov. 1980).

Sarrel, P., and W. Masters. "Sexual Molestation of Men by Women." *Archives of Sexual Behavior* 11:2 (April 1982): 117–31.

Scherzer, L., and L. Padma. "Sexual Offenses Committed against Children." *Clinical Pediatrics* 19 (1980): 670–85.

Schiff, A.F. "Examination and Treatment of the Male Rape Victim." *Southern Medical Journal* 73 (1980).

Schneck, J. "Zooerasty and Incest Fantasy." *International Journal of Clinical and Experimental Hypnosis* 11:4 (1974): 199–302.

Schultz, L. "The Child Sex Victim: Social, Psychological and Legal Perspectives." *Child Welfare* 41:3 (March 1973).

Schultz, L., ed. *The Sexual Victimology of Youth*. Springfield, Ill.: Thomas, 1980.

Schultz, R. Address at the Second International Conference on Multiple Personality/Dissociative States, Chicago, Ill., 1986.

Schwartzman, J. "The Individual, Incest and Exogamy." *Psychiatry* 37 (May 1974).

Seligman, M., and S. Maier. "Failure to Escape Traumatic Shock." *Journal of Experimental Psychology* 74 (1967): 1–9.

Sgroi, S. "Sexual Molestation of Children: The Last Frontier in Child Abuse." *Children Today* 44 (1975): 18–21.

Sherfey, M. *The Nature and Evolution of Female Sexuality*. New York: Random House, 1972.

Showers, J., E. Farber, J. Joseph, L. Oshins, and C. Johnson. "The Sexual Victimization of Boys: A Three Year Survey." *Health Values: Achieving High Level Wellness* 7:4 (July–Aug. 1983): 15–18.

Silbert, M., and A. Pines. "Child Sexual Abuse as an Antecedent to Prostitution." *Child Abuse and Neglect* 5 (1981): 407–11.

Silver, R., C. Boon, and M. Stones. "Searching for Meaning in Misfortune: Making Sense of Incest." *Journal of Social Issues* 39:2 (1983): 81–102.

Simari, C., and D. Baskin. "Incestuous Experiences within Homosexual Populations: A Preliminary Study." *Archives of Sexual Behavior* 11 (1982): 329–44.

Simpson, C., and G. Porter. "Self-Mutilation in Children and Adolescents." *Bulletin of the Menninger Clinic* 45:5 (July 1981): 428–38.

Sloane, P., and E. Karpinski. "Effects of Incest on the Participants." *American Journal of Orthopsychiatry* 12 (1942): 666–73.

Soules, M., S. Steward, and K. Brown. "The Spectrum of Alleged Rape." *Journal of Reproductive Medicine* 20 (1978): 33–39.

Spencer, J. "Father-Daughter Incest: A Clinical View from the Corrections Field." *Child Welfare* 3:9 (Nov. 1978).

Sroufe, L., and M. Ward. "Seductive Behavior of Mothers and Toddlers: Occurrence, Correlates and Family Origins." *Child Development* 51 (1980): 1222–29.

Steele, B., and H. Alexander. "Long-term Effects of Sexual Abuse in Childhood." In *Sexually Abused Children and Their Families*, edited by P. Mrazek and C. Kempe. Oxford: Pergamon Press, 1981.

Stringer, G., and Deanna Rants-Rodriguez. *So What's It to Me? Sexual Assault Information for Guys*. King County Rape Relief, 1987.

Summit, R. "The Child Sexual Abuse Accommodation Syndrome." *Child Abuse and Neglect* 7:2 (1983): 177–93.

Summit, R., and J. Kryso. "Sexual Abuse of Children: A Clinical Spectrum." *American Journal of Orthopsychiatry* 48:2 (April 1978): 237–51.

Swift, C. "Sexual Victimization of Children: An Urban Mental Health Center Survey." *Victimology: An International Journal* 2:2 (Summer 1977): 322–27.

Swink, K., and A. Leveille. "From Victim to Survivor: A New Look at the Issues and Recovery Process for Adult Incest Survivors." *Women and Therapy* 5 (Summer/Fall 1986): 119–41.

Symonds, M. "The 'Second Injury' to Victims." *Evaluation and Change* (1980): 36–38.

Tick, E. "Male Child Sexual Abuse: The Best Kept Secret." *Voices* (Fall 1984).

Tilelli, J., D. Turek, and A. Jaffe. "Sexual Abuse of Children." *New England Journal of Medicine* 302:6 (1980): 319–23.

Tormes, Y. *Child Victims of Incest*. Denver: American Humane Association, 1968.

Tsai, M., S. Feldman-Summers, and M. Edgar. "Childhood Molestaton: Variables Related to Differential Impact on Psychological Functioning in Adult Women." *Journal of Abnormal Psychology* 88 (1979): 407–17.

Tsai, M., and N. Wagner. "Therapy Groups for Women Sexually Molested as Children." *Archives of Sexual Behavior* 7 (1978): 417–27.

Van Buren, A. "Boy's Early Sex Life Disturbing to Mother." *Star Tribune*, July 6, 1986.

van der Kolk, B. *Psychological Trauma*. Washington D.C.: American Psychiatric Press, 1987.

Van Ness, S. "Rape as Instrumental Violence: A Study of Youth Offenders." *Journal of Offender Counseling, Services and Rehabilitation* 9:1–2 (Fall-Winter 1984): 161–70.

Virkkunen, M. "Victim-Precipitated Pedophilia Offences." *British Journal of Criminology* 14 (1975).

Vredevelt, P., and K. Rodriguez. *Surviving the Secret: Healing the Hurts of Sexual Abuse.* Old Tappan, N.J.: Revell, 1988.

Wahl, C. "The Psychodynamics of Consummated Maternal Incest." *Archives of General Psychiatry* 3:2 (Aug. 1960): 188–93.

Wald, E., C. Woodward, G. Marston, and L. Gilbert. "Gonorrheal Disease among Children in a University Hospital." *Sexually Transmitted Diseases* 7:2 (April–June 1980): 41–43.

Walker, B., E. Somerfeld, and R. Robinson. "One-Night Stands: A Challenge for Family Therapists." *Family Therapy* 5:3 (1978): 259–65.

Walsh, C.P. The Self-concept and Sex-role Orientation of Adult Females in Therapy with and without Incest History. Ph.D. diss., University of Florida, Gainesville, 1986.

Walters, David. *Physical and Sexual Abuse of Children: Causes and Treatment.* Bloomington: Indiana University Press, 1975.

Webster's Third New International Dictionary. Springfield, Mass.: Merriam, 1971.

Weinberg, S.K. *Incest Behavior.* New York: Citadel, 1955.

Weiner, I. "A Clinical Perspective on Incest." *American Journal of Disabled Children* 132 (Feb. 1978).

Weiss, J., E. Rogers, M. Darwin, and C. Dutton. "A Study of Girl Sex Victims." *Psychiatric Quarterly* 29 (1955): 1–27.

Werman, D. "On the Occurrence of Incest Fantasies." *Psychoanalytic Quarterly* 46:1 (1977).

Westerlund, E. "Counseling Women with Histories of Incest." *Women and Therapy* 2 (1983): 17–30.

Wolvert, R., and N. Barron. "Parents United of Oregon: A Natural History of a Self-help Group for Sexually Abusive Families." *Prevention in Human Services* 1:3 (Spring 1982): 99—109.

Yates, A. "Children Eroticized by Incest." *American Journal of Psychiatry* 139 (1982): 482–85.

Yorukoglu, A., and J. Kemph. "Children Not Severely Damaged by Incest with a Parent." *Journal of the American Academy of Child Psychiatry* 5 (1966): 11–24.

Yates, M., and K. Pawley. "Utilizing Imagery and the Unconscious to Explore and Resolve the Trauma of Sexual Abuse." *Art Therapy* 3 (1987): 36–41.

Zaphiris, A. "The Sexually Abused Boy." *Preventing Sexual Abuse* (Spring 1986): 1–4.

Zuckerman, D. "The Hurt That Keeps on Hurting." *Psychology Today* 18:11 (Nov. 1984).

Index

About the Author

MIC HUNTER received his bachlor of arts degree magna cum laude in psychology from Macalester College. After finishing the Chemical Dependency Counseling Program at the University of Minnesota, St. Paul, and getting certified as a chemical dependency practitioner, he began working as a case manager in an intermediate care facility for chemically dependent men and women. He went on to complete a master's degree in education from the Psychology Department of the University of Wisconsin, Superior, where his thesis was entitled "The Demographics of the Self-help Group Sex Addicts Anonymous." He then earned a master's degree in human development from Saint Mary's College, Winona, where his position paper was on treatment issues related to male sexual abuse; this paper led to the writing of this book. He is also the author of *What Is Sex Addiction* and *The Twelve Steps and Shame,* and is coauthor of *The First Step for People in Relationships with Sex Addicts.* He recently completed the Two-Year Intensive Postgraduate Training Program at the Gestalt Institute of the Twin Cities. Mic Hunter is certified as a chemical dependency counselor and is licensed both as a psychologist and a marriage and family therapist. He practices in St. Paul, Minnesota. He is currently editing two volumes for therapists who work with male sexual abuse survivors, *The Sexually Abused Male,* Volumes 1 and 2, which will be published by Lexington Books in 1990.

Please remember that this is a library book,
and that it belongs only temporarily to each
person who uses it. Be considerate. Do
not write in this, or any, library book.